THE COMFORT OF THINGS

THE COMFORT OF THINGS

DANIEL MILLER

polity

First published in 2008 by Polity Press
Reprinted 2010 (three times), 2011 (three times),
2012 (three times), 2013 (twice), 2015, 2016, 2017, 2018

Polity Press
65 Bridge Street
Cambridge CB2 1UR, UK.

Polity Press
350 Main Street
Malden, MA 02148, USA

ISBN-13: 978-07456-4403-5
ISBN-13: 978-07456-4404-2 (pb)

A catalogue record for this book is available from the British Library.

Typeset in 10.75 on 14 pt Adobe Janson
by Servis Filmsetting Ltd, Manchester
Printed and bound in the United States
by LSC Communications

For further information on Polity, visit our website: www.polity.co.uk

To Rickie, Rachel and David

CONTENTS

ACKNOWLEDGEMENTS

My first acknowledgement has to be to my co-researcher, Fiona Parrott. All the material on which this book is based derives from research carried out in direct collaboration with her. The success of the project came in large measure from the effective rapport we developed in our fieldwork. We also discussed the interpretation of each household during our fieldwork, which no doubt has informed my writing about them. This book would simply not have been possible, or would at least be a great deal poorer, without the quality of her contribution. But in turn I am sure we would both wish to thank the many, many people who gave to us the considerable gift of their time and patience in order to help with our research. We hope that, eventually, they have not regretted that they did not do the obvious London thing and slam the door on us, and that we were not too tiresome. I hope that through this and subsequent publications they will feel that their stories have contributed to something worthwhile. I also acknowledge the considerable amount of time and effort that my wife, Rickie Burman, gave towards helping me with the manuscript. I would like to thank the following for comments on an earlier draft: Mukulika Banerjee, Barbara Bender, Haidy Geismar, Martin Holbraad, Rachel Miller, Marjorie Murray, Anna Pertierra and Michael Rowlands. I am grateful to John Thompson and Polity for taking on this project. Finally my thanks go to Olga Neva for designing the book cover and for including our cat.

PROLOGUE

This book is the story of thirty people, almost all from a single street in South London. They are selected from one hundred individuals and households studied over seventeen months by myself and Fiona Parrott, a PhD student in my discipline of Anthropology. It is also a book about how people express themselves through their possessions, and what these tell us about their lives. It explores the role of objects in our relationships, both to each other and to ourselves. We live today in a world of ever more stuff – what sometimes seems a deluge of goods and shopping. We tend to assume that this has two results: that we are more superficial, and that we are more materialistic, our relationships to things coming at the expense of our relationships to people. We make such assumptions, we speak in clichés, but we have rarely tried to put these assumptions to the test. By the time you finish this book you will discover that, in many ways, the opposite is true; that possessions often remain profound and usually the closer our relationships are with objects, the closer our relationships are with people. This is why the first two portraits are called 'Empty' and 'Full'.

The diversity of contemporary London is extraordinary, and begs to be better understood. But, increasingly, people's lives take place behind the closed doors of private houses. How can we gain an insight into what those lives are like today: people's feelings, frustrations, aspirations, tragedies and delights? Not television characters, not celebrities, but real people. How could one ever come to know such things about perfect strangers? We could try and knock on doors and ask to talk with them, to hear their stories. If you can persuade them you are not selling anything, not Jehovah's Witnesses, they might let you in – they did let us in. But asking people about themselves is by no means straightforward. English people, in particular, often seem embarrassed by direct questions about their intimate lives and relationships. Sometimes people from other countries embarrass us in turn, by gushing forth these detailed accounts of their lives. Yet often you feel you are listening to a script; something readily prepared for such an encounter. They sound as much a justification or self-therapy as an account. Language is often defensive, restricted and carefully constructed as narrative. You can ask people about themselves, but the results are often much less informative than one would like.

This book takes you on a different route towards this goal. The questions were not only put directly to the people who opened their doors. We also put our questions to the interior of the house. We asked what decorations hung on the walls, what the people who greeted us were wearing, what we were asked to sit on, what style of bathroom we peed in, whose photographs were on display, what collections were arrayed on mantelpieces. This might seem a rather absurd thing to do. How can one ask questions of things that cannot speak for themselves?

Objects surely don't talk. Or do they? The person in that living-room gives an account of themselves by responding to questions. But every object in that room is equally a form by which they have chosen to express themselves. They put up ornaments; they laid down carpets. They selected furnishing and got dressed that morning. Some things may be gifts or objects retained from the past, but they have decided to live with them, to place them in lines or higgledy-piggledy; they made the room minimalist or crammed to the gills. These things are not a random collection. They have been gradually accumulated as an expression of that person or household. Surely if we can learn to listen to these things we have access to an authentic other voice. Yes, also contrived, but in a different way from that of language. I don't pretend to be Sherlock Holmes or Poirot, let alone CSI sleuthing for clues to solve a puzzle. The detectives and forensics tend to look at the inadvertent, while in this book I feel I am paying proper respect to that which some people have themselves crafted as patiently as any artist, as an outward expression of themselves. The original painters of these portraits are the people who appear in this book.

And what pictures they painted. Our only hypothesis in starting this work was that we had no idea what we would find on this entirely ordinary-looking street. This proved correct. Could I have imagined that one morning we would meet a man who was responsible for the death of dozens of innocent people, and, on the very same afternoon, a woman who had fostered dozens of the most deprived children of the area? I didn't expect to participate in the most charmed Christmas since *Fanny and Alexander*, or to hear how a CD collection helped someone overcome heroin. I didn't know you could find vintage Fisher Price toys on eBay or expect to hear such a convincing paean to the wonderful world of McDonald's Happy Meals. I had no reason to see a logical connection between a laptop and the customs of Australian Aboriginals. I hadn't thought of Estonia as an outer London suburb, or understood the potential of tattoos for controlling memory. I had no reason to expect this ordinary London street to include such sexual exhibitionism, or the tyranny of Feng Shui. I didn't know one could care for a dog with quite such tenderness, or really find life starting at sixty. I hadn't registered quite how devastating divorce can be for children; I had underestimated the vast range of objects that people collect and why exactly they collect them. I wouldn't have guessed that teaching sociology might fit well with wrestling, or anticipated that image of goats looking amazed at basketball champions. I hadn't predicted that I would get such an opportunity to share my affection for John Peel, or learn about prostitutes and custard. Above all, I sort of expected, but couldn't really fully imagine, the sadness of lives and the comfort of things.

This is also a book about Londoners. The people of London deserve something better than the categories we generally use to describe them. London is unprecedented. Never before have so many people from such diverse backgrounds been free to mix, and not to mix, in close proximity to each other. At first this was described in terms of Londoners and others: the multi-culturalism of the Greater London Council; the recognition of specific populations from the Caribbean or South Asia. But London today has moved well beyond ethnic minorities. Indeed, it was even then the case that the Londoner next door might have been from Greece or the United States. Yes, there is a huge increase in people from Eastern Europe, but the neighbour today might also be from South Korea, Brazil or South Africa as well as Irish, Pakistani or Jewish. Maybe it is better to start by seeing the typical London household as a Norwegian married to an Algerian. What, then, is typical? What can lead us beyond such categories?

Nor is this just a problem concerned with place of birth. Gender isn't what it used to be. Being gay came to form another minority, but this labelling, too, fails to do justice to the range of people we meet. There are quite a few gay people present in this book, but it wasn't clear by the end that they had a whole lot in common other than being gay. Similarly with class; one man seemed to convey the stereotype of a masculine worker propping up the bar at the pub; who would have little in common with an acupuncturist; and yet it was the latter who turned out to come from working-class Romford, while the former was doing summer work while at university. Categories create assumptions. But older people now want to keep on clubbing, middle classes have an affectation for cockney. Is that the *au pair* or your wife?

Nevertheless, London is most definitely not a free for all. People may still suffer from crushing constraints. Class can still be a creature of limited educational possibilities. People are still stereotyped by racism. Men and women still make derogatory remarks and have problematic expectations about each other. But still, London seems to be a place where people can confound and confuse expectations, and for me, observing London, perhaps the healthiest option is to acknowledge generalisations and categories when they emerge, but to at least try and not to start from these. Because it just may be that the generalisations emerge best, not from place of origin or gender, but around an orientation to science or celebrity, gardening or church.

This book is an experiment designed to find people without recourse to such categories. Not to research them by picking them in the first place as tokens of 'man', 'Asian', or 'working class'. Instead, this book has acknowledged and exploited the unprecedented nature of modern London. That not just a few streets, but most streets today contain a mixture of homes – some, housing association; some, privately owned; big houses divided into maisonettes; and some smaller houses being gentrified. That where migrants once settled in particular areas, they have now tended to disperse widely. And because most people can't even tell you the names of their neighbours, there is little pressure to homogenise around a neighbourhood. So this book is about a random street that I had no reason to choose. It was undertaken in that liberal spirit of taking people as you find them and letting them emerge as they would.

To do that, we had to pick one random street in the first place, and then try to persuade the people to let you into their homes. This wasn't easy, but, by dint of spending seventeen months on a single street, we reached our goal of one hundred individuals and households and had only eight final refusals, providing what may be as close to a genuine slice of London as one is ever going to reach. In fact the street turned out to match well our lack of expectations. Only twenty-three per cent were actually born in London, and there were no minorities more significant than any others. People came from everywhere and anywhere, and they were old, young, very gendered and sort of gendered, well off, badly off, and mainly sort of OK off. But this is what is special about London, and what this book is about: thirty portraits which pay respect to whoever these people happen to be and which, between them, paint a bigger portrait that starts to emerge as an image of the modern world. They are presented here not in sequence but juxtaposed, in the same manner that they live together on this street. One house gives no clue at all as to what you will find in the next and there is rarely much orientation to the street itself.

I call these chapters portraits because I employ an approach that may have become somewhat passé in mainstream anthropology, a form of holism. A feeling that, in many cases, there is an overall logic to the pattern of these relationships to both persons and things, for which I use the word 'aesthetic'. By choosing this term I don't mean anything technical or artistic, and certainly I hope nothing pretentious. It simply helps convey something of the overall desire for harmony, order and balance that may be discerned in certain cases – and also dissonance, contradiction and irony in others. In learning anthropology, I had been taught to look for such an overarching sense of order in relation to the much wider study of society or culture. On this street it seemed useful to see individuals and individual households as somehow analogous to a society. So each of these portraits is sketched, and then filled in, according to what seemed to be the style of those sitting for their portrait: some comic, some tragic, some cubist, some impressionist, some bleak and some exuberant. You can read this book as you might move through a gallery. You should pay attention to the details, but then consider each composition as a whole, and finally ponder how each contributes to the pattern represented by the book as a whole. This is not Hogarth or Goya; there is no satire or parody, no horrors I set out to expose. I am an academic, trying to listen to and learn from the same materials that are here on exhibition.

In the conclusion I return to my more familiar academic style and consider the wider picture that emerges when you take the array of portraits as an entry into understanding modern life. I start by acknowledging that these contemporary London households bear little relation to the assumed objects of social science. This is not a society or culture, a neighbourhood or a community. Yet at the same time this is not a picture of the fragmentation, individualism and anomie that were assumed to follow from the absence of societies and neighbourhoods. Instead I focus on what seems to matter most to the people themselves: their ability to form relationships, and the nature of those relationships. Relationships which flow constantly between persons and things. Using illustrations from these portraits, I discuss the way people create this aesthetic; that is an order, or style, which can be discerned across a range of quite different types of relationship. I conclude that there is a hitherto unsuspected way in which an anthropological, rather than psychological, approach can be found appropriate for such an analysis of individual households. This follows from seeing the street as a fieldsite on a par with New Guinea: a diverse collection of societies, each to be respected as a cosmological order in its own right. Just as we have traditionally learnt from the study of the diversity of societies, so also we can learn from the diversity of these microcosms. But, to do this, we need to respect their authenticity and not to dismiss them as superficial.

Anthropology is the discipline which tries to engage with the minutiae of everyday life while retaining a commitment to understanding humanity as a whole. This book tries to remain consistent with that ambition by bringing together these general questions as to the nature of modern life, with an ethnographic immersion in, and a wonder at, the world of small things and intimate relationships that fill out our lives.

At this point you are invited to turn to the portraits themselves. Each is designed around two aims: an experiment in learning how to read people through their possessions; and to help us appreciate the diversity and creativity of contemporary Londoners. But if you would like to know more about how this study was done, and important issues of selection, ethics and anonymity, then please turn to the Appendix first.

Portrait 1

EMPTY

George's flat was disorienting not because of anything that was in it, but precisely because it contained nothing at all, beyond the most basic carpet and furniture. Absence of a degree doesn't particularly disturb. A place can be minimalist, or there can be a single plant or poster that gathers presence precisely through contrast with the lack of any other resting place for the eye. But there is always something: a little china ornament, a postcard from a trip somewhere, an image of a friend or relative, even an old ticket stub or label. What I can barely ever remember encountering is a habitation entirely devoid of any form of decoration. There is a violence to such emptiness. Faced with nothing, one's gaze is not returned, attention is not circumscribed. There is a loss of shape, discernment and integrity. There is no sense of the person as the other, who defines one's own boundary and extent. I was trying to concentrate on what he was saying, but I was disturbed by the sheer completeness of this void. I began to feel we simply had to visit the other rooms in his house, his bedroom and his bathroom, in the hope that they would not replicate this chilling absence. But when, during a subsequent visit we did take opportunities to glance around these other rooms, they proved just as empty.

This emptiness in someone's surroundings, that leaches away one's own sense of being, was only enhanced by our experience of George himself. Even a space this empty wouldn't have felt quite so disturbing if it had become filled with the presence of the man. His stories, his attachments and relationships could have re-populated the space, turned this room back into a living-room. But, from the time he started speaking, it was evident that there was no counterbalance between person and place, rather that the flat was the man. It was the way he responded to each thing said to him. Usually when one speaks to another person there is an automatic moment of introspection, a sense that a person has looked inside themselves for the answer, interrogated themselves; so instantly and so obviously that we rarely think of that process. But with George there is the feeling that, at least in the first instance, he seeks to answer each question by interrogating the shape and form of the question itself. He presumes that all questions are formulaic, derived from those bureaucratic situations which have made up the bulk of his encounters with the outside world. Such questions merely seek appropriate answers; they don't want their time wasted with detailed and irrelevant information about an actual person. They demand an answer that instantly confirms one of the three or six categories of answer that can be used as bureaucratic data.

So George ponders what it is that this question is formulated to obtain. If every animal trap has a highly specific shape designed to catch some particular animal, then what kind of trap is this question, what shape or form should George transform into to satisfy it? He never answers quickly, he ponders. With us there is an additional worry because our questions and conversation tend not to fit his previous experiences. They don't sound as straightforward as the usual questions of officialdom, but they don't have that comfortable emptiness of polite English questions designed merely to prevent the impoliteness of silence; questions about the weather or what's on television. But often, after a while, George shifts from looking anxious to a broad deep smile, and it is clear that he has decided what category of question this is and what the appropriate response should be.

There is a mechanical, impersonal quality in his measured replies that makes one aware of the materiality of sound. He speaks always in complete sentences. He will talk about himself, but it is as though he is describing this external person to another. Two examples may help:

'I do not have a motorcar. If I had a motorcar someone would vandalise it. In a way I don't want a car because of this type of thing. I do not want to go outside, and find something's gone wrong. I don't want anything of that nature.'

The other refers to the only picture we eventually found on display in the entire flat.

'No. I've not been, but that picture's of the Scilly Isles, off the coast of Cornwall. This is an atlas of the world. I've always been interested in world-type geography. This is my best atlas, my book of world geography. If you don't want to look, I understand, but to me geography was one of my favourite subjects when I was at school. This is what I used to look at. If the subject was geography this was one of the books I used to look at.'

Often, when he has finished speaking, he will ask: 'Does this satisfy you?' Or before saying anything else, he will first ask: 'Can I just say something?' Often, instead of elaborating, he will think for a while and then simply say, 'I think the answer to that is no', or 'I think I shall answer yes to that question'. He seems anxious that the answer given is complete, that no one is muddled, that any additional information could complicate things.

This way of speaking is matched by the deliberate precision in his appearance. A seventy-five-year-old for whom dressing has the aura of an obligatory routine. The black creased and ironed trousers, the clean knitted jersey, the striped socks matched to the slippers. One can imagine him dressing incredibly slowly and carefully, moving up his shirt from one button to the next, putting on his tie with great care, perhaps several times over, until it was just right. This is a man for whom putting on the second sock would be an entirely separate activity from putting on the first sock.

The immediate temptation is to classify George as lacking something in himself. As being slow on the uptake, or whatever the appropriate medical term would have been. Actually that phrase, 'slow on the uptake', seems to fit his manner perfectly. But, as we listen to him carefully, I increasingly feel that this would be wrong. As George's story unfolds, something else emerges: that there is nothing innately slow about George, but rather he has become what we encounter as a result of all that has, or more importantly has not, happened to him. There is something else not going on here. Just putting a label on him would be to substitute effect for cause.

Notwithstanding the emptiness of his own surroundings, George remembers places that had their own decoration. His grandmother had 'proper' pictures on the wall, ones that, he reckons, were worth something. His father had pictures of birds – 'English type birds, not foreign birds'. He remembers his grandmother's house as a big house. He had no siblings. What he seems to have had from the beginning was a sense of tyranny, of being completely under the control of an authority. All later authority became a copy of the original and most total exemplification of authority, which was his parents. It appears that every time he might have been allowed to do something or go somewhere, or become somebody, his parents prevented it and he was powerless to do other than their will. When the war broke out he was supposed to be sent away from home, but his mother desperately tried to fight this. When she failed and he had to leave, he became sick immediately, to the extent that the officials relented and he returned to spend the war in London with his mother. Similarly, although he passed his examinations such that he could have stayed on at school, his parents took him out of school and refused to allow him to continue. He worked from 16 to 18 and then passed a test to go into the navy, but this was countermanded by his father, who sent him to the army. These references to his ability to pass examinations and tests don't seem to suggest any intrinsic slowness of thought.

George describes such events without any evident rancour or bitterness, but in his typical slow descriptive monologue. But he seems entirely aware of the constant unfairness and constraints in his life, an example being the impact of his parents. At one time he was in the army. He never saw active service, something he attributed to his parents: 'No I never left the British Isles. That's another thing. My father and mother have always said "You are not to go outside the borders of the British Isles".' In fact when he was twenty-one he did eventually go on a trip organised by his evening class to Sweden, but that was the nearest point he ever seems to have come to an actual revolt against his parents' wishes. He never again went abroad. At one point he noted 'my father was even worse than my mother'.

School clearly made quite an impression on George as a social environment outside his home. He still thinks of much of life in terms of subjects that are taught at school, such as geography. He has clear memories of his time at school, wearing short trousers, serving in the church. Teachers seem to have captured something of his parents' authoritarian role. In turn, this sense of authority was transferred to his encounters with employers, and now increasingly with bureaucrats. After the war he obtained work as a clerk in a large company. He worked there until he was fifty-five, when he was retired under protest, since he wanted to continue at least to sixty. He continued to look for employment, turning up regularly at the employment exchange, but this was to be his last job. He has been in this enforced retirement for twenty-one years. The decades at work seem to occupy very little space in his life. Yet one could easily imagine him in one of those black and white newsreels which show an Edwardian vista of offices with rows and rows and rows of identical looking men filling in identical looking ledgers. In meeting George, it felt as though one was meeting the last of those clerks.

On our first visit it was probably clear we were searching around for material things to talk about, and so when we returned he had carefully gone through his possessions and finally found in a drawer a postcard from a lady in Spain. There was a story attached. He had been asked:

'Would I be willing to meet her at the airport and take her to the house where she was going to live. I'd never met her before. I said how can I recognise a lady at the airport like that? I was told I was to go to an address in Fulham where the lady was going to live. I'd never been to the road before. So when the day came I was told to go to London airport and sit on the chair outside the entrance to number 4. I had to find number 4 and sit in the chair and wait for the lady to come up and speak to me. I wouldn't recognise her. She was supposed to come up and speak to me. I sat there for hours. I was wondering if the whole thing had been cancelled when suddenly a young lady came up and spoke to me, told me what her name was and said now are you going to take me to the house in Fulham? So I took her.'

It seemed as though any request to take responsibility for an action was quite exceptional. That he had been singled out, taken from a row of desks and asked as an individual to do something. One could still feel his fear of that responsibility. Almost the only memories that stand out from that period are the deaths of his parents, and the responsibilities he had for the funerals. It sounded as though the terrifying prospect of having to deal with the funerals was as memorable as the deaths themselves. Maybe George had then, or has now, some form of mental retardation. But what I sensed was more a fear of having to act as an agent of his own fate. His account suggested that, for some reason, his parents used him, their only child, to give themselves a singular experience of total authority. An authority that sucked out his core, the basis for any expression of his own will, leaving him ever after dependent upon authority, teachers, employers and always also a dependency upon the officialdom of the state. The flat was empty, completely empty, because its occupant had no independent capacity to place something decorative or ornamental within it.

In order to be in range of his work, George went to live at a YMCA, which provided care for him in the way his own home had. He really couldn't imagine staying anywhere else. But, finally, at the age of thirty-three, it was clear that he no longer counted as 'young', and he was told he would have to move out. The manager helped him find another hostel, which lasted around five years, after which he was moved to the hostel he had stayed in right until the time he was moved to his present flat. Just a year before we met him, this hostel was closed down. He simply assumed he would be moved to yet another hostel. He was told to apply for one. As he put it. 'And I filled in four different forms, transfer forms, and they altered them. They were checked by members of staff. And I ended up nowhere.' As often when George talks, there is that terrible sadness in his particular phrasing that makes it completely clear that George knows that on every such occasion he could only ever have been considered as an afterthought. He watched as each occupant left for a new place. He talks about them being taken away in a motor-car. The last one left in a minicab. No one thought to give him a forwarding address, so there would be no way he could keep in touch with any of them in the future. Finally there was no one left but him. Even then, no one seems to have been concerned with George. It was only the care-taker/support worker who was confronted with the fact that he had to be dealt with when she wanted to take a holiday. At that point she informed him that he would be moved to the flat he now occupies. 'But I did not want to live alone by myself. But these people, all these experts, said this was the only suitable and available place for me. So here I am.'

A van was supposed to pick him up at midday. It broke down. He waited. Eventually at 3.00 p.m. another van came for him. They packed up his things. Not even the support worker came with him to this new flat – just the two removal men. They brought him and moved his possessions, first to the pavement, then to the flat itself. The sofa couldn't go up the stairs. It had to be brought in by ladder through the window. It was George's first ever sofa. Even if he had no ornaments, he still needed basic carpet and furnishing. But no one had given thought to this. All the good furnishings went somewhere else. Finally there were a few seconds and leftovers remaining, and he was asked to select from these – which is exactly what he has in his flat today. They came from the lounge of his hostel. His sofa matched another one there, and he requested both, but he was turned down.

So, for the first time in his life at the age of seventy-five, George found himself alone in a flat of his own, without any company at all. Even worse for George was that, for the very first time, he was expected to learn to look after himself. That was excessively hard for him, as he puts it:

'I don't like shopping. I had to pull myself together and do it for myself otherwise I'd have no food to start with. So I pulled myself together and do all my own shopping. I do all my shopping myself. Nobody does cooking for me. That's my worst subject. Whether I like it or not I've had to get on with it, I've had to learn how to do it.'

This phrase, that cooking is 'my worst subject', comes up many times in George's conversation.

George was dumped into his new flat ten days before Christmas. The date was significant. There had been nine people in the hostel during the previous year; two of those went away before Christmas and the remainder stayed on for a Christmas dinner together, surrounded by Christmas decorations. That, at least, had been company. This year, at Christmas, George was alone, just as he had been for the rest of the year. So now we can see why George's flat remained empty. Because, even supposing that George had had the will, the sense of his own ability to take objects or images and use them to decorate this flat; supposing that he felt the psychological strength to do such a thing – in fact, even if the whole bloody flat was stuffed to the gills with inconsequential paraphernalia – it would still have been a completely empty flat. An emptiness without that at one with the emptiness within himself. This was the other reason there were no decorations. There was just no point.

George has now settled into some sort of routine. He goes out about three times a month into central London. He refers to this as going there on business, for example to pay a tax. These expeditions have become major reference points in his life. He may also go out for a haircut. His one point of social contact is with a meeting of Old Age Pensioners at a church hall he attends from time to time. He simply observes that they are mainly female, that they are all poor, that they are all old, but above all that they are not at all happy. His only other outing has been to his one distant relative with whom he remains in touch, a market gardener. He has been to visit their farm a few times over his life. His description of his most recent visit is typically frustrating. It was clear that on some previous occasion he had been taken to see the breeding pigs on a nearby farm. This made a huge impression upon him and he was desperate to see them again. Throughout the visit he had been waiting and hoping that this experience would be repeated, but, being George, he had never actually asked his hosts or indicated his desire. As a result, although he had been taken to see the cows, he was not on this occasion given the opportunity to re-visit the pigs. The way he talks, in some awe, about the 'lady pigs' suggests that maybe an earlier visit was one of the very few occasions when he has directly witnessed any kind of sexual activity. This inability to act for himself in the world is especially evident when it comes to discussion of those things he would most wish to do. One of his prime ambitions is to visit Kew Gardens. He has been there three times, but the last visit was some thirty years before. When we ask where he would most like to live, he can only think of the YMCA.

By far the most important of the outings he does manage for himself is to view Royal pageantry, especially the Trooping of the Colour. He has gone to this ceremony annually for the last twenty-five years. He cannot usually go to the key ceremonies, because these days he finds them too crowded and noisy, and if there is a ticket required, he cannot afford it. So the highlight of his life is most likely to be a rehearsal of the Trooping of the Colour. George is more than simply a royalist. One could imagine the appeal for him of a movement such as fascism, itself an experiment in aesthetics. Fascism attempted to attach to itself individual identity through the participation of each person in its aesthetics. From the Nuremberg rallies to the charisma and oratory of its leaders, fascism spoke directly to every member of that society in a manner that entranced and made them feel like a pixel in a picture – a picture which was beautiful in its completeness and superior to anything that mere individuals could accomplish by themselves.

George had nothing to mediate this direct relationship between himself and the state. The state has become his mother and father, his teacher and his bureaucrat. The constant oppressor who determines his fate and his only resource – the one that feeds him, clothes him, accommodates him and otherwise ignores him in its own sheer unimaginable superiority to him. It would not even condescend to find out about him anything in excess of what it needs to know in order to deal with him. No wonder, then, that, when the state appears in its full majesty, an unbearable but unrefusable beauty, it draws him like a moth to fire. This exquisite, violent, regal glory that constitutes British history before him and will last forever after him, and which justifies the sheer inconsequential lack of his mere being. Why should he matter in front of Her Majesty parading down the Mall? It was his greatest privilege merely to bear witness and be in thrall to this power, this majestic procession of red and gold and bayonets. He needed to be there to justify all that he was and all that he wasn't.

Not surprisingly, over the years this pure form of authority has started to become an interiorised vision, often reducible to the expression 'them'. One of the most common ways for George to finish his replies is with the expression 'we will leave it at that' with a wry smile. It seems as though on these occasions he knows there is more, he has located something about himself that could have formed part of the response, but sagely he has opted for discretion. Because, on occasion, when something does slip through and he starts to talk beyond the answer, it turns out that this was not the result of introspection but of paranoia. On those occasions he has decided to share with us something of what he knows about 'them': the force outside, that which would be displeased to know that we have come to visit him, that which is watching us and him, that which we should be alerted to and careful of. The particular things they don't like, such as him going to visit some place or the presence of loud music, suggest that 'they' began in his head as admonishing statements by hostel staff. Being unanswerable and repressed, they hardened like gallstones into permanent and painful interior voices that can no longer be dislodged. Often his statements are not couched as opinions but as something that 'everyone' would say: a generic disapproval of loud noises, or of gossiping with neighbours, where his own voice has become merely an expression of 'the voices'. Perhaps this is why he will watch television but doesn't have a radio. Its disembodied voice is perhaps too close to his unrelenting experience of the voices within.

No doubt George will continue his encounter with the state, from its most lowly officials to its most refined and pure aesthetic. But from now on there is really only one more event that has yet to take place for George, and even that is simply a repetition of the same event that had occurred to his parents. He speaks of his one remaining distant cousin, the one with the farm:

'She knows exactly where I'm to be buried. That's where my mother and father are. When I die she'll come to London, pick up the body and take it to F . . . Then they can decide what to do with it. There's a church in F . . . It will most likely go straight to S . . . crematorium and every-body will go back to F . . . and that'll be the end of it. I'll be cremated.' George has had a will made up. He was once told that people get very excited if they are mentioned in a will. His cousin is the only person George knows, so this is the person to whom George will leave . . . absolutely nothing.

During our time on this street we heard and encountered many tragedies, people who faced all manners of diseases and degradations, who nearly died, who actually died, whose children had been killed. There is no escaping the horror and tragedy in the interior of people's lives. But it was particularly after meeting George that we found our-selves in tears after leaving his flat. Because in every other instance there was a sense that, at least, that person had once lived. With George, by contrast, one simply couldn't escape the conclusion that this was a man, more or less waiting for his time on earth to be over, but who at age of seventy-six had never yet seen his life actually begin. And, worse still, he knew it.

Portrait 2

FULL

The curtain opens on a scene from the *The Nutcracker*; a lounge and drawing-room resplendent with Christmas decorations. In the bay window is the most perfect Christmas tree, topped by a fairy whose clear features and hand-made white net costume provides the apex to the array of silver and gold baubles and delicately crafted ornaments that adorn every branch and indent the tree offers for decoration. None is too large or gaudy, there is nothing plastic or vulgar. At the foot of the tree larger presents lie scattered. On a table in front of the tree is a nativity scene, unusual in that both crib and figures are of plain unpainted wood, tall austere kings looming over the cradle. They seem unimpressed by the glitter and sparkle of the myriad lights reflected in the silver tinsel which occupies any spare niche of wall and ceiling that lends itself to additional adornment.

From the centre of each ceiling there hangs an elaborate contrivance of circles and spokes from which are suspended a hundred tiny little parcels, wrapped up in green and red crepe. The diversity of shapes discernible through the wrapping promises an array of presents, each individually selected. Collected over the year, they might be a wooden ornament, a cigarette lighter, or, sometimes, just a lump of coal. The shapes have become only partly discernible in their careful wrapping, enhancing the sense of mystery and promise. Each one is designated by a small number stuck onto the surface. Green tinsel weaves its way along these lines and circles of parcels, punctuated by small lights. Tinsel and lights extend from the centre of each room to the corners and in additional arcs along the walls, from corner to corner. On closer inspection, the lights are found to be small antique glass in the shape of miniature Chinese lanterns, with hand-painted designs. Between the two rooms there must be close on a hundred of them. They are neither dull nor bright, but simply sufficient to diffuse a generous sprinkling of light that seems to come from everywhere.

In one corner sits a portly and elderly gentleman, stooped over a desk. In one hand he holds pliers with which he deftly works many lines of gold cord, together with ornaments and lights; repairing, setting, arranging and lovingly creating additional pieces still to be set, though at first there seems to be no place left that could yet bear them. The combination of patience and precision suggests a craftsman, who brings to this task years of experience garnered from professional work. One senses that this task is one he has given himself year after year, decade after decade. This tradition, so far from making the task seem dull or repetitive, has rather enshrined this particular time of the year as the climax, as a period of feverish excitement against which the rest of the year pales, creating a grey background to highlight the colour and splendour of the season. This seems to be his moment. Just as years of repetition and experimentation lie behind the integrity of the room decorations, which now appear as a natural and ideal fit to the interior space; so his skills of concentration and fingerwork have developed to fit perfectly to this task – which more than any paid labour, so fully expresses the person.

For, in truth, this is not a scene from a *Nutcracker*; no dancers are waiting in the wings, no curtain has opened. It is just another ordinary terraced house in an ordinary terraced street. And yet no childhood memory of the *Nutcracker*, no lithograph of Cratchit and his family, no West End store window or specialist Christmas shop in Alsace or National Trust recreation has ever appealed as this lounge and dining-room setting of Christmas. Only Bergman's film *Fanny and Alexander* seems to capture its significance. It is the product of a century of devotion to the cultivation of Christmas itself. There are no plastic baubles. The Chinese lights were first collected by the father of the man now working the gold threads. The original collection grew until these Chinese lanterns were no longer for sale as a result of the Second World War. Each year since has added its own contributions of other ornaments. The hand-crafted wooden nativity scene is from the Philippines, bought on a visit fifteen years ago. This year's contributions include some blue glass discs with painted Christmas scenes, suspended as part of the ceiling decoration. They were purchased a few months earlier from a shop specialising in Christmas decorations in Prague. The only other innovation of the current year is a rearrangement of some of the lighting in the hall. That is sufficient. Changes are slight and careful, tested for a year or two and then incorporated or rejected. The house has been adapted through this same gradual evolution, so that now the chandelier slides across to make way for the hanging of the numbered gifts, and there has been extensive re-wiring with many additional fitments, such that no part of the room is excluded from its contribution to the season.

Behind this labour of love lies the labour which is love, something that becomes evident as soon as one is able to observe how this Christmas scene fulfils its ultimate purpose: when it shifts from foreground to background; and becomes merely the setting to celebration, to conviviality, chatter, drinking, feasting, gossiping and re-acquainting. During this season of family visiting there will be careful acknowledgement of all that has happened in the year past, celebrating what each individual who passes through this scene has in turn contributed. If young enough, they will take their presents from beneath the tree. But at the same time their own experiences and achievements of that year are brought and laid at the foot of the tree in the form of conversation, listening and appreciation.

While the elderly man has been bent over his work, his wife has been busy in the kitchen. This year there are eighty-one home-made mince pies as well as bowls of fruit salad, and many supermarket goodies, from puddings to stilton. These have to be unrefusably good, since she knows that they will be encountered by family and friends already stuffed with the turkey, ham and other savouries that she has also prepared. The single most important marking of the season for this couple is that every one of their-five children and ten grandchildren, the latter ranging from five to twenty five, will at some stage come and partake of their Christmas festivities. And this year they will achieve this goal.

Most, but not all, will appear on Christmas Day itself. For, in truth, no in-laws have ever managed to put up serious competition to this year-long devotion to the one season. Usually those who cannot make it on the day itself arrive during the subsequent days, until, four days after Christmas, all are accounted for, bulked up by friends, neighbours and other seasonal visitors – this year even anthropologists. No meal lasts less than three to four hours. A century or more of accumulation has somehow been transmuted into the holism of the scene itself, just as generations of experience and expertise have gone into this cultivation of sociability – that sociability which is the front stage to these celebrations. The connection between this devotion to persons and to things is nothing obvious or intrusive; rather, it flows so naturally that it may take a certain academic, critical distance just to come to an awareness of its being there at all.

It was there at the moment when Mrs Clarke interrupts her conversation with you abruptly because she has caught sight of one of the children who is just about to open a parcel. At first she says nothing to the child; she merely makes sure that the parents do not miss the implications. Do they want the present opened now; will they ensure a record is kept of whom it is from so that its receipt can be properly acknowledged; is there a sense of occasion appropriate to the opening? Otherwise the social meaning will be lost. A child cares little about the whos and the whys and merely latches onto a – now anonymous – toy with the naked greed and hedonism of childhood. But that would be the kind of waste which is most abhorred in this family: the waste of an opportunity for social appreciation.

That sociability is there, again, when Mr Clarke seems to know exactly how to choreograph the provision of drinks without as much as turning around. The low, base notes of ordinary white wine, tea and fizzy drinks need to be punctuated by special high notes. A bottle of champagne should never just be opened; it must occasion squeals of delight and be bubbly in its conviviality as well as in its consumption. An old port should only be opened when those who drink it will appreciate its particular and special nature. This means that it won't emerge at all this Christmas, no one is in that kind of mood; they are too flippant and the banter is too light. But that doesn't matter – it doesn't even matter that port is out of fashion right now. It lies upstairs and will come down in ten years, if need be, at any rate only when Mr Clarke has a sense that a moment of proper appreciation would follow upon its entrance. So, when the party is on an even keel, it needs simply to be kept supplied; but when it needs some extra sparkle either he or his wife know that there is something special, some little extra firelighter to rekindle any embers already starting to lose their power to keep winter at bay.

But, more than food and drink, what they are alert to is achievement: any conversation that happens to mention what this or that person has managed for themselves or for others during the course of the year. The single most important ingredient to this recipe of love is appreciation. No one is less important than another, no one should have to claim credit for themselves. When any new visitor arrives, they will hear an ever-growing list: of this one, who has gained a place at Nottingham to study physics, and of that one, who did better than expected at their GCSE exams (or would have done, but for the unfortunate coincidence of illness or a poor teacher). Everyone can be excited by the promise of the new job that a nephew is about to start, surely more interesting and less oppressive than the one he is now due – or rather overdue – to leave. Did the visitor miss the story about this grandson's holiday in Morocco, or that this granddaughter is starting to go out with someone more regularly? These too are little lights, hand-crafted, none outshining another, all patiently collected and displayed, all contributing to the col-lectivity that is family and friendship – the twin spirits of Christmas pre-sent.

Christmas is the festival which unites the general and the particular; it is the most universal in the sense that everyone, in a hundred coun-tries – today, even non-Christian countries – is imagined to be cele-brating the same thing on the same day. Yet it is simultaneously the most specific of all the festivals, since no one else ever celebrates Christmas in the way 'we' celebrate it. The festival brings the majesty of the greatest to the least. The traditional English Christmas moves, during the day, from the divine family to the royal family to our own family. Each celebrant brings their own unique traditions.

And this family is no exception. Take, for example, those little parcels, wrapped up and suspended by string at the centre of each ceiling. Each visitor picks a number from a hat which corresponds to a number on one of the parcels, and this is then theirs to harvest. In this manner, the background decorations enter into the foreground of social interaction, to be consumed along with the food and drink, so that everyone ends the day feeling bloated with consideration and company.

This book contains thirty portraits selected from a hundred households, but, if I recall one moment of greatest pleasure, it was in the presence of this family. This happened not in the year when we participated in their Christmas celebration, but in the following year, when we arrived in their house during the decoration of the tree. At that point we were confronted by these same objects in their other aspect, as one of the family collections. There were well over eight hundred ornaments designated just for the tree alone, now laid out on the carpet and tables – from foot-long spikes to delicate traceries of glass angels. Arrays in every hue of metallic colour, reminiscent of the reflections and fragility of bubbles; accompanied by filigrees of wire; with tiny scenes, such as a crèche indented in a cave-like space within a sphere. Hundreds of distorted versions of oneself reflected in silver and gold balls and baubles. Choristers and fairies; sea-horses and miniature ribboned parcels; the commonplace and the rare. That was the occasion when we heard the many stories of how they had been accumulated from shops in the neighbourhood to sites all around the world. The highlight was when we were allowed to hang some of the decorations on the tree ourselves. Although Jewish, I was brought up with a full English Christmas; to be granted back my own eight-year-old self so unexpectedly and effectively, in the middle of fieldwork, was sheer delight.

What was remarkable about the Clarkes was the scope of their sensitivity. It somehow managed to include so many people and so many things and yet always to give full consideration and care to that specific person or thing. It was a gradual refinement in the skills of knowing just what would comfort this person, or supplement that collection, or be precisely the right time to offer a particular thought. The source of this particular form of sensitivity lies in the relationship between Mr and Mrs Clarke, the sense that no two people could possibly know more about each other; and this made them only more interested in, and appreciative of, the smallest possible detail of each other's lives. It's evident in the banter between them. Each is constantly correcting the other, adding details, making sure the date is accurate, often flatly contradicting the other. In some couples, this would imply getting at each other; in others, it would be merely correcting. But in their case it becomes clear after a while that they are actually perfecting each other. They are gifting each other the mutual integrity of their own sense of truth. Something this close could never have developed without what was, most likely, some manner of division and difficulty between them in the past, perhaps over decades. This is not some seamless blending of two smooth surfaces – such powerfully bonded love never is. It is the much stronger and gradual meshing over decades of what once must have included jagged edges and mismatched bits of personality.

But today, in the tightness of their own relationship, they form a safety net which can then protect an increasing number of relatives, friends and others they feel responsible for. As it has expanded, more and more people have come to rely on it. This is the couple who would volunteer to take school outings to the seaside, to intervene in a problem in the locality, to look after a child whose parents needed to be away, to act as school governors or to organise a celebration. Typically, with their own family they manage to keep things complex rather than simple. Unlike most families, they have not been reduced to individual relationships with each separate descendant. Something happens, say, to a pet, to a grandchild, or in relation to the repair of a windowpane – and, somehow, several different family members will be involved, giving of their time, labour, money or advice, so that bonds develop between their descendants and not just vertically, with the older generation. But it is hard to isolate the mechanism behind all this. There is a generosity of spirit whose virtue lies partly in not drawing attention to itself – in particular, in remaining hidden to its recipient. If you want to observe the precision and delicacy of their care, it is better to start by observing their attention to things.

Take for example Mr Clarke and his stamp collection. This is merely one in a series of collections which include the Christmas ornaments, toys like Meccano sets, clocks and glass. The collection that probably represents his greatest passion is that of old cars that he can renovate, and there are countless summer days when, walking up and down the street – an activity which took up much of our time in this study – we have seen him outside his house, pottering around a vintage car he was bringing back to the land of the almost living. But it may well be the stamp collection that absorbs most of his time. Started when he was eight, it now consists of many albums, mainly based on British and Commonwealth/ Empire stamps, plus little satellites such as a collection of Russian stamps. More unusually, he also has a passion for what he calls 'Cinderella' stamps: those never formally used for postage, for instance the stamps representing various taxes paid. He is also fond of his collection of propaganda stamps from both Britain and Germany, which formed part of their respective war efforts.

In most of his collecting and repairing Mr Clarke starts from the skills he developed in his work, from his initial training as a chemist to his subsequent work with cars and, more generally, in engineering. For Mr Clarke all activities, whether caring for a child or caring for a collection, expand from the moral centre of seeing a job well done. The skill of care is always painstaking and technical in its application. So his stamp-collecting is light years away from my memories of just opening up envelopes of assorted colourful and curious items and re-ordering them according to half-remembered geography lessons. Mr Clarke has here a whole tray of solvents, specialist tools, and lights and instruments for detecting rare watermarks or evidence of counterfeiting. As we observe him, he is patiently removing inappropriate hinges from the back of stamps and other, damaging effects of the old methods of storage.

The connection between the way he cares for stamps or Christmas ornaments and the way he has cared for people throughout his life is not just one of analogy. Both activities are properly described as care work in the broadest sense because both are saturated with moral principles – which, if anything, are more explicit in the relation to objects. This is evident in his ambivalence as to the potential financial worth of a stamp collection. He may know that his present action of removing the signs of inappropriate previous treatment would enhance the value of these stamps, but he would be aghast at any suggestion that this is the reason behind his actions. He is scornful of those who collect in the hope of making money, pointing out how their search for commemorative stamps or sheets of stamps tends to undermine value precisely by increasing their popularity: which leaves them worth less than the paper they are printed on. He would never expect a dealer to give you back more than a tenth of what you paid for a stamp. If anything, he has gone

out of his way to make sure his collection is not financially valuable –
which, he is aware would have made him protective or insecure about
its presence. This was never going to be that kind of investment. By contrast, he creates value through the patient juxtaposition of knowledge.
He can talk for hours about the relationship between forms of printing
used on the stamps and other media, or about the way a series reflects
some transformation in the way nature was being appreciated in a particular country at that time. Yet he is not an academic, since his knowledge is not a part of his career or a form of self-presentation, a
testimonial to his being clever or having more knowledge than another.
It is, rather, a natural accoutrement of the act of collecting, the high
degree of professionalism found in all great amateurs.

His morality determines even what he chooses to collect. He scorns
the degree to which stamps become valuable because of a technical mistake, such as when they have been printed backwards or with some rare
fault. He has no interest in such stamps. A friend collects stamps which
have come from the post office of the House of Commons; he sees this
as of limited interest. Because, for him, attention to the craft of collecting – or consuming – these stamps is a direct extension of their history
as craft production, which he fully appreciates in its own right, as both
a chemist and engineer. Intentionality, not happenstance, is the source
of the human value to which he wishes to devote himself. With his magnifying glass, he can show appreciation for the miniature two-tone
scenes that form the centrepiece of many Edwardian and Georgian
stamps or reveal the poignancy of an event – for instance the St Helena
stamps overstamped with the resettlement of Tristan de Cunha, which
followed the volcanic eruption.

A casual observer tends to think of stamp-collecting as a kind of
obsessive, what academics like to call fetishistic, pursuit. But Mr Clarke
is always sensitive to the social relations of the activity itself. He goes to
occasional stamp-collection meetings or to the annual exhibition at
Olympia, but he could never be seen as the kind of stamp geek who
reduces relationships to this one pursuit or, worse still, collects objects
in lieu of a devotion to relationships with people. On the contrary, he
does his best to make sure that each of his descendants has at least the
opportunity to develop a serious interest in the craft, but without ever
pressurising them beyond what seemed to be the natural length of their

interest. So, while currently he spends much of the time devoted to his collection with an eleven-year-old grandchild, he is quite aware that, for the child, this may only be a passing phase. The person he most respected and learnt from was an uncle who was chair of the civil service stamp collection, whose interest was largely due to the meaningful relationship he found there to the history of colonial government. He and his wife do not visit countries specifically because they are represented in his stamp collection but he will use holidays as occasions for visiting stamp shops.

Stamps remain an active conduit to wider knowledge of history and geography, as does his love of cars. He has probably now visited most of the world's leading car museums. While he can apply some of his work skills to stamp-collecting, the real backbone to his integration of work and leisure is the restoration of old cars, since for much of his life he has worked with cars. The car at the front of the house is his second, out of only seven that were made at the time. The other is being restored for him in the US by a specialist who is simply better than anyone currently available in the UK. When it is finished, he will make a formal application for the original number plate.

To see the bridge between concern for objects and concern for people in Mr Clarke requires listening carefully and putting together different stories. After watching him with stamps and with cars, one can observe how careful, patient and crafted is his care for people. This is easier to observe in the case of Mrs Clarke, whose conversation rarely strays from her constant concern with a vast number of friends and relatives. Her collection of people is much more overt, and makes use of many genres associated with being a woman. After a very short time, Fiona starts to feel like an adopted daughter of the house. But it soon becomes apparent how much their practice of care is centred on the way they combine their strengths, and that it always was like this. Some of their best stories about cars relate to their early days, when they were camping or running a youth club for twenty-four children who otherwise would not have been able to afford a summer holiday. Two of their own children met their partners at this club, just as they themselves had originally met at a Catholic youth club. Then there was the occasion when a dozen children would have been left stranded on the beach, but for Mr Clarke's connection with a local bookie and, through him, with someone back in

London who had the right spare part – so that they could repair the vehicle and keep the holiday literally on the road.

Mrs Clarke has her own means of using this expressive relationship to objects as an instrument of her care for people, as is evident at Christmas. Other people, even pets, can also become a means of extending the fundamental love they share. For example, when Mr Clarke was going to hospital for an operation, they both managed constantly to steer conversation towards the plight of their cat, who was due to have a lump removed at more or less the same time. With respect to the cat they could show their emotions, endlessly petting and combing her and showing their affection by calling her, with the utmost tenderness, a 'horrible old scruffy cat'. Mr Clarke would join in telling the cat: 'you'd better be out of hospital when I am out'.

This refusal of self-centredness, even with respect to such important and anxious events as a forthcoming operation, could be taken as mere reticence, an English denial of, or an embarrassment towards, sentiment. Indeed there are other families where that is all it is, and it can quickly become debilitating and even ridiculous. But in the case of the Clarkes, as with everything else about them, reticence was never going to become something shallow, or an affectation that detracted from their humanity. Rather, it is part of their integrity and their depth. Because, for them, this self-effacement forms part of a larger truth which they would never let themselves forget, and comes from their deep religious faith. That what they represent in life comes in large measure from previous generations and needs to live beyond them to pass on to the future. It is this faith that represents for them the ultimate source of their values.

Just as the collection of Christmas lights started in the generation that preceded them, so do many of the traditions that they treasure. Mrs Clarke is happy to recall what she inherited, whether in skills of cooking or in skills of sociability. Christmas ideally is, simply, what it always has been and always should be. This becomes very clear subsequently, when we meet and carry out our research with some of their children. They fondly remember their Gran's house mostly as it was at Christmas; the lights, the baby grand piano, the playing games. But, once again, Christmas merely stands out as the epitome of a much wider set of continuities. In turn, the children are starting to create their own

Christmas, though in truth this is one area where their autonomy is somewhat stymied by the centripetal pull of the Clarkes' celebrations. But, in time, they will achieve it. Already in so many other respects, these children stand out in more or less precisely the same way that their parents do. Even though they married, for all the influence of their partners and of their partners' families, there persists an extraordinary power of continuity that comes across as a direct legacy of Mr and Mrs Clarke.

For the street as a whole, what is shocking is how few households have any relationship to a wider community, let alone giving service to one. So continuity, to this degree of altruistic commitment, is very clearly something inter-generational. It is the Clarkes' children who, in turn, become school governors, serve their time on the committees of gym clubs or wine societies, keep an eye on neighbours' pets and children and generally give of their labour and their time, and not just out of their pocket, to the service of the wider community. Yet they are no clones; different children take up particular aspects of these features of the Clarkes. One child inherits a love of collections; another has no such interests but is quite passionate in his love and devotion to pets.

So while there is continuity, it is always through a kind of creative re-configuration of their inheritance. There is a lovely image of one of the Clarkes' sons who used to get his daughter to sleep with long descriptions of the workings of four-cylinder stroke engines, especially the details of the compression cycle. Yet another successful use of engineering, entirely worthy of Mr Clarke himself. Often these legacies come back together in unexpected ways. One of the children has ended up restoring a car, just like his father. But quite unintentionally. It arrived from an elderly and retired teacher. He had always been the one to fix her car and, at the time when she probably knew that she was dying, she insisted that he keep the car, on the promise of keeping it roadworthy. It was the sort of request that he couldn't refuse and now, after her death, feels is even more unrefusable. So, even though it's a pain to do and in spite of not having much idea of what will become of it, he is in fact restoring it. This is a testimonial to his most important inheritance: the aesthetics of care, which he applies equally and indiscriminately to objects and persons, since one always turns out to be the vehicle for the other. Fortunately, he has also inherited his father's appreciation of the intricacies of machine technologies.

A daughter, by contrast, seems to have inherited her mother's penchant for stuff saturated with the creativity of her own children. A house that seemed almost like one giant dressing up box; full of photographs, bits of material, boxes of cards, school reports and record collections, even a full-size mannequin. But, once again, there is nothing here that could be dismissed as mere mess, in the sense of material left around after its usage is complete. This is stuff left around in ready anticipation of being used, to be imaginatively transformed by some future action. It is a material expression of the breadth and depth of the relationships within that family, and also of the kind of home where you just know that lonely neighbours or less confident schoolfriends of her children will be inexorably drawn in, to try and gain some purchase on this wealth of humanity.

Mostly this continuity is created by example, but, on occasion, even the relationship between the generations can be engineered. Given the sheer accumulation of collections and other materials, it is a job just to conceive of how the Clarkes could manage the inheritance of their possessions to their children. Between them, of course, they developed a whole series of original and imaginative solutions. Even when they were little, the five children had been designated a colour, which helped them to organise themselves at the time and to prevent arguments over flannels and hats and toothbrushes. One of their sons recalled another advantage. When times where hard and the Christmas presents could be little more than a hand-knitted egg-cup warmer, at least they were each given one in their respective colours, which made them seem personal. Recently, each of the children have been invited in turn to put tiny stickers of their respective colour onto any of the furniture and other possessions in the house that one day they would wish to inherit. As with everything in the family, no sense of seriousness is allowed to intrude into what has successfully turned into a game. They can lark around, joke about it, and in the process actually learn to share and retain an overall sense of fairness. They can also express their desire for particular objects such as a canteen of cutlery, in such a manner that it enhances rather than sidelines the care for persons, inseparable from those attachments. This was the Clarkes' way of making a will. Instead of a ponderous sharing out of assets, it was a fun recalling of things which had, over the years, become evocative and therefore valuable to each specific person.

In a similar spirit, the Clarkes often use Christmas for another set of gifts. Although the children may have left home decades before, this is not a family who throws away anything that can be cherished. There are lofts full of childhood toys and other objects, because, however much the children have come and taken their own belongings, there are always more left behind. So now, for one Christmas, the Clarkes may have taken all the old school reports and bundled them up in sacks with ribbons of the respective colours of their children and given them to each, together with the other Christmas presents. Or it may be some of the old toys such as Muffin the Mule or teddy bears. One year it was their medical records; all those little books one tends to be given on visits to the children's clinic. Another year, it was their art works from primary school. Once again, the Clarkes' divestment from things had become almost imperceptibly integrated into the dominant Christmas traditions of gift-giving and playing of games.

The Clarkes are one of the reasons why, as well as writing an academic text in the future, I wanted to paint these portraits. To convey something of the sense of ethnography as enchantment, as a privileged access to such private beauty. As in all these portraits, it has been possible to record and include only a few fragments of what there is to learn from the Clarkes. But I have to hope that there is enough here to convey a sense of their extraordinary craftsmanship and of the central role of their material culture. From this family one learns the artisanal form of love, care and devotion, performed with such subtle grace, creativity and imagination that the ways persons become objects of care and objects become subjects of relationships blend imperceptibly with each other in the overall fullness and artistry of these lives.

PORTRAIT 3

A POROUS VESSEL

Using the term 'aesthetic' to describe some people's orientation to material culture could in some cases seem pretentious and inappropriate, but with Elia it feels quite natural. It speaks, first, to the vibrancy and colour in the life she has crafted. This is not some dull landscape of a person. There are vivid swirls of emotion, from intense joy to anger and bitterness. There is constant rhythm and flow and movement. This is no simple realist portrait, because the picture is full of half-discernible shapes that move between the worlds of the living and the dead, of the tangible and the ineffable. It is the image of a person who is extraordinarily porous: on the one hand, a rock that has taken more than its fair share of buffeting and is left isolated in loneliness and dependent on its own strength and stability – but also a permeable rock, which constantly absorbs the outside world, its compliments and its insults, and at the same time gives out in the form of relationships, concerns and gifting.

One doesn't just converse with Elia. She is a storyteller and, more than that, a conjurer. As she talks, her body is never still. Her hands dance the tales she tells and through some sleight of hand a ghost suddenly appears and dominates the room for a while, before fading back into some furniture or piece of clothing that has become its home in her world. There are many such ghosts who talk, not only to her and through her but to each other, crowding the room with their admon-

ishings and comforts, stroking her back to soothe her, or blaming her
for some slight. At the head of this pantheon from the other world
stands a serene figure, an avatar of divine imagery, a model of sagacity –
her grandfather. Much of the time he is at rest in the little table in the
corner of her room, which he crafted when he was alive and has been
part of her life since she was a child. The table stands for the generations past and those to come. The sanctity of his memory is no bar to it
becoming the place where her own grandchildren play, storing their
toys next to it, and even marking it with green paint and scratches.
Because, for her, this is their proper inscription on a monument; their
activity ensures the table's ability to unite her family across four generations.

When needed, her grandfather emerges. Although he died when Elia
was ten, he remains a much more active figure in her life than many who
have died since, or are even formally alive still. He was, and is, a wise
and philosophical man, who once told her fantastic stories about the
Greek heroes. And today it is he who can find the answer to every problem. She admits that the whole family revere him as an ancestor: 'we've
canonised him'. She has photographs of him displayed prominently in
her living-room, next to herself as a small girl. 'He's in my head, he's in
my soul, he's in my spirit, he's within me, he's within the love within me.
If I have a problem I will actually ask him and I will myself go into his
psyche and see what he would have done, see what he would have said
to me and it would have always been something very gentle. When you
are really, really sad, when I have a great problem, when I've done something, when I've lived through something I shouldn't have lived
through, I would ask him how to get me out of it.'

This is not some vague transcendent presence. Recently she had
begun to feel her age and the loss of all that she felt could no longer be
part of her life. Then one day, travelling on the London underground,
she noticed opposite her a handsome Greek man, half her age.
Astonishingly, he continued to look at her with some intensity, until the
lines in the book she was reading started to dance around before her.
Then, as she breathlessly left the train, he followed and finally introduced himself to her. This was the start of what, for her, was a rather
wonderful relationship. It couldn't last more than a month, since he
had to return to Greece, but during that time she found a soul mate, an

intelligent, sensitive and respectful man who gave her back precisely what she seemed so sure she had lost in life. The age discrepancy worried her at first, but she somehow felt better when she discovered that his mother would have been approximately the same age as herself. She never doubted that this man was a gift from her grandfather. Indeed she met him on her way back from a ballroom dancing session where, much to her surprise, they had suddenly played a piece of music that was her grandfather's favourite. It was he who understood her fear of getting older and appeared to have found this beautiful means of showing her how much life could still offer. 'I thought that was my granddad giving me the kick and boost that I need for this part of my life. To send me off on a new wave. So he really did love me, didn't he?'

Her grandfather had lived around the corner, along with a range of great aunts and uncles, all of whom worked in the flower business. First in markets and then in shops, but they also did general building work when it was available. He loved dancing and cooking, as she does today. Not all of these figures became active ancestors and took up a place in her house, but her grandfather is certainly not alone there. Her mother is a very strong presence, especially within her clothing wardrobe, as is her Aunt Dimitra, who personally made many of these clothes. 'I call on them all up there, they must get earache up there. It's just the way I am, but I know other people are like me. So in fact what you just have is a great love and that love never ever dies and that's the inheritance you have from such persons.' There are other places where she can commune with them. On one occasion we accompanied Elia to visit the graves of her ancestors, a rather beautiful site where she seeks solace and advice, and continues to lavish care on the stones and flowers that are their grave sites. These figures of the past are not all benign; there are some she retains an intense relationship with because she still has scores to settle and she may never entirely forgive them for the hurts they inflicted upon her.

Elia's world is that of magical realism; it is not just the ghosts that are conjured, but also the way she shifts one out of a grounding in an ordinary, plain, rational and often colourless world; the extremely sensual way she uses her hands, fingers in particular, often drawing arcs in the air or tracing on the surface of the sofa, in wave-like motions which make her tales of love and emotion appear as shapes and bodies in themselves. This movement is not just directed at audiences. Elia's kitchen faces onto the street, and sometime passers-by are amazed. Because, for Elia, to cook is also to dance. As with everything else in her life, the genres blur naturally into each other. 'You have to have rhythm, without rhythm you can't work, no matter what you are doing, you have to have a flow of movement, your hand has to have a touch and it has to have that rhythm in it . . . I have always danced because I love the movement with the music. I was here one night and it was before Mummy died and I was very, very sad and Zorba was on and I just got up and danced with him in the film. Right at the end he does the dance and it just lets all the sadness out and it's a marvellous, marvellous medium for when you are happy or sad.'

The way emotion itself ebbs and flows with the movement of her body reflects and reinforces her sense of permeability to the effects of others. For example, when her grandmother was dying of cancer and had bad headaches, 'she said "my head, my head, my head", and when I got home I had caught her headache and the headache was hers and it was awful and I had to call the doctor the next day because I was very ill.' When she describes going out dancing, it is as though she casts herself into the world like a net. The clothes she chooses draw attention and comments from others; hopefully she can land some compliment, that will flow back into her, offering her sustenance and defence against any unwelcome contents in her evening's trawl: insults and (perhaps worse) the attitude of people who don't or won't see her presence in their world. With Elia, the expression 'fishing for compliments' changes from its usual, disparaging meaning, to convey an image of her astride an Aegean rock, casting out her net to see what glittering phrase or subtle praise can be lifted from the dark ocean.

She describes this permeability herself, mostly in relation to her experience of dancing: 'you feel all the sadness here and you bring it out from yourself, you just stretch it out, which is all in your head, you visualise it coming out and then you're moving your body with how you are feeling, whether it be sad or whatever you are going to do. And you are using your hands, your body, your feet, everything'. For her, this movement out in the world may be caught in a relationship that may not even be with her as much as with the emotion or sensuality she has projected into her dance. 'He's a sod and I love him and we will do a really evocative dance which is very simple, but our bodies will move to the music, all of the time beautifully, just complete. You are on the same wavelength, your feet are the same and you are moving like that and that is very beautiful in itself. Then afterwards people think we are having it away, but we are not. There is nothing else between us, but on the dance floor we are lovers.'

Each deceased relative represents a different facet of her inheritance. Grandfather gave her wisdom, grandmother – her humour and character. Aunt Dimitra made Christmas special with presents that seemed real luxuries at the time: special foods such as marron glacé, drinks such as advocaat and cherry brandy. Another aunt showed her that you don't just buy children presents and hand them over, but you actively play with them. If you give a paint set, you also gift them the time of painting together with them. Yet another relative bequeathed her the skills of how to approach people, which Elia took up when dealing with clients in her own flower business: how to reassure people, make them feel that they made the right choice and that things can look beautiful. Above all from Aunt Dimitra she learnt the art of praise.

In Elia's world, three kinds of object, in particular, are in constant movement with each other: relationships, things and emotions. That they are inseparable parts of her material culture is evident in the contents of her wardrobe. Almost all her clothes represent not just things to wear but integral aspects of her relationships with others. Two of her most present ancestral ghosts reside within this wardrobe: her Aunt Dimitra and her mother. Many of the garments were made originally by Dimitra, often in the first instance for her mother. As one goes through the wardrobe, garment by garment, a high proportion of them speaks to some relationship. Quite apart from all those she has inherited, there are those from a friend who has since died. Another was lent by someone she really can't stand, and therefore, after ten years, she still can't dispose of it (even though she would never wear it) – just in case that person were ever to ask for it back. Then there are those given by significant partners, for instance the leopard-print nightie from a boyfriend.

Often the relationship is mediated through her initial understanding of clothes, that came from watching Aunt Dimitra make them. So a dress is complimented on how sensibly the seams have been placed; which contrasts with horror stories she can tell of women wearing modern clothing that has split apart in the most embarrassing situations. Other clothes represent a critical relationship to one set of her relatives, who are extremely wealthy and can spend hundreds, if not thousands, on a single garment. This is matched by the way Elia demonstrates how she, by contrast, can make quite inexpensive clothes appear elegant and resonant of other, superior values, than mere price. Her own choices create another sense of good value. The garment that is really worth spending money on is a high quality bra, or a slip that lets the dress fall properly – or, as for so many women, there is value in the sheer chutz-pah of finding a dress for £8 at Primark that can still attract compliments against rivals a hundred times the cost. Such comparisons are not lim-ited to price. She also contrasts herself with those who try to be mutton dressed as lamb, with all those 'dingle-dangles' and clothes which leave one's bosom hanging out or show any lumps that don't happen to fit. She, on the other hand, displays the clothes she wore for her recent young man: simple long black skirts that won more than just his respect. Although she mainly entertained him in her home, she always dressed carefully, as though they were going out to a restaurant.

Then there are the clothes, and especially the shoes, which are an essential part of her ballroom dancing. There is the obligatory *diamante*, the fishnet tights she will wear just when everyone regards her as some-one who can't, but also what she describes as the 'wrecked silver or gold super-dance Latin shoes, which cost a fiver but I can dance in them all night'. Many of her clothes will never be worn again, but they give her wardrobe a double function as a kind of museum: the dress she bought when she was just eighteen; the furs; the black dress with scarlet flow-ers; the blue satin with its gold and silver brocade; above all, the fine Janet Reger underwear. These are lovingly stored away with other trea-sures of memory such as the bedcover that her great-grandmother made on her Greek island. Even though her children spilt paint on it, she can't throw away something which she can imagine this ancestor actually weaving, perhaps a hundred and thirty years ago.

With some other people, one would look at this array of clothes and see each as representing a person, or an event. But the word 'represent' doesn't capture Elia's sense of objects as forms that actually mediate and transfer substance and emotion between people. When she wears a bor-rowed dress to a dance, the compliments she receives are also flowing to the friend, not just to herself. It's the same when she sits on a gravestone and feels the love which that person once bore her rise again and embrace her from within the stone; or when the presence of an inlaid jewellery box reminds her of the time she was dangerously ill, and her grandparent cried at the end of the bed and she sensed that this box was removing the burden of tears from her. Objects store and possess, take in and breathe out the emotions with which they have been associated. Not surprisingly, to clear and tidy this room is for her the means to clear and tidy her head and – a term which is important to her – her soul.

For Elia, the way objects, relationships and emotions flow is also part of what she sees as her Greek ethos of sharing. It starts with her memory of family meals as a child, around furniture that her grandparents had actually made. But in her stories people commonly take a burden from others or give it to them. A typical story revolves around a distant relative who called in a debt just when Elia's mother was dying and the business was having some temporary difficulty. This wealthy relative, with a second home, treated her not just with unkindness, but with such an undisguised attitude of disdain and exclusion that it continues to rankle today. Being family, she knew exactly what insults would really hurt, how to twist the knife. 'I was stunned, absolutely stunned and my head just went haywire with migraine. It just took over my whole body. I can't believe that anybody can kick anyone so deep when one is on the ground. The next day I couldn't carry the sadness about, I couldn't carry the hurt. I went to church and gave it to God because I couldn't carry it.'

The sharing of burdens between people and transcendent realms is also evident in Elia's reflections upon Christmas. As always, this is partly a way to commune with her ghosts, and when she finds especially good ingredients, she offers them on behalf of her grandmother who would so much have enjoyed cooking with them. But then Christmas is a time when one can bring back the past and make it live again. For a long time the advocaat and cherry brandy were despised as old-fashioned. But now a new generation has arisen with no point of reference and, when she re-introduced these, they took to them as a delight and an innovation. This is the time for old recipes, the grinding up of the nuts and anchovies for her pasta sauce, or her own particular panna cotta. Eventually, though, her reputation for Christmas hospitality ended with her being burdened with catering for forty-three relatives.

Yet it is the very same sense of sharing and giving associated with Christmas that can make this also the cruellest and the loneliest time of year. 'And the saddest thing was, there used to be long Christmas holidays at that time when the shops weren't open and everything. Boxing Day and the day after I would be completely alone, completely alone. Everybody had their families and I had nowhere to go. I would be here for forty-eight hours, all on my own, because I wouldn't knock on anyone's door, I wouldn't phone anyone up, because I thought they knew I am on my own. That was so sad, being on your own, and I used to die for Christmas to be finished, and you had had all those people in your house and fed them and cleaned after them and it cost you God knows how much. You can't believe it, can you? The loneliness is horrendous, awful, wicked and you can't believe that you entertain all those people and nobody cares about you after. No one thinks of you.' This is the other side to Elia's extraordinary permeability as a person. The same quality that extends her and that allows her to flow outwards to other people, that one can feel in her presence, is also what makes her vulnerable to insult and – in equal measure – to a sense of emptiness if what she gives out is not matched by a love, or at least consideration, flowing back in her direction.

The sheer strength of her emotions and the way they flow is felt by Elia to be something very Greek. Her memories of her Greek relatives are constantly contrasted with another branch of the family, which is English and lives in Dorking. She remembers her astonishment and confusion when going to visit them at Christmas and finding that they had actually put food away in the cupboard, to keep it from the children. She felt they treated her Greek relatives as though they were gypsies, and sees them today as cold and bigoted. Before she returned to the family flower-business, she was sent to a hotel management course, but she couldn't stand the sense of hierarchy, the way you were supposed to talk to receptionists one way and to the managers another. She fled and took up waitressing for a while, where at least she felt removed from this cold harsh world where she lived but could not feel that she belonged.

In *His Dark Materials* by Phillip Pullman, characters can use knives to cut a bridge between one world and another. There are hundreds of such other worlds all around, if one could find ways to link them. This is Elia's aesthetic. For her, the Greek universe is one that mixes

mythological figures with the living and the dead. So she can still dance
her way into the imagination of past lovers and share again with them
her world and the burden of its hurts and insults. She infuses food with
ancestry and brings into her body other people's pain, but equally
becomes saturated with the sense of love that protects her from pain.
Objects are magical, talismans that ward off evil, bottles within which
are found genies: clothes that take away her age and enchant even the
sceptics; furniture inscribed by grandparents and then grandchildren.
Such is the sheer power and scale of her emotions. Sitting with Elia one
sees heights of joy and depths of despair that make one feel she comes
from a land of mountains, while we inhabit mere hills.

The events surrounding death and her experience of it have a significant place in Elia's corpus of storytelling. The narratives usually begin
some time before the death itself. For example, she talks of a premonition that her grandfather was going to die, and 'so I took him all in visually'. She remembers counting the seventy-two wreaths at the funeral
and seeing it as clear evidence of how much he was loved. By contrast,
her memory of her own mother's death is one of bitter failure.
She recalls her oath to her mother that she wouldn't die in hospital, and
her frustration when that was precisely where her father took her. She
recalls precise details of the food she had prepared for her mother's
return home, which was never to be eaten.

There is a constant leitmotif in her discussion of several deaths: the
way she felt let down by others during the initial mourning. In Greek
tradition, participation in public mourning is important; but at her
grandfather's death, for example, she was sent to school instead. She
could see the intense grieving of others, the way they collapsed when
distraught, the way they were acknowledged and supported by others.
But, as she recalls, 'I was on my own there, it made me realise something, I have mainly done my grieving on my own. I have never had any
support in grieving.' She had wanted to be with the coffin, to share this
grief with the mourners, but people disregarded this young girl. When
her favourite Aunt Dimitra died, she wanted to go back to the Greek
island of her origin 'and sit on a rock and put my feet in the water and
I would have been OK'. But she had no money to do this, and her husband wouldn't let her go. On each occasion, the loss of the relative was
exacerbated by the way others didn't seem to see or understand her grief.

She hated it when, at a recent anniversary of a death, the others were chatting about a television programme and refused to give her the attention she needed; because, for her, grief itself needs to be acknowledged by others and thereby sanctified.

At least she does grieve. There are lessons from the failures of others in that regard. Relatives who never seem able to cry and give acknowledgement of grief seem to her to become cold, isolated and bitter, because the burden is not shared. They cannot come to terms with their own regrets about the person who has died. She can see how her own view of public mourning, the deepest expression of loss, has somehow become almost embarrassing in this modern English context. That perhaps one of the reasons people seem to avoid her and leave her in loneliness is that they are afraid of someone they regard as 'larger than life', who lives in terms of these grand emotions, and who therefore can be seen as emotionally demanding a state others seem increasingly ill equipped to cope with or respond to. The English talk of emotional blackmail, the mere idea that you should have to contemplate the feelings of others, becomes a threat to personal freedom. So generosity, kindness and consideration are all transformed into the curse of emotional blackmail. For Elia, by contrast, feelings are gifts which, when expressed, help other people to share and come to terms with their own. But even in the depths of mourning, other people fall short in this basic humanity and leave her stranded.

She is aware of the way rituals of the church are useful in helping to transform the dead into ancestors. She notes the comfort she received, for instance, from the anniversary rites of the Greek Orthodox Church. She also notes the way her grandmother in effect created a shrine to her deceased husband, putting lights around to illuminate his picture and setting up flowers in front. She contrasts this construction of ancestors with the way she can simply repudiate and forget others as the merely dead. For example her English family, who, in life, were as cold as a corpse – so that death made little difference. She neither knows where they are buried nor cares much either.

She naturally brackets together different experiences of loss: the death of her mother and aunt, children growing up and leaving home, her divorce, getting older herself. All of these things require some form of mourning. She feels she was really helped in that regard by a radio psychiatrist, who told her: 'All you women out there who have got children of thirteen or fourteen. Get out of that kitchen, get on a course, get yourself something to be interested in. Because in a few years time your children will be off and you will be made redundant.' She took this advice and started first on pottery, then cake decoration and other courses. At present she is on a writing course, where she learns to express the same stories she tells us, only in another form.

In this process, material culture plays a central role. The way Elia relates to loss and bereavement can best be seen in the comparison between three genres of object: clothing, graves and jewellery. The most suitable and successful instrument of bereavement has been clothing, the most difficult has been jewellery, and the most poignant has been the cemetery. Many of her clothes have a double resonance, since not only were they inherited from her mother, but they had been made by her beloved Aunt Dimitra. At first she stored them in a box at the base of her cupboard. But some she gradually gave away to others. This was done very carefully; the recipients had to be 'lovely' people as well as needing these clothes for some reason or another. The circumstances and origins were made very clear to them, and they were expected to receive them with a sense of reverence.

Then, after some fifteen years, Elia felt she could wear the clothes herself. At first she wore them privately within the house, but not so that anyone else could see her. Then she started to wear them for occasions. These had to be special occasions. 'It has to be a posh one, where I can carry it off; whereas everyone else is wearing £500 to £600 dresses, I am wearing one of these.' There would be occasions which cried out for such usage: for instance her own son's wedding, at which she wore a dress and shawl made by her aunt and worn by her mother. Now it is more that there is always something of her mother's about her when she goes to various functions – be it a handbag or a scarf. Such things bring the dead and the living into a state of immediacy with each other. So, thanks to the clothes, she can serve her mother again: 'you find ways to bring her into social ways and events and family events and of giving her a good time'.

The completion of this process has come with the feeling that she no longer has to acknowledge the point of origin of an item of clothing when she wears it. Today, through her wardrobe, she has assimilated something of what was mourned, then lost through the process of bereavement itself. That does not preclude the explicit return to rituals of bereavement, for which clothes can still play a role in evoking the sense of loss. 'I would say to people "would you like to see my mother's dress?" and there would be a showing. Sometimes I might look at them, but I would be crying, if I was on my own and I would be cuddling them and things like that, I would be crying for those two wonderful women, both for Aunty and for Mummy.'

Jewellery does not seem to be amenable to the same sense of gradual incorporation as clothing. Partly this may be on account of its very materiality. Clothing is not forever, it changes and fades and can take on something of the corporality of its wearer. It has features which are gentle and encouraging of this gradual assimilation of one person into another. By contrast, jewellery stands immutable, in a more abstract relation to the person. The point of gold and diamonds is that they don't change or fade, they resist humanity. This is reinforced by their monetary value which, again, pitches them back into a more abstract form of value, so that they tend to be a colder, sharper instrument of transmission than clothing. Certainly Elia's relationship to bracelets stands in stark contrast to that of clothing. They have become her testimony to the irreconcilable.

Six weeks before her death, her mother sorted out her jewellery and allocated a diamond bracelet to Elia. But, within a month her uncle took it from her and gave it to one of his own in-laws with whom he wanted to keep in favour. She had not forgiven that uncle by the time of his own death. It rankled, just like the fact that her own family property had gone to the sons, in accordance with Greek tradition, although she was the one who had constantly sacrificed herself and given time and energy to the family. But for her it is not the property, but the bracelet, that comes up time and again, in terms of her own bitterness. A feeling which returned to her recently, when the engagement of one of her relatives involved passing on one of the diamonds from that original bracelet. As often in Elia's case, it took an intervention from the shades of her ancestors, listening directly to their advice, to reconcile her to attending the wedding in question.

One of the places where Elia can still give vent to her abiding sense of hurt is the cemetery. This is where she can express herself directly to the souls of the departed. She sits by her uncle's grave and asks aloud: 'What did you do it for, what did you do it for, why did you do it to me?', and she knows that, in heaven, her aunt is giving him a 'right telling off'. She loves the photos, which are an integral part of Greek gravestones. There she is, her other aunt Dimitra, with her broad smile 'she always sends me off with a smile, she would say "come along, be happy darling, find happiness", and once I was up there and I actually sat on the stone and felt the love they had for me, and I put it into myself. I got all this love that they had, how they felt for me and I took it all in and I left the cemetery.'

A visit to the cemetery means putting on her lipstick and looking appropriate for this greeting of relatives, for whom such things mattered a good deal. As usual she has stories about the graves themselves. The quarrels between brothers, which meant that none of them took responsibility for a particular grave – so that it therefore lacked a proper inscription. Her sadness when she sees a grave that carries only the word 'husband', not 'loving husband', as it should. The mystery of a grave where the family all died at the same time. And the curious motifs and pictures on graves that speak to the profession or accomplishments of the deceased – mostly people she knows nothing of apart from these graves. Sometimes, when she has good news, she will tell her deceased grandmother when she is in the kitchen. But when it's exceptionally good news, she feels she should come to the cemetery and tell her in person. Once there, she becomes concerned with cleaning and maintenance: everything should look cared for. Fortunately these Greek graves have the look of a carefully tended garden, unlike most cemeteries.

While some feel that the graves are a place for ritual and prayer, Elia feels that this would get in the way of her personal relationships. She avoids prayers and indeed any kind of formal acknowledgement. For her, this is a time to chat, quarrel and fuss around with a scrubbing brush or pulling out grass, showing her care for people who have lost little of their individuality or ability to answer back through their relative insubstantiation. She tells us that, whatever you bring in to the cemetery, you come out with peace and you know that you are alive.

The cemetery acts in a complementary capacity to the clothing in relation to her bereavement. In effect, this is the place where her ancestors remain unchanged, where one can commune with them as they had been in life, whereas the clothes are allowed gradually to fade and become absorbed into herself. The cemetery is also a tragic space, which reminds her that children can be taken away at an early age and that death gives perspective to life. The clothes, by contrast, seem constantly in motion, like so much of her own life, providing different ways she might be – new relationships, possible alterations and alternatives. Elia is eloquent about the process by which clothing helps her come to terms with her loss. How wearing their clothes helps the dead take part in life, how she is taking her mother back into herself. How, as a result, her mother is now 'in a good place', as is she. Elia sees in things what I see in her: the importance of permeability as the core to her aesthetic of life. The cold imperviousness of jewellery, the emotional porosity of graves, but above all the active permeability of clothes, now embroidered with the ghosts of the departed, who can embrace you as easily as you can embrace them.

STARRY GREEN PLASTIC DUCKS

We are chatting, as always, about stuff around the house, and one of us, I forget which, remarks on the numbers of CDs we can see. Simon then tells us he has some 15,000 records and 2,000 CDs in storage. At first we just continue chatting. Then suddenly I feel as though something has just got stuck in my brain. I had started to visualise what 15,000 records in storage might actually look like. Fortunately Simon is only too happy to elaborate on this remark. Simon is a treat in that respect. He is one of the most expansive talkers we have come across, and almost all his conversation is about the thing we are primarily interested in, which is Simon. 'Music for me is memory . . . it's very very evocative . . . people are always saying to me: "why don't you sell them you could make . . . money" and I once threw away some records out of pretentiousness, threw away some very very cheesy records, and I've never regretted anything so much in all my life . . .'

Simon's tastes are eclectic. There are very old dance records. One of them is 'An instrumental flamenco-y dance record and it's beautiful, it's absolutely exquisite in its construction, very very evocative. And then at the other end I have extremely cheesy records that, no matter how much of a bad mood I'm in, it's impossible to stay in a bad mood when they're on . . . they're just so silly.' This eclecticism starts to emerge as really very important to Simon. The first step in appreciating this collection is to understand the way he relates music to emotion. Although we give labels to emotions: anger, love, fear and so forth, the semantics are quite clumsy. It's mainly these few words. For Simon, music is vastly richer than words as a means to express the variety of emotions. This in turn means you cannot just experience them; you also gain a sense of what they are and what they are good for. Music has become the form and repertoire of his feelings.

Once music has taken on this role as the external manifestation of Simon's emotional repertoire, it becomes available as a means for self-control and self-expression. He doesn't just put on music to suit the mood he is in, which is probably the most common use of music by the rest of us. He is much more active and manipulative in his deliberate choice of sound. He will use music to calm himself down, to prepare himself for something such as going out or meeting someone, but also to tease himself with, or to challenge himself. From thumping hard rock to lyrical ballads, from Bjork to trance, there is so much that can be constructed, so many instruments around to orchestrate one's emotions. Simon is more like a chef skilled with cuisine. He enjoys imagining a series of emotive sounds and their order or combination. This is a use of music which is perhaps becoming more common today, as people sequence iPod repertoires, but Simon has been doing this for ages. When he gets it right, he finds he can savour this arrangement and sequence of emotive forms the way other people savour meals.

This leads to the third stage in Simon's use of music, which is to stimulate that which is creative in him. Often, while music is playing, he will develop a 'music video' in his head. Unlike most music videos, these are not based on the lyrics of the song. It is something developed out of the beat, the mood of the music. Typically, the visuals come from fantasy worlds; there are princesses and dwarves and magic, figures cavorting, plotting, falling in love. Sometimes Simon writes fantasy stories based on these 'videos' he has imagined under the influence of music, which for him is more efficacious than any drug experience – though he has tried most of those too. Both his parents were involved in art and design, and for Simon it is important to take an active role, a creative role, which brings into play his own imagination and not just that of others. When he reads books – and he reads a great deal – Simon doesn't really appreciate it when there is a considerable and rich description of a character.

He tends to skip or skim those passages, because he wants to be involved in that creative act himself, to flesh out and visualise for himself who the person in question might be. An implication from Foucault or Barthes – the death of the author is the birth of the reader. To be creative as a consumer he has to resist the intentions of writers. Similarly with film: what excites him is not so much the content of the film but its consequences for him; what it makes him think about, or question or do. So music, with its evocative but incomplete objectifications which seem to demand that one takes them further, is perfect.

Simon is never content simply with the stimulation of an inner world of imagination. He is always wanting to make this manifest in an outer world, increasingly populated by his visions and envisioning. While most people will occasionally give voice to an opinion, a sensation or an acknowledgement of something seen or heard, Simon, given the opportunity, provides a kind of running commentary on what he is thinking. The fact that he talks about himself so much may not mean that he is particularly narcissistic; very possibly, most people spend most of their time thinking about themselves. It's just that one has the feeling that a much higher proportion of Simon's thoughts is being laid out in front of you. He does this in large measure because he finds that, as with the music, having his feelings expressed and putting them outside of himself has many benefits. He is able to consider them more fully. Does he agree with his own statement, or was that just bullshit, now evidently so because he has said it? All this is also a way of driving himself forward. Once he says he is going to be or do something, the very public presence of that claim commits him to it.

Simon doesn't want this external aspect of himself to become dissipated or distant. He wants to keep it at hand, to use it in composing and constructing himself on a continual basis. That's why it's important to him to have the music physically out there, as vinyl and CDs. To possess it, ideally to see it within reach, so that, like a cook's ingredients, they are all at hand when he needs them. It's desperately sad that so much has to be in storage at present, but one day there will be shelf after shelf of these ingredients of life, ready for him to mix and savour. Simon would never understand it, if someone claimed that he must be materialistic to want to possess so many things. It appears to him as merely the natural way an individual grows in life, becomes more, with age and experience, than he or she was before. Accumulation is simply what you are, and in his case it must take an external form. It is Simon's own version of his Protestant tradition, which was constantly looking for some outward sign that a person was one of the saved. Simon has lost the religious underpinnings, but has been left with a restless search for such signs of himself. One also senses that Simon is someone for whom, if things are not evidently going forward into the light, they would soon be slipping backwards into the dark. He could easily become fearful, morose and despondent. But Simon is not, in practice, given much to such dark moods. Simply because he now knows himself pretty well, and he knows the means and skills of staying positive, of moving forward, of accumulating. When things threaten otherwise, Simon has the right music to put his life back on track.

There is, however, one part of life where Simon rejects music and finds it unsuitable, even threatening – an indicative refusal. Simon does not at all like to have music on during sex. Because he has a quite specific relationship to sex. He could not be more at ease with the basic issue of being gay as a sexual orientation. He was going to gay clubs when he was thirteen. If anything, he feels privileged and enthusiastic about the emotional and sexual possibilities which, for him, are part of who he unequivocally is. But what does trouble Simon is some of the other connotations of being 'out there': the endless stereotyping of how gay men are expected and supposed to be; the 'out there' of style and the body.

So Simon systematically repudiates the expressive repertoire that is most closely associated with being a gay man. He has no interest whatsoever in body lotions, skin treatments and the cosmetic industry now available to gay culture. He is not particularly interested in clothes of any kind, nor indeed in shopping, more generally. He doesn't go to the gym and he would never take steroids. He is ambiguous about the whole gay-club scene. The problem is that, in London, the club scene is simply too good. If you are looking for the best time, the most relaxed, inventive, fun time, then you have no choice but to orient yourself around the gay-club scene . . . even if you are not actually gay. But Simon always has to add the caveat that he is there because it's the best, and not simply because he is allowing himself to be ghettoised as gay. So Simon will constantly berate what he takes to be the worst side of gay culture. His *bête noire* is what he claims to be the mistreatment of good-looking women, who are exploited as mere fashion accessories by gay men – I suppress the obvious retort that straight men are not known for being significantly different in this respect.

For Simon, this repudiation of stereotypes about gay men is much more than simply an affectation. He is serious and committed to this independent control of who and what he is, in sexuality as in music. The degree of that commitment can be very impressive. He detests the culture and the assumptions about promiscuity which have become central to that stereotype. For six years, until he met Jacques, Simon abstained completely from sex. He had reached a point where he thought he was destined never to enjoy a proper and fulfilling relationship, something from which Jacques has rescued him.

Simon also knew that this was not entirely about his own choices and his own sense of integrity. He also has his fears and concerns, where the self behind his self-confidence could easily drain away. The one thing he could hardly bear to see externalised was the image of his own body. He was fine collecting photographs for his own records and memories. Indeed his constant concern with his own self-development meant that it was important for him to be able to view the different stages of his life; this helped him to understand where he was coming from and who he could be. He has loads of such images stored away in albums. Images from parties, with his parents, of all his friends and of many good times in the past. He even keeps those sets of photos taken in booths, in underground stations. What freaked him was the idea of a photo of himself put on display, put into the public domain. He couldn't help having that gnawing consciousness that, although Jacques was seven years older than his own thirty, he himself never has been and never would be as good-looking as Jacques. And he didn't particularly want a reminder of this. Sure, he could have covered over the mere self with that garish, camp externalisation which is open to gay men in a way it is not to straight men. But this is where the body was the opposite of music. Simon simply refused the assumption that cultivating the external appearance of the self was actually the way to cultivate the self. It was like a huge mistake, a misunderstanding of where and what a person was. Simon is the person that Simon creates, through his mind, his music and his countless acts of self-development. Why should this almost fortuitous symbol of himself, the looks he just happens to have been born with, the rough physiognomy – the appearance people judge by – be the sign that others take actually to be him? There certainly was neither justice nor truth in that.

Instead, Simon returns to all that is positive in his life and all that he can make of it. In relentless fourth gear, he refuses to dwell upon the body, change and loss. First of all, that is just spilt milk. In any case, nothing is ever really lost. He always finds a way to focus on continuity and attachment rather than loss. When one of his favourite plants died, one he had nurtured for twelve years, Simon insisted on planting something new right on top of it, sure that there would be some re-birth thereby. It's the same with past friendships. Especially when he was a teenager, Simon always re-invented himself, and that often meant developing new relationships and relinquishing older ones. But he always tried to maintain some kind of contact with those he was leaving behind: at least a Christmas card, or a postcard, or an occasional message. People, like things, should never be completely lost or discarded.

He even extended this to family. As with many young men, there were strains and tensions at times in his relationship to his parents. But Simon took the initiative. At one stage he persuaded his mother to develop an entirely new relationship with him, based on letters. He insisted that these should not be letters from her as his mother but from her as an acquaintance, a newly developing friendship. This ruse was completely successful, and the subsequent letters from these years have become one of his most treasured possessions. Even when a relationship went badly and ended, he kept the photographs and other detritus from the wreck. He could still turn mistakes and tragedies into lessons to be used in building his life. Simon loves many types of literature, and managed to secure a signed copy of a novel from Isabelle Allende. But it's hard to resist a smile when Simon admits that his all-time favourite tale is *The Never-Ending Story*: it could be the title of his autobiography.

It is not hard to imagine how people might misunderstand Simon. This relentless self-expression, this endless positive could become wearing. Simon spends so much of his time pointing out something bright and interesting in the world around him, always insisting that others should then acknowledge and agree. He can sound in constant need of reassurance. There may well be something insufferable in Simon's refusal to acknowledge that other people are not always in the mood for this kind of effervescing; in his demand that they, too, at this particular instant, give voice to the joys of the world. There are so many times when other people would rather be grumpy, or complaisant, or, simply, relaxed into a steady, more contemplative mood. This expressive engagement can also seem superficial in its restlessness and sensuality. Yet I confess that I couldn't help identifying with Simon, suspecting that I also share something of this immaturity of the bright eye: the same desire to externalise a vision of the world in the hope that other people will savour it. Simon and I got on very well.

Of course, Jacques is exactly what one would expect, given Simon. Jacques is relaxed, clam and pretty unflappable; a simple melody that eschews these high and low emotional notes in favour of a slow but appealing rhythm. Jacques has much less problem conforming to some stereotype, and, if one's vision of the Frenchman is someone who manages to spend four hours over a single meal appreciating the subtleties of the cuisine and the comforting languor of one's companions, then Jacques would have no issue with it at all. It is the thing he really misses in London: when other people are sent arrays of gifts, Jacques only ever really wants one thing from his native land, and that is good food and drink – which is precisely what his mother will always send him, whether for birthdays, Christmas or just to show how much she misses him.

In return, Jacques sends his mother the reassurance that he is well and enjoying himself and moving gradually forward in his own life. He will often email pictures showing him having a good time at parties, or trying on the uniform in his new job, so she can see there is no reason to be anxious on his behalf. Jacques enjoys looking through these pictures himself, increasingly on the computer, where images have been ordered into files he can browse: family, city, plants, animals, France, my birthday. While for Simon photos need to be printed out, to be there as external objects, Jacques enjoys the new possibilities of digital images stored on the computer itself. Jacques' room is overrun with house plants. Somehow he has managed to find unlimited alcoves and niches in this small space, and within each flourishes sometimes quite large dark green foliage, so that one almost expects a black panther to be prowling around the bed.

Just as the photos of himself are those that Simon hides from public view, it is photos of Jacques that adorn their rooms. But there is no sense that Jacques is conceited; they are there together with photos of his mother, his friends, or places of which he is fond. They convey, rather, a sense of relative unconcern. A picture might be there because of the subject, or it might just match the wallpaper. In neither case is he much concerned about what it might say about him. There are also items from his growing collection of beer glasses from around the world, trophies he has nicked from many good pubs and clubs in his time. For Jacques, it's not things in themselves that he can cultivate, but processes and techniques: looking after the plants; slow cooking and the preparation of meals; even with these glasses, it's the nicking that counts at least as much as the having. While Simon confronts, cultivates and explores the possibilities of emotion as a thing, Jacques simply does things with feeling.

Simon worries about his age, wondering whether thirty represents a sort of obligation to be a certain kind of person. Jacques has no such problem. If anything, he was always looking forward to being older. His sense of himself as calm and mature is not new, it's something that took hold quite early. He couldn't wait to be twenty and then thirty, because in himself he felt he was already of that age, and that he needed his formal age to catch up with him. He is now looking forward to being forty. He has decided he will celebrate with some grand drunken party, in a farmhouse near Paris he will rent for the occasion. He just hopes that Simon can come to share something of his own relaxed acceptance of life as a matter-of-fact development that happens to you and doesn't always have to be worked on.

It is food rather than music that Jacques tends to find evocative – and also smell. The one other item that Jacques exports from France are the toiletries which are found clustered in the bathroom. For example, the perfume by Thierry Mugler, which reminds him of a woman he once stayed with. Unlike Simon, he hasn't accumulated that much over the years, mainly what he can take with him from place to place. It's not that he is restless; he, too, has only had one major relationship prior to meeting Simon. He has simply never felt the same need for a relationship to a body of things, or seen their accumulation as a vicarious sign of his own growth.

Simon and Jacques fully recognise the degree to which their complementary natures make them so suited to each other. But, typically, Simon makes this explicit and thinks it is something to work on. Simon plans their future together, their ever increasing closeness and integration, and, characteristically, he does so through finding some external form that will make it evident to both of them that this is the case. In particular, he focuses on the fact that they are moving into a new shared flat. He has already worked out which rooms will be largely dominated by Simon, which by Jacques, and which shared. He assumes they still need their own autonomous space. When they do move, Simon carefully monitors his possessions, to ensure they fit within this plan. After a few days, however, Jacques' possessions start to migrate into non-designated terrain. Both of them know that this is not some territorial gambit. Jacques is simply more relaxed about space, less concerned with any precise order, sees such things as inconsequential. So, if Simon chooses to put things back where they had been while Jacques is on shift work, it's not aggression or an 'issue'. It is simply that Simon can be bothered, while Jacques cannot.

Fortunately, they both share a delight in many aspects of the new flat. They admire its retention of various Art Deco features. An ideal setting for their large poster by Tamara de Lempika. They admire the tiles, the silver banisters and the view of the London skyline at night. The flat fits their joint image of themselves as a kind of 'boho lefty'. Certain features that had defined them separately now blend. The jungle has been tamed, as plants scatter through the flat, taking their place on the mantelpiece along with candlesticks and other assorted ornaments. Jacques' French toiletries have made friends with their rather more lowly English counterparts. Plenty of stuff didn't make it. They enjoyed partaking in the London tradition of leaving unwanted furniture on the pavement and watching how quickly it disappeared. They found it particularly amusing that their neighbours knocked on the door and asked if they were giving anything else away, since it was the very first time these neighbours had ever spoken to them.

One reason why the new flat works is that it is not viewed as any more than a stepping-stone. They are still renting. There is no way they can afford otherwise, given prices in London. But they share a dream of the house they will finally own together. One very different from these

South London flats. Their dream house, which sounds like something from one of Simon's fantasy tales, is in fact a farmhouse on the outskirts of Tallinn in Estonia. Yet the logic that has produced this dream as an outcome is wonderfully pedestrian. Like almost every other young couple in similar surroundings, they have been faced with this inability to afford their own property in London itself. Almost all such couples set their sights on some place further and further from the centre, until it looks affordable. Simon and Jacques simply extended this process until it reached the outer limits of the new Europe that, given their own mixed nationalities, became their more obvious point of common reference. They speak of Estonia basically as a kind of very, very outer London suburb. It is far enough from the centre for the property to be cheap. It has a great party and club scene, including a decent sprinkling of gay bars and clubs. They agree it is a bit provincial; they compare the gay scene with Portsmouth. But, given the choice between Portsmouth and Tallinn, there is surely no contest. Tallinn seems to combine a growing reputation as a place of the future with the authenticity of a traditional capital city.

The dream farmhouse is also important because, in their joint imagination, it gives them the one thing the present apartment lacks, namely sufficient space to bring out their various collections. In Tallinn every one of Jacques' fifty beer glasses would find its proper place, and, until they can be displayed properly, Jacques would rather keep them in boxes. Simon could finally bring back his vast collection of music, which is only expected to grow still further in the future. With a space such as this farmhouse, issues of autonomy would naturally be resolved, since there would be plenty of room to express both their togetherness and their differences. By now Jacques fully understands Simon's need to make things tangible, including their developing relationship. He is not surprised that their fiftieth day in the new apartment, for example, becomes the occasion for champagne and celebration. Simon fusses and worries. At a restaurant, Simon becomes concerned when he wants to order the same dish as Jacques. Does it mean that he is now just copying his partner? Jacques reassures him that Simon's choice is still Simon's, and nothing is lost by their increasing sharing of taste.

In this manner a couple forms. Every day some little discussion about some little thing – negotiations, arguments, appreciations of little touches and gifts. Just as Simon accumulates music as his emotional repertoire, so his growth in the relationship with Jacques needs to manifest itself in accumulation. But they must be the right things. Some things that made him uneasy, such as the photos of Jacques' previous boyfriends, and especially the bed itself – the place Jacques had once had sex with others. Gradually such sources of anxiety are displaced. Jacques has even persuaded Simon to live with one particular striking photograph of himself on public display, one in which even Simon has to agree he looks pretty good. Not everything is agreed upon straightaway. Simon was totally affronted by the gift from a mutual friend of an armchair which, with its pink motifs, was too 'out there', in far too conspicuously gay style. But, as Jacques pointed out, 'for fuck's sake, we *are* gay', and after a while Simon seems to have got used to it. At least he has never yet bought that rug he was threatening to cover it with.

There is one set of objects which remains decidedly Simon's and which has worked as part of their relationship because it can become part of the gift exchange between them. Simon cannot buy a beer glass for Jacques because the whole point of that collection is that they have been individually filched from places where they both have drunk. But the one thing Jacques can buy for Simon is another of his extraordinary plastic ducks, which now populate their bathroom like some gaudy suburban pond. These are by no means just your average yellow-bodied, red-billed bath ducks, or Disneyfied cartoon ducks. Here are ducks in black uniforms with badges, ducks with devil horns or seductive eyelashes, ducks wearing camouflage, or at least sunglasses, green ducks covered in stars. Mostly confined to the bathroom, but occasionally wandering into the kitchen, in the form of casserole dishes, or onto the walls as photographs. Looking at them *en masse*, I have to tell you, Simon, whether you like it or not, those ducks are most definitely 'out there'.

Portrait 5

LEARNING LOVE

In truth it had been a pretty dreadful morning. Marjorie was quite sure she wasn't having this kid back. She had been picked up by social services and that was the end of it. The little terror certainly knew how to hurt you. She had tried to flush the photos of Marjorie's own children down the loo, along with the ones Marjorie had taken of her. Although nothing had been said, she knew just how much Marjorie loved her children. This child, in her own suffering, had an acute sense of this one quality in other people's lives that was absent from her own. In any case it was obvious from everything around the room. She also knew that Marjorie could have given her something of that love too. Just meeting Marjorie would have told her that. But it wasn't enough. However hard Marjorie tried to bring her into her circle of care and affection, this kid knew the difference between love for a foster child – there for a while and then gone – and the love a mother has for her own child. Her reaction was to try and destroy the lot. If she couldn't have the same, she didn't want any. And for all her experience from more than forty previous foster children, there were limits even to Marjorie's ability to create this illusion of equality.

She had certainly tried. The room was testimony to the care and attention to detail in her strategies. Sure, there were loads of pictures of Marjorie's children scattered around the room, but they included her adopted as well as her own children. They included grandchildren, they also included friends, caricatures of well-known people, pictures from Marjorie's own past. The sheer quantity and diversity of these images seemed deliberately designed so that others wouldn't be able to pick out the special nature of her relationship to her own children as the only type of love available in this room. There was such a gradation of care and affection, such a diffusion of so many moods and nuances. There was silly love, romantic love, embarrassed love, fleeting love. Surely each foster child could find some point of attachment or empathy among this profusion of possibilities. Perhaps they would feel some affinity for those pictures of Marjorie in her youth. One couldn't really be intimidated or threatened by the Austin Powers Sixties silliness of mini skirts and polka dots. The way so many of these pictures poked fun at the person they portrayed, in a manner that showed the solidity of respect they could still take for granted. All of this should have made it easier for these unconfident, suspicious newcomers, looking for the slightest sign that they were being denigrated or *dissed*, or that they were not really welcome. Surely a family that didn't take itself seriously, where even photographs were a kind of banter, a gentle pricking of pomposity and pretentiousness, could offer a home, however deep the despair. Usually it could, but not that morning.

Marjorie knew the limits to these ideals of integration. She knew that, even with the best will in the world, not everyone could be redeemed, included or comforted. Such was her own experience, her own confidence, that when, as now, it was obvious that she had failed, she accepted failure without a sense of hurt or defeat, and certainly without recrimination. There was that security which comes from having had over forty foster children through over forty years. It was simply a situation that was not resolvable; someone who needed something she did not have to offer. It wouldn't for a moment stop her being top of the list for the next child in need of a temporary home, a child who, this time, would probably respond positively to Marjorie's careful cultivation of this her home. She would continue to prepare the ground, so that any fragile seedling could be transplanted and have a pretty good hope of flourishing under her warmth and care.

This child may have been able to resist Marjorie's embrace, but I couldn't. Almost immediately I felt at least some kind of love for this woman. Our encounter with Marjorie was fleeting. She never formed part of the larger ethnography, in that we only ever met her for a couple of interviews. Yet it took about ten minutes before I felt those rigidities of resistance to the stranger soften, then melt away and be replaced by the desire for proximity, for her company. There were other aspects to this attraction. Although nearly seventy, Marjorie was also just extraordinarily good-looking. The radiance of the place was clearly sourced in her own face and mannerisms. That face was remarkably unlined, but it certainly had depth that made the maturing of her looks more beautiful rather than less. By comparison, the entirely smooth looks of the young seem pasty, superficial, unformed and even ugly. One wanted to touch and feel Marjorie's face, and, if that was inappropriate (which it most certainly would have been), one wanted to appreciate the depth that lay behind the smile and the eye.

Marjorie was attractive not because she was older, but because she was thereby deeper and more expressive. This was a form of beauty, where an erotic attraction was entirely compatible with her embodiment of a maternal and moral ideal. Marjorie was the meeting point of good and good-looking. Most of all, though, I felt that, to understand Marjorie, I had to adapt to a different sense of scale. It was a bit like watching Doctor Who and his Tardis: one felt that behind this quite petite figure lay something or someone massive. After a while it dawned on me that to understand Marjorie required something really quite simple. This was merely to comprehend that a human being has a capacity to keep on growing, not physically yet actually. Marjorie had never stopped and never would stop growing, until her demise. She made one realise how rare this is in human beings and how impressive when one meets it face to face.

One of the first clues lay in those same photos of herself. Many were silly, self-disparaging and intended to give her a range of identities for people to connect with. But they also revealed a woman who was constantly re-fashioning herself; constantly changing the style and colour of her hair, her clothes, her make-up, her looks; not as a form of aging, but as a positive and constant self-transformation. In this respect she was as much a teenager in her sixties as in her actual teens. So many individuals find that one period of their life – the time they were adolescents, or first in love, or settled into the role of mother – that one moment becomes the particular self which they subsequently fix on as their true identity. It becomes an image of themselves which they can return to for comfort, or mourn as its appearance is lost. It exists over and above the present. But Marjorie never succumbed to the temptation of that kind of stability, never needed one self that was more true of herself than any other. She simply continued to explore the new possibilities that every age of her body, her ever changing relationships and London itself created for her. These developments were just as exciting, fresh and adventurous as ever. In a couple of years, that vivacious blond or metallic copper-redhead might well be Marjorie.

This constant and continual growth couldn't be expressed in her body, except through this subtle conveying of depth in an unlined face. But it could find a much more evident outlet through her use of her own house. The house was the site where she could expand through constant accumulation, where her size, her history, her continual adding to herself took a material form. In truth her house was pretty large. It went up a couple of floors and then some, with the loft. It was also, in one sense, empty, as her children had moved on and had children of their own. Yet it was entirely clear that Marjorie needed a bigger house; that, whatever its apparent size, it was hardly enough to contain her; that she could happily and rapidly have consumed a mansion. Dorian Gray in reverse, hidden in Marjorie's attic was a portrait of youth and dynamism that belied the false aging of the merely physical self.

Marjorie's house is where everything is kept, pretty much by everybody. There may be photos in every nook and cranny in her living-room, but they are nothing compared to the three suitcases of photos that she keeps upstairs. Although she has produced and given away a special collection to each of her children, these merely skim the surface of what she retains. But it's not just the photographs; it's the clothes, the keepsakes, the prizes, the toys, the souvenirs from holidays, the para-phernalia of fads – from keeping-fit fads to collecting fads. Of course some are kept more in hope than anything else. No one is really going to want to ride that bicycle again, it's too rusty and the later models are much better, but it remains as likely to evoke some childhood escapade as any rocking horse. Then there are all her own clothes; the ones she keeps in case they come into fashion again, but also the skinny size-eight dress: there is no chance of her wearing it again even if it does come back into fashion, but it is important to retain it as an object and not just as an image within those sixties photographs. In any case, almost everyone who ever could keeps at least one size-eight dress.

Marjorie shows how limited our understanding of such storage remains. We have inherited our misunderstanding from the founding myth of modern consumption, the one we have to watch once a year: the image of Scrooge and Cratchit. During that festival of gifting when consumption and relationships are reunited under the tree, we denounce the mean-eyed accumulation of base coin and celebrate the spending out of resources in the rich celebrations of turkey and crackers. But actually neither Scrooge nor Cratchit help us to appreciate the kind of accumulation practised by Marjorie. Scrooge represents pure storage, the frozen potential of money. Cratchit's warmth thaws out that potential and allows it to take all the diverse forms of food and cheer. But there is another kind of storage, the one that accumulates things in their fullness of shape and diversity, gilded with the patina of relationships. Marjorie endlessly accumulates such material possessions, but they never lose their rapport with the present; they are not being protected from use but preserved for use. She does change her photos, watch again the old videos. She does bring out clothes which come back into fashion, if she can still wear them. The stored possessions of her children flow out to them when they have a new house or a child of her own, who can be entertained with the toys they themselves once played with. But then they can return them again when those children are past the appropriate age, or when someone has to move to a smaller place or becomes unable to take care of their own things. Above all, the sheer number of things can grow and still be part of her because she too continues to grow.

The house exists in a series of cycles of time reflected, again in the images of her living-room. There are the classic possessions of her early life; these rarely change, but even they can be put away or brought out during some major re-ordering. Then there are the possessions related to recent events, the last holidays or the latest visit by a grandchild – most of which will not stay on display for long, although a few will earn their keep and remain in place. Between the two are shorter and longer-term cycles of replacement and refurbishment that move in and out of display and storage. But nothing is so static, or so hallowed, as to escape its duty to be judged by the present because ultimately, for Marjorie, the point is to

remain dynamic, and available to the future. She neither simply stores like
Scrooge nor simply consumes like Cratchit; rather, she manages an ever
growing resource.

This richness of use is also developed by having as many registers of
use as possible. For many people, things are either on display or they are
not, and the genres of display are limited. But Marjorie doesn't just have
an extraordinary range of content in her photographs, her figures, her
ornaments and her decorations. She also manages to exploit the multitude of ways in which these can be displayed. The humour and banter
can be extended through a playful technique of alternating order and
disorder. So a serious-looking, quite glamorous image, professionally
framed, is disturbed, say, by a newspaper clipping or some related old,
frayed sepia print, stuck into the frame and disrupting its posture of
philosophical solitude: the serious square, with the jaunty intruder stuck
in at an angle. There are clipboards, sequences of images, postcards,
things torn from magazines. Some images are half-hidden behind
others, some are hidden completely. The same layering that one can
sense by looking at Marjorie herself is made that much clearer in the aesthetics of her display. There are photos over photos over photos. A
white ceramic Chinese figure of Serenity is coupled with a plastic fart-
ing fish. Real flowers must compete with plastic ones, and with all the
mirrors and clocks and things that seem to be waiting to find a lasting
place of rest. No one would suggest that this was the result of order or
strategy. It seems the perfect sign of mere haphazard accumulation,
things gradually displaced and re-configured by new things which
needed to be shown when there was no free spot where they could be
placed. Yet this, too, is a kind of order, a refusal to allow anything to be
privileged and protected from the vagaries of the future. In most other
living-rooms, inertia itself commands increasing power. A thing and its
place matter merely by virtue of the time it has remained in that place.
It gains the deepened authenticity of time, respected merely for its own
laziness. But not in Marjorie's living-room. Here, what doesn't continue
to contribute to love isn't worthy of respect. What doesn't grow fades.
There is nothing gained here by mere inertia.

Equally resisted is the tyranny of conventional aesthetics. Nothing at
all in this room is designed to 'go' with anything else: not the furniture,
not the ornaments, nor the displays. There is no place for colour, shape

or texture to claim an abstract regard for itself, as though it could transcend its true service to humanity. In this room humanity and materialism are found to be one and the same: an unlimited respect for the capacity of people expressed through things. Marjorie knows how much a person lacks when they lack material things. Those foster children who come without a single image either of themselves or of anyone they knew, and with almost nothing else besides – not even an old frayed soft toy. She is aghast at the naked emptiness of their lives. Without anything to possess, what chance have they got to possess themselves? Marjorie knows much more than most what it is both to have nothing and to be nothing.

Marjorie also understands that what matters is the presence of the person, not their particular form. Nor is any particular genre especially worthy. A person may be here as a photo of their face, a drawing they did as a child, a framed piece of clothing, their name in wooden letters, a present they brought back to Marjorie from holiday, a prize they won playing snooker, a book they recommended, a fluffy animal or their wish that this old chair be placed here rather than there. It doesn't matter if this is evident to anyone other than the person it speaks to or speaks of. All that matters is that feelings are respected and placed here, in some form or other, with feeling. This is a living living-room; an animated scrapbook of juxtaposed relationships.

In this display, no one can be embarrassed by what they are, have been, or can be turned into by others. That little penis on the then three-year-old looks like it could still pee out of its photo, to the consternation of the now six-foot lanky lad, who is there to be teased. That shy young lady looks ridiculously glamorous and unfeasibly beautiful in the specially crafted studio portrait: it has become the final evidence which forces her to admit that she can be every inch as beautiful as everyone tells her, although she has always denied it. The pavement caricaturist gave that huge elongated chin with a dimple to a neighbour; and a friend can't pretend that it was anyone else who gave Marjorie that lurid liquid in a glass slipper bought in Tenerife. After all, they are all prepared to enjoy the scene of Marjorie's suspenders, displayed when she tripped on a paving stone in her twenties; or the photo taken when she was off guard, where her expression makes her look like a constipated aristocrat. Much of this is personal, but there is one value expressed throughout that is not spoken about and yet is instantly evident. Marjorie and all her family proudly claim their long roots in the South London working class through their accents, their choice of dialect, and this constant defrocking of the pretensions of those who would seek to place themselves on a higher plane. Amidst the images one finds celebrities, from the Beatles to TV newscasters. But these are likely to be present in the spirit of those magazine pictures of celebrities caught at their least prepossessing rather than in their crafted glamour. And in Marjorie's living-room, they mix as free and easy as you like, with Marjorie herself, her relatives and her friends.

The visual display is always complemented by the possibility of a story, an anecdote, which mixes in equal measure embarrassment and achievement. The child who won this award, or was brilliant at that sport, is also the one who was too shy to take the stage at the school play, or who came downstairs with this or that undone. All those stories associated with holidays in the caravan at the seaside – the same place where so many of the photos were taken. And then, as the children grew up, stories about what they did in places she never expected they would have the chance to visit. Stories about the wooden elephant they brought back from Kenya, or the merry mooning drunk from Australia. Sometimes a story can be so admirably self-effacing that she writes it up and puts it on display itself; for instance, the story of the child who asked what she was doing and, when told that Marjorie was 'making herself look beautiful', replied: 'But I like you ugly.' Sometimes these stories are there to shock, like the one about the child who screamed every kind of profanity at a department store Santa Claus because he didn't have the right present in stock; or the quite unrepeatable story about the elderly neighbour, the prostitute and the tin of custard. Several of these stories mock not just people but circumstances. Death enjoys little respect or protection in stories such as the one about the man who forgot there were ashes in the urn, or the phone that rang from the coffin. Such stories may seem an indirect route to self-respect; they come from generations of south Londoners who laughed behind the faces of the toffs and snobs they served and who found their humanity in the levelling process by which anything and anyone could become a good story.

It's not that Marjorie is inured to the terror of life and mortality. These foster children can come with horror in their eyes, images of

needles and blood and corpses drowned in their own vomit, which
Marjorie too had at one time confronted as a routine part of her working life. Marjorie has a kind of moral fatalism. She sees how many of
these children are the victims of other people's fate and has little time
for blame or credit unless it's genuinely due. Stuff happens, and in the
meantime she is happy to enjoy and accumulate stuff. She has no interest in religion, but she likes to talk about spooky coincidences, because
spooky mixes serious and silly in Marjorie's own style. On her shelf is
Nick Hornby's novel *How to be Good*, a text which appeals to her sense
that even being good, when taken too far, is completely silly. For all her
fostering and commitment, Marjorie wouldn't be seen dead transposed
as the ponderous lady philanthropist of the upper-class.

To understand Marjorie one had to appreciate that there is almost no
fit between the place she started from and the place she ended up in.
There were difficulties in her relationship to her mother, though we
hear little about these. More to the point, her relationship to her first
child was anything but successful. She was struggling with failures in her
relationship to her partner, and this made things very difficult at a time
when she would have wanted to focus on the relationship to her child.
In the event, there was separation as much as bonding in this first
attempt at parental relationships. Marjorie's case reveals something
quite different from the generalisations one tends to pick up from the
writings of psychoanalysts such as John Bowlby and from subsequent
studies of attachment and loss. In these writings there is a presumption
that the ability of persons to form deep and important attachments later
in life is largely dependent upon the quality of their first attachments,
above all those with their parents, although in this literature it is almost
always their mother. In general, in psychoanalysis, mothers seem to get
an awful lot of blame and credit. But Marjorie very likely neither gave
her first child what these analysts call 'a secure base', nor had one for
herself. But later relationships do not necessarily reproduce the state of
attachment of earlier relationships. This doesn't allow for the possibility which is so striking in Marjorie's case: that she simply gets better
over time at creating relationships, and particularly at parenting. The
psychoanalytical literature that followed from Bowlby seems to give relatively little consideration to the evidence that, for a person such as
Marjorie, the failures of early attempts at being a parent might be the

stimulus which creates the drive to become a better and better one in the future.

I strongly suspect that this is the key to Marjorie and to the constancy of her growth. I think it was precisely that things did not work well for her at first, that the love she initially experienced from others and in turn gave out to others was pretty unrefined and had many failings and gaps. The conditions she lived in were at first hard and harsh and didn't provide this idealised base, to which all subsequent love somehow returns. A rough and stony love, it gave merely a hint that, if sufficiently polished, worked on, smoothed and refined, it could eventually reveal something that would dazzle the world. But, from that difficult start, Marjorie found the opportunity to learn how to do love better. She had more children, she had other relatives, she had grandchildren for some of whom she had to be the primary caretaker, she adopted children, then she fostered children, dozens of them. She had her own personal relationships, the men that clicked for a while and those that didn't. One that lasted for twenty years, others for two.

When one has reached one's late sixties, there is the possibility that, as in this case, one has had a hell of a lot of close intense relationships – even those life-defining, life-determining relationships to children or a husband. Many people do not learn to get better at relationships; they lose rather than gain confidence, they repeat their mistakes. But Marjorie fed off her own life. She certainly learnt, she developed her skills – even professional ones, which social services had helped introduce as part of the fostering network. But, most of all, those skills came from learning from her own early mistakes, and then increasingly from her accumulation of successes. By now, there were many people who owed a good deal to the blessing of Marjorie's skilled and experienced love. By now, she was phenomenally good at it – which is precisely why, within ten minutes of meeting her, I too fell, just a little bit, under that most benign of spells.

PORTRAIT 6

THE ABORIGINAL LAPTOP

Malcolm has been coming to London for eight years, though his longest continuous stay was for three. His relationship to the flat he lives in is quite complex, but complex in a way that is becoming quite common for people in their thirties. It is one of those informal arrangements of sub-letting that can take place when people buy their own property. In this instance it was a Council property which was something of a bargain for that reason. But then the buyers found that their work was sending them off to another country, and the apartment was given over to a network of friends and friends of friends who somehow kept it occupied and rented. Malcolm is one of those friends of friends, with no formal claim to the place yet with a certain, acknowledged sense of rights, simply through length of association with the people and the place. Actually, it is his personal furniture that occupies the flat for the most part. On the other hand, many of his possessions lie in boxes in various sites around Australia and the UK. This partly reflects the fact that he has changed his mind several times as to whether he wants to settle in Australia or in the UK for the longer term. It's not at all that he is a particularly vacil-lating character; quite the contrary. It is more that changing job possi-bilities seem constantly to re-tilt the balance of opportunity, and he has a mature sense of respect for life's opportunities.

So Malcolm has developed a relationship to a flat which is a little bit his own in usage, even if it can never be his in ownership. But, given that he moves from place to place, it isn't really his home. The nearest thing to a real home for Malcolm is found in a rather unexpected place. It is his laptop. This is the place within which he leaves himself and finds himself, creates order, tidies up, furnishes, dusts and returns to for comfort. It can't subsume everything in its outer structure of keyboard and screen, or inside these incredible silicon chips, which every year, we are told, have become thinner and smaller and yet will hold even more of our lives. The laptop sort of spills out into other materials such as the back-up discs, his certificates, his thesis, and especially his photographs. Yet all of these are orchestrated by their relationship to the one core object that is Malcolm's home – the laptop itself.

Malcolm is a digital man to the core. But he has become one not because of any particular technological interest or predilection towards the latest gimmicks and possibilities. What he relates to and cultivates is nothing to do with the mechanical quality of the thing. It comes from his discovery that the laptop can facilitate the quality of order out of which he has built his relationship to people, and most especially his relationship to himself. Malcolm has a passion for keeping himself in order, through a process we could call self-archiving. Malcolm is constantly concerned that the record he stores of who he is and what he has done is kept up to date. His emails must be in proper folders, edited, tidied, and in every respect sorted. Both his friendships and his work are largely organised by email, and this is where, in many respects, 'his head is'. All his personal materials are contained and controlled in much the same way on his laptop. Photographs are ordered, filed and sorted with contextual information. So is his music. Ideally, extraneous material is eliminated. Bank statements no longer required are shredded.

Malcolm thereby keeps his home in order. But there is another quality that makes this term 'home' an appropriate one. It is the simple realisation that, given his mobility, there is only one address that seems to have much by way of permanence; and that is not a place of bricks and mortar, but his email address. Because the email address has established itself as the place where everyone can always find him, and he is always at home. For a friend or relative who has no idea where he is, even what country he might be living in, this is the one address that does not change over the years. He also prefers to keep the same mobile phone number, but this doesn't have the same sense of becoming the core to his life as does email, because it does not attach itself to the same cultivation of order in life. It is only email that seems aesthetically to form an integral part of that home-making process which resides in the laptop itself, snug within all his other internet tastes and tasks.

The fact that Malcolm is moving between two opposite ends of the planet is a reasonable enough explanation for his identification with the constancy of his email address. But it doesn't explain his embrace of the laptop as his home in this much wider sense, of a place he furnishes carefully and which in turn furnishes him with the order of his life. To understand why he constantly keeps himself up to date as a kind of living archive, we need to appreciate how much of his life has been devoted to the archiving of others. Malcolm is keenly interested in one side of his family which represents his Australian Aboriginal ancestry. For many years now he has sought to recover the traces of their tribal origins in the area near Alice Springs. From this experience he has become concerned with how a future archivist would be able to deal with the evidence for his own life. As he puts it, one is 'tidying things up, as you progress in life, tidying things up along the way'. Much of what he does is assumed to be for the benefit of some putative descendant, on the assumption that such a person would be just as keen on archiving their ancestor as he is. He often considers who this descendant might be, and he is quite clear about certain relatives who, clearly, will never give such devotion to the task. He thinks his brother's child might be just such a person, even though this archivist in the making is currently aged four. As a result, he takes on the work himself; the sorting, the editing, making sure that there is sufficient context. He constantly strives to keep himself encapsulated within some neat package that could be posted into history.

The roots of this specific relationship to the ordering of the past are various, including both Aboriginal and non-Aboriginal influences. On the one hand, he is driven to continue a quest began by his mother. As an Aboriginal, she suffered the traumas of colonial transitions, with three of her older siblings taken away from her own parents. She became involved in a personal quest to recover information about these lost brothers and sisters. She, and then in turn her son, also felt aggrieved by the way Australian Aboriginal history has become so much attached to less savoury repositories such as police archives. Malcolm's ambition is to complete this process of archiving his mother's lineage and, subsequently, his own life, finally depositing the information in an Australian State Archive – which is where, he hopes, Aboriginal lives would be treated with proper respect. When his mother died, the documentary materials were gradually pared down by him to a set of box files. Despite being quite young himself, death is often uppermost in his mind. Not from any depressive cause, but more because it positively reminds him both of his responsibility and of his attachment to his sense of lineage, notwithstanding that he himself has no children. So his own documents, just as those of his mother, have gradually accumulated into six box files. These, too, have been stored with a more sedentary relative.

For an anthropologist, there is an obvious link here to a literature I encountered as a student. For example, how identity in Australian Aboriginal life is constructed in large measure through a concern for lineage. More especially, as the anthropologist Fred Myers has noted with respect to the Pintupi peoples, many Aboriginal groups radically dissociate themselves from material possessions related to the deceased and preclude direct transmission of their identity through such possessions. All Malcolm's mother's material belongings, such as her clothing, were systematically destroyed at her death. From that experience, Malcolm has generalised a larger antipathy to the storage of material things. He has given away almost all the possessions he had once stored, even quite valuable antiques, many of which he ended up giving to a single mother in need. He recognises that this has become integral to who he is: 'I think I've set myself up to be out of touch with objects and things, so . . . there's probably something psychological behind that.' He is constantly throwing things out that others would have hung on to – just in case they might use them again or store them as memorabilia. If his mother's legacy and his own mobility were not enough, he also detects an influence from a quite different source. His father, so far from avoiding material possessions, avidly collected them, as an antique dealer. This meant that their home was stuffed full of things. But, as he recalls, the consequence was that just as he was getting attached to something which had become part of their home furnishing, it would inevitably be sold. So here, too, he learnt a lesson about how not to become too attached to particular things. The legacy from his father, the possibly valuable antiques, he later gave away.

For Malcolm, the emergence of the digital resolves his basic contradiction of materiality. How can he, at one and the same time, both keep things and dispense with them as objects? Digital media compress all the sensual objects of the world and reduce them to an other-worldly domain, where they remain a virtual presence. But that other world has its own order and aesthetics. It is not merely an alternative medium for the creation of self-archiving. Digital media creates its own sensual field, of text complemented by visual materials and sound. It can respect the larger integrity of connections between the media it incorporates. His concern is always that photographs should be accompanied by text which contextualises them, and this can be accomplished most easily within his laptop. He gets worried when he sees people throwing photographs away that might be important to their family history in the future. He understands that people become overwhelmed by the profusion of images which something like a digital camera can create. But he sees the laptop as the solution to such problems, because it makes it possible to order, archive, prioritise, select and give context. So what could be disorder becomes here formalised and controlled. Many things are archived in the very instant they are created. This is both a private and a public duty. Malcolm also keeps his own version of a blog. An updated website with pictures and text related to himself.

Malcolm loves the very actions and processes involved in becoming a digital man. The way you can now discard the materiality of music and just download it to the laptop, 'CD covers – woosh yeah out they go, it's just more crap to carry around'. Even books which are integral to his work he has given away – something quite exceptional in our experience of fieldwork on the street. As he puts it, 'I read novels, like I'll buy books, but then I'll give them away. I believe more than one person should read them.' As so often, the aesthetics of his order is replete with moral, functional arguments that are an integral part of their aesthetic quality. If the legitimacy for what you are doing fits neatly and crisply with the action itself, then it looks better and feels better.

The epitome of this process, and the digital form he is most enthusiastic about, is email. Because, for him, this is not just a means of communication, but the medium for organising relationships. He was just in the middle of sorting emails when we met him. As a result, he picked up on twenty friends he should have been in contact with but hadn't

recently. He immediately sent them all emails about his latest movements. The very process of sorting becomes his re-acquaintance with his
social network. It registers, but then updates, his relationships to people.
The laptop is where he meets his friends to chat, reminisce, make plans,
gossip, form relationships and end relationships.

Yet not even his laptop can resolve all Malcolm's contradictions.
There is one he is constantly aware of and knows will never be resolved.
The contradiction that lies at the heart of a life devoted to self-storage
and self-archiving. Because he is undertaking this task himself, he determines what shall remain and what shall be discarded. It is his selection
that decides what people in the future will regard as having been worth
keeping from their ancestry. Yet this runs against the archivist in him,
who deals with the past and may find invaluable precisely that which the
people of the time regarded as ephemeral or uninteresting. Should he
keep records of his tax receipts, for example? Ultimately, who is he to
determine who he is and forever will be? Then, while the laptop gives
him some measure of control, he worries about people. Because, for all
his use of the laptop in effect to take responsibility for himself, he will
still, eventually, depend on others to take responsibility for storing him,
in the way he takes responsibility for archiving his mother. Finally, not
even the laptop itself is worry-free. He recognises that digital forms are
not always the perfect solution. He worries about whether one day the
formats might become redundant and everything he has invested in
would thereby be lost. The laptop seems almost perfect as the solution
to his ambitions in life; as the contemporary completion of a cosmological tussle with materiality which was once central to the lives of his aboriginal ancestors. But there is now an awful lot of cosmological eggs in
that one basket, and in the end the basket itself looks a little fragile.

PORTRAIT **7**

HOME AND HOMELAND

Mrs Stone first came to settle in London from Jamaica in 1956, and to this house in Stuart Street in 1958. The house in Stuart Street has the feel of one long inhabited by a family. It has lost any pretension to an architectural or decorative style, rather, it echoes back the intense network of family relationships of which Mrs Stone is now the apex, having twenty-three grandchildren and, while we were visiting her, her first great grandchild. The house is occupied by two main classes of material. One consists of items such as books, music and pictures which relate to her Christian faith; the other, an abundance of photographs and cards representing her extended family. The significance of these cards will emerge later on. Mostly, while Mrs Stone talks to us at length about weddings, holidays and trips to Jamaica and the doings of her grandchildren, her second husband sits in the corner. Having suffered a stroke, he is severely limited in his ability to communicate. But, although he cannot talk, he can certainly understand, and there is a breadth to his smile, an enthusiasm to his supportive nods that has become an integral part of the warmth of this friendly living-room.

For the birth of her first two children, Mrs Stone returned to Jamaica, where her own mother supervised the arrangements. Then she did not return for over a decade, and her next four children were born in London. After this, she started to visit Jamaica at least once a year, and she has now made some thirty return trips. In 1987 she decided to return permanently to Jamaica, to a house she had built in Christiana, one of the coolest and highest sites on the island. She was not alone; many of the original migrants from the island, some of whom had settled in Stuart Street, had also returned around that time. Neither was Mrs Stone alone in her experience of the failure of this enterprise. For her, this was primarily a result of the difficult relationships between her first husband and his relatives in Jamaica. Eventually, in 1991, she felt she had had enough and, with a single suitcase and a few clothes, she left her husband and returned to the house in Stuart Street, which fortunately had not been sold in the meantime.

One might think that that would be enough: the project of making a home in Jamaica would have ended with this failure. But Mrs Stone could not abandon her ambition. Since her return in 1991 she had gone to court, in a dispute with her first husband over both houses – in Jamaica and in Stuart Street. In 2005, when the case was finally resolved, the first thing she did with the money she received was to build another house back in Jamaica. Almost everything about this project spelled out the word contradiction. One of the foundations for the relationship Jamaicans feel between home and homeland lies in the tradition of family land, as opposed to personal or private ownership. That is, land was always jointly owned by the extended family, all of whose members retained rights to it so that it therefore could not be sold. Yet the money for building this new property came from what is now a very common practice in Jamaica, namely that of splitting up such family land between individual owners. In Mrs Stone's case she then sold all but the three lots she retained for building her own house and perhaps later on others, for her children. In this manner the long tradition of family land is finally coming to an end.

Recently Mrs Stone went to the Ideal Home exhibition, where she fell in love with some expensive Italian furniture, which she purchased for her new house in Jamaica. By contrast, her house in Stuart Street is furnished entirely with very modest materials, which nowhere match the standard she has set for her Jamaican home. This division between the place she earns her money and the place she spends it on goes back to earlier generations. Her own father worked in the US before the war and, with that money, created a middle-class lifestyle in Jamaica, with a farm and enough cattle for Mrs Stone to claim one could 'bathe in milk'. She fondly recalls that, even when going around the farm, he would sport a massive diamond tie-pin and his velvet hat. So she, in turn, having made her living in London, can only imagine a fine house as something belonging to Jamaica.

Mrs Stone describes the house she has just been building in Jamaica: 'the two lounges, one is upstairs and one is downstairs and three en-suite. You just go into your bedroom and that's it, everything is in there, your bathroom and stuff. The ground floor has the master bedroom and the en-suite and the powder-room. It's got space. You can put what you want where you want. Then there's a garage, as you can see, there's a door that takes you right in front of the garage into the house there. Then you get a kitchen, a long kitchen there and one upstairs.' This is the house for her new Italian furniture; just as her father had a glass-topped table and a fine roll-top sofa that they would put out under the mango tree for him to relax on. Her main memory as a child is the end-less polishing of the fine silverware. By contrast, the ornaments in her house in Stuart Street are generally inexpensive and functional.

Yet there is another contradiction. Mrs Stone cannot match this continuity of commitment to the house itself with any personal com-mitment to actually live there. For one thing, given her husband's cir-cumstances, she is well aware of the advantages of the National Health Service, as she says 'you can't get it nowhere, you can't get it in America. Here is best.' But there is also her own personal affection for England, notwithstanding the prejudices she suffered during her early years. She knows full well that 'I can't give up England . . . I think it's because I spent all my other years in England so it's not so easy . . . I'll have to come back here. So everything is just going to be running back to Britain, running back to my home, to my mother country, that's what it is you know. Yes, run back to my mother country.'

As a result, she is now quite unclear what to do with the house that she has built. She says: 'When I was up there, because we went up there, the person who was looking after the house told me that the house is sort of nearly finished and everything and what do I want to do with it because it has to be occupied. Because people might just, you know . . . So he said what do I want to do with it. If I wanted to rent it. And I said no, I don't want to rent it, I want to go in my house. So I'll have to take care of that.' In the end Mrs Stone decided that her brother could live in it. So, for now, she is in the slightly bizarre position of paying the electricity and the taxes on the house, with no particular prospect of actually living there.

In all this, the relationship to Jamaica is ambivalent and contradictory; but in other respects it's equally surprising in its smooth and seamless continuity. The ubiquity of the mobile phone in Jamaica certainly helps here. Today she can be in constant communication with her relatives. Mrs Stone discusses prices for goods in London and Jamaica as though talking about two ends of the same high street. Recently I published a book together with Heather Horst, on the impact of mobile phones on low-income families in Jamaica. As part of our research, we would go through every name in an individual's mobile phone address-book (obviously keeping these names strictly anonymous). Almost inevitably, these contacts included Jamaicans living abroad: relatives and friends who have become the source of increased remittances. For the rural area where we lived, we concluded that the land would probably be depopulated but for this support from remittances. Mrs Stone's children regularly meet up with her for holidays in Jamaica; sometimes they hire a mini-bus as a family, and it is clear that several of them were thinking along the lines of having a second home in Jamaica in the longer term. So in some ways Mrs Stone and her family regard the two sites as though they were part of one. But this is not always the case. Another Jamaican family we worked with in Stuart Street launched one of the most angry and resentful diatribes I have ever heard against the treatment they received from their relatives when they had returned to visit.

There is not a single object in this house in Stuart Street that I can recognise as having come directly from Jamaica. Mrs Stone explains that it would be pointless to have souvenirs, given how often she is there. Furniture only travels in the other direction. Mainly, what she brings back and distributes amongst her family is Jamaican food. Items such as tamarind balls which, even if you find them in London, are really not the same as the homemade ones from Jamaica. Food seems a more personal and appropriate mode of remaining Jamaican. For her son's wedding, even the cake is being split between an English-style tier and two Jamaican-style tiers. The only material objects she misses are the certificates of all her previous qualifications: school exams, naturalisation papers and secretarial courses. Her husband never returned these to her from that first house in Jamaica. Such certificates tend to be seen as hugely important to people from the Caribbean, wherever they are living. In parallel with the house itself, they form the material evidence for one's life, its achievements and the sense that gradually, over the years, one has become a person of substance.

In listening to Mrs Stone's story I could not help but relate it to a recent PhD thesis I had supervised, by Heather Horst, on the topic of Jamaican migrants returning to their homeland. If her work were to be published with a frontispiece, it would have to depict one of the graves she later showed me in rural central Jamaica. The gravestone in question took the form of a miniature concrete house complete with doors, windows and gables. It looked more like something to put dolls in than something to lay a corpse beneath. Some of these graves are surrounded by ironwork identical in style to that which surrounds actual houses. She interprets these gravestones as marking the end of a long journey. For most Jamaicans, the project of building a house is not a one-off act. Traditionally most people could only afford to build their own house in stages. As money accumulates, one might lay a foundation for a new room, or complete the tiling of another. Building the home of one's aspirations is often a life's work. The house was always the primary mode by which life itself was marked as a progression. Despite all the pressure from the church, it wasn't having children that usually led people to marry. It was only when one could demonstrate one's ability to have some sort of house of one's own that marriage was seen as proper.

This close association between building a life and a home is obviously complicated when a Jamaican migrates to London. The move creates an ambiguous relationship between home and homeland. Most migrants intended to return to Jamaica at least in retirement; an intention often reinforced when they experience a rejection of their initial assumption that they would be fully accepted as British. But if they do return to Jamaica they face a second, even more unexpected, rejection, as Heather has documented in her thesis. Those who never left see these returned migrants principally as 'English' and may worry that, with their greater wealth, they will lay claim to land and authority at their expense.

Furthermore, returned migrants have grown an affection for certain elements of English life such as an English-style garden and forms of behaviour, so that they have a sense of ambivalence about who they are. As
such, they may feel they are no more at home in Jamaica than they were
in London.

These two paths come together as returned migrants attempt to
create their sense of homeland though building their dream retirement
home. One of the principal incentives behind the initial migration to
London was that it would become a means to afford the kind of home
they aspired to but could not expect to construct on local incomes. The
primary form of re-location in Jamaica is through building and furnishing. As 'The English', returned Jamaicans tend to migrate to the cooler
uplands of central Jamaica and build homes which any Jamaican recognises both from scale and from style, as houses of returnees. So in the
first instance the project of returning to Jamaican identity through resettlement is inevitably a failure: they are no longer considered to be
Jamaicans. Heather found in her study that many of these returned
migrants increasingly spend their time going to, or being involved in,
the organisation of what become highly elaborate funerals. Because it is
only in death, interred beneath these miniature models of the perfect
house, and interred in the Jamaican earth itself, that the final return to
Jamaica is successfully completed. A return blessed by deep religious
faith in another final resting place.

So Mrs Stone is living in one home, but feels strongly the pull of two
other ideal homes: that in Jamaica and that in heaven. She is always
aware that beyond the everyday secular life there is another place where
one's heart and soul must dwell. Although this living-room has plenty of
books and music, not one of them is secular. Similarly, all the decorations on the wall that are not family photographs are religious images.
Mrs Stone plays the organ at her local church, and many of her family
attend church every Sunday. When the new house was finished in
Jamaica, the most important task was to organise its blessing. This was
arranged in Jamaica, through the local church and returnee residence
association. She played the organ and fed around forty guests for a ceremony which inaugurated the house as a proper – that is, a blessed –
house.

It is clear, though, that, when Mrs Stone counts her blessings and

appreciates how far they outweigh her tribulations, she need not dif-
ferentiate between those that come directly from on high and those
she can see around her in her family. Apart from photographs, the
most significant material expression of these relationships comes in
the form of cards. Cards on mantelpieces, cards on table tops, cards in
bundles tied with strings or rubber bands and kept in plastic bags. Her
children might have preferred to introduce more modern forms of
communication. Her daughter bought her a computer, which sits in
the corner of the room, almost completely covered in crocheted lace,
topped with a smiley stuffed animal. Her daughter may have subsequently complained, in exasperated tones, 'Mum, this is not for knit-
ting on', but Mrs Stone doesn't even know if it is connected to the
internet or not.

By contrast, her relationship with these cards is deep and full. She
reads out some of the messages they contain, both those pre-printed on
the cards and the hand-written additions. 'For a very special grandma.'
'When I think about the things you have done for me over the years I
know that you're not only a wonderful mum but also a unique person.'
'So many things that have brought me happiness and comfort have been
gifts from you. Things like encouragement, advice and kindness.'
'Mum, have a wonderful mother's day, love you loads thanks for remembering me in my times of need.' These cards clearly derive from a
common stylistic tradition. They are manufactured with paper so heavily drenched in sentiment that they feel as though if you squeezed them
tight, they would flood the floor with tears.

One of my (no doubt many) prejudices is that I detest the English
attitude to sentimentality. If I happen to listen to a programme such as
'Critic's forum' on Radio Four, I can more or less predict that at some
point a critic will comment on how excellent a film or book is because
it doesn't contain a shred of sentimentality. Sado-masochistic violence
of practically any form is entirely appropriate for aesthetic creation,
but God forbid that something might contain a trace of sentimentality; this would forfeit any claim to artistic merit. By contrast, I
will sometimes seek out a Bollywood family musical or a Hollywood
version of *Little Women*, knowing full well that I will start crying as
soon as the scene is set and continue through to the credits at the end.
Given the national stereotypes about the English inability to express

emotion and the way this constrains relationships, one can't help thinking that the abhorrence of sentiment is in some respects a systematic denial of something that the English are in need of rather more than most.

I admit I find it hard to relate immediately to messages such as:

Your kind and caring ways I hope you always share,
your patience and understanding are far beyond compare

or:

To thank you for the memories and all the lovely ways,
    you have of bringing special joy to ordinary days.
To thank you for your thoughtfulness and for your special love,
    and to wish you all the happiness you're so deserving of.

Yet overcoming this distance and condescension is essential. The primary grounds for the practice of anthropology is empathy, the ability to see the world from perspectives other than one's own, and empathy is not a million miles from sentimentality – it is the generic as opposed to the personal expression of feeling. One has to start therefore from the undeniable observation that, like many others, Mrs Stone clearly finds the precise phrases used in these cards to be highly significant and meaningful. Certainly they are manufactured commodities, but then so are chocolates, or films, or flowers.

When Mrs Stone buys cards for her relatives, she doesn't simply select the first she comes to; she will read a dozen different such cards until she finds one that expresses what she feels. With so many relatives, a good deal of her own time is spent finding the right message. She has become a connoisseur of what some may regard as doggerel but which, through the labour of her selection, becomes profound. 'I like to read the cards, and sometimes they ask me – where did I get these cards from. Someone told me recently: "Grandma, I think you might have your own printer." Because they don't see those things anywhere. They are so special – so, you know, I try to get special cards for them and I know they do the same thing for me.' Her aim is to make someone feel that they are cherished, and in turn she assumes that, when she receives a card, it signifies the careful selection of a rhyming message that conveys the degree to which she is cherished.

Mrs Stone's problem is that she simply cannot bring herself to throw these cards away, however many there are and however much they accumulate. 'Some of my cards are up for months. Sometimes it's a thank you and I like to look at some of the thank yous. I see there is a pretty thank you and I think, let me see who's sent it to me. "I've got to hand it to you, I've always known you were thoughtful, but this time you have outdone yourself." So when you read thank you cards like this, I don't want to get rid of them straight away, you don't really want to. "It's nice to know that there are still people who take so much pleasure in doing special things and making others feel good and I just had to thank you and let you know that I think you're someone very special." You can't throw away things like this. It's these two little ones, they can barely write: "Dear grandma, really sorry we are so late getting back to you, we have been waiting for some photos to come back so we could send you a card with them."'

She does want to clear some of the cards out, but, when she starts on one of the bundles and reads the content, she just hasn't the heart to part with them. 'Some people give you a card and you know it is coming from the heart. So I definitely keep those cards. So many happy things mean I can't throw them away.' I have got lots of them over the years, I try to throw them away sometimes but can't!' Between birthdays, and Christmas and perhaps above all Mother's Day, it is hardly surprising that the house seems to be drowning in cards. But nothing else speaks so directly to what makes Mrs Stone's life worthwhile.

A middle-class person may spend just as much time going through cards published by the Victoria and Albert Museum or Oxfam to find a visual image that is appropriate because it isn't sentimental, but so perfectly tasteful that in its own way it, too, demonstrates the labour of concern that has gone into its selection. The difference is merely one of class. While the middle class avoid direct reference to what they wish to convey because they consider it vulgar; others, who have not been socialised into a system of aesthetic distancing from the immediacy of emotions, go directly to the message itself. Mrs Stone is quite sure and surely right, that her feelings of cherishing and love will be shared by many other people and that her individual feelings can therefore be properly conveyed by this generic form. This speaks to a common humanity and she is entirely comfortable with the explicit open sharing of that humanity.

> So Mrs Stone I want to say, I appreciate all you are.
> I think your home is beautiful and to your family you're a star.
> I hope the house in Jamaica is really a dream come true.
> And for all your help with our research here is a big thank you.

PORTRAIT 8

TATTOO

Charlotte is in her early twenties; she is highly sociable and clearly prefers to be in company rather than on her own. She is also very open, to a degree that is slightly troubling. Troubling because one can't help wondering if it implies an almost inappropriate innocence or naivety; then wondering in turn whether this simply reflects our own loss of the capacity to accept such openness at face value, without suspicion that it must be other than it seems. One reason, though, for her openness is simply that our project is dear to her heart. Perhaps of all the people we encountered in our research, she has the most consistent and systematic set of ideas about how to work with, how to control and how to benefit from the technologies of attachment. She is also someone who clearly enjoys expounding her 'philosophy' of such things. Not that she is immodest. It is simply something that deeply interests her and she has, quite evidently, made a huge commitment to this very topic.

The evidence for this lies in her single most obvious attribute to a passing stranger: the sheer abundance of piercings and tattoos that she displays. At the time we met her, she was in the middle of having her legs tattooed more or less in their entirety. In part, this was her gift to the tattooist, a friend over the past eighteen months. To become a professional tattooist one needs first to demonstrate one's skill through application to volunteers. Such a substantial tattoo will take months to complete and represents a major commitment from the one to the other – something that Charlotte welcomes in certain respects. For Charlotte's philosophy of the tattoo includes the way deep friendships can, in this manner, confidently leave their indelible mark. Clearly, also, such grand designs are the culmination of a devotion to this body art which shows itself in a number of other tattoos, from her arms and back to her neck, and piercings evident on ears, nose and belly. All in addition to those on more intimate parts of her body, not shown to the general public.

Merely the possession of this body decoration, however, would not have signalled anything in particular to us. There must be countless reasons, from boredom to exhibitionism, why people choose to have piercings and tattoos. Before talking to her we would never have guessed the degree to which she has embarked on a quest so close to our own, although through very different means. We merely had a vague premonition that marking the body in such a manner could be yet another genre through which attachment becomes inscribed, and therefore we welcomed a chance to discuss this at some point in our research with a relevant subject.

It turned out that there were precedents for tattooing in Charlotte's family, but not such that would have led one to expect them to re-surface on her own body. Her grandfather had tattoos from his youth which now, late in his life, he bitterly regretted. Indeed one imagines that most people who resist the lure of tattooing do so for precisely this reason: the fear that an act of the moment in effect leaves scars for life. On the other hand, it was with her mother's connivance that she first set foot on this path, with a single ear-piercing when she was eleven. It was a jeweller, a friend of her mother's, who pierced both her ear and that of her twin. He then lent the gun to her mother, who intended to pierce the other ear while Charlotte slept but couldn't summon up the courage to do it. As a result, Charlotte sported a single earring at a time when this was not common, which led to a trend at her school that her mother felt guilty for having started.

Her second piercing, at the age of fifteen, emerged simply from a desire to have the other ear done because she wanted to look more like the other girls of her age. Her third, in her nose, at seventeen, actually failed. It was done with an earring gun and didn't heal until she took the stud out, after a year. So any further developments took place despite warnings and difficulties. Nevertheless she persevered, and soon was marking all the key moments in her life with piercings in the ears, belly and elsewhere. She developed such a passion for these that at one point she was adding new piercings almost weekly. Some of this was associated with moving out from parental control and the classic teenage assertion 'you don't know who I am, now I've moved out'.

These new piercings marked all manner of events. For example, about one in her ear she says it recalls the time 'I had met one of my very good friends in Camden Town and this person had sort of introduced me to Camden Town and made me feel like actually I can go there and not feel like everyone else looks better. That symbolises to me that I had sort of made it in the group. It had got to the stage where people would talk to *you*, and not because you are wearing all the labels under the sun. It's actually because they want to talk to you, because you're a good person. So I would be upset if this piercing was to close, because that would be very difficult.'

Since she was by then an older teenager, this coincided with a sense of wanting to have more control over her relationship to her mother and what she regarded as the requisite autonomy. For example, when her mother started to complain 'oh, but you're just trying to be the same as everyone else', she responded by seeking out the most extreme and different piercings, so as to be in a position to answer back: 'I've got a piercing, but not because everyone else has that, but because nobody does actually.' It's possible that this balance between copying and separation was established first in relation to her mother; but even more because she had a twin. She wanted to be like her, but then she also wanted to be very different. The same process develops in her relationship with her friends. She starts by copying them, but then she finds ways of marking out her individual self through differences.

As one might expect with piercings and tattoos; there is a strong element of what could be termed the conventionally transgressive; for example, those Camden Town strategies of trying to see just how many piercings she could get away with, or what makes for a radically different piercing. She doesn't always win her battles with society. Not long ago, the management in her workplace changed and she was forced to remove many of her earrings. 'That felt like they were taking my whole soul from me, it really did. Because everyone knew me for those earrings, they were the happy earrings. And when she made me take them out I did cry. It was absolutely awful, because I felt it wasn't me any more. They had taken away a big part of what I had made myself.' She consoled herself a little by keeping all that was removed in a drawer. She also started to accentuate piercings on areas of her body that are covered up, such as her belly, which began to sprout some really large and obtrusive rings.

One of her strategies is simply accumulation, as in the quantity of piercings. Unlike other members of her family, she is seen as someone who likes to accumulate things from her past. She is not at all ashamed of all the stuff that she retains from the days when she was a devotee of a boy band. She keeps travel cards, photo albums, concert programmes – all to the annoyance of her mother, who sees it as clutter and is looking forward to Charlotte taking the stuff away to her own place (something she is planning to do soon). The other strategy is to use piercings as a means of turning memories into an object-like form, which can be attached and detached from the body and thereby controlled. She always favoured things she can attach as memory to her body: a half-a-heart necklace she had from a boy and wore for six years until she lost it, or the ring her mother gave her when she was twenty-one.

So the jewellery was an early means of attaching memory, and it is as though from this period on she has been experimenting with the specific advantages and disadvantages of various forms of externalised memory. This desire for control is not applied just to things. She also starts to develop memory as a kind of fiction. Although born in London, she has developed an imagined association with Brazil, the place of origin of her lover. When we met her, we simply couldn't place her in terms of her accent, which turned out to be because she is mastering accent as another means of embodying the sense that Brazil is where she is *really* from. You don't expect to meet a fake Brazilian-in-London accent, even in my work. So, as with the jewellery and the piercings, she is exploring unexpected ways in which associations can be made attachable and detachable, and above all inalienable – something she will finally achieve with the tattoo.

Every single piercing or tattoo represents a highly specific memory she can look at to remind herself of its origin. Those on her back are photographed, so she can see them more easily at her own convenience.

At first, piercings were, simply, significant memories. Then, as things started to improve for her socially, she became more insistent that they represent specifically happy memories. 'I called them happy piercings because I put in colours instead, because at that point they were plain. Then I started putting in purple and different fun things because I was happy. When we used to go out of a night I got confidence whilst I was there, so I started doing colour.' The memory can be of a friend, or a fabulous party, or sometimes a party which was actually held in order to have the piercing done, along with friends devoted to the same purpose. She is ambivalent about memories that are not clearly happy. For example, she has happy photographs on the wall, but the one dating from the time when her lover returned to Brazil lies in a little box on the top of the wardrobe which she can't reach. She just knows that it is there.

Most people think of memory as something we possess inside our heads and we control from within. When we talk of reflection on things, we tend to think, first, in terms of the medium of language and thought. But Charlotte has seen that a memory can also be treated as a thing, an artefact. Some can be thrown away like old clothes when you are tired of them; some become a life-long commitment. Her self-reflection is rather external and visual. I can only surmise, but it may be that particular individuals find it hard to control the way memories bubble to the surface within their head – problematic as well as happy ones. They may conclude that externalisation provides a better means of controlling memory, keeping them separated into clear categories of good and bad. This talk of happy and bad times may seem too simplistic – the ideal that we can keep the good and expel the bad could seem infantile, an unwillingness to face up to contradictions. But actually Charlotte's strategies are much more subtle. What she cultivates are gradations of materiality. These help her avoid thinking in terms of degrees of goodness and badness. She prefers to use the qualities of different material forms to create her own gradations between permanence and letting go.

And this provides the context for understanding her movement from piercings to tattoos. Because, ultimately, the advantage of the tattoo is that it is completely inalienable, something that cannot be separated from its possessor. So, in her philosophy of memory and attachment, the tattoo is quite precise and linked to specific qualities and potentials. When her lover went back to Brazil, she had a particularly large ear-piercing, carried out to create a hole that was stretched and could never close, to symbolise the impossibility of closure in the relationship itself. This was a quality further embodied in tattoos.

Some people clearly regard tattooing as a kind of irresponsible, immature act by people who haven't thought through the consequences. But for Charlotte it is quite the opposite. She has gradually progressed through other possibilities – through music, photographs, clothes, jewellery and piercings, and she has worked through the precise way in which each can be employed as a technology of attachment. The piercings are to a degree reversible. One time, when she moved to a different part of London, she systematically took out a series of bottom rings from her ear as a means of clearing out some older memories and other 'rubbish' that she now felt she wanted to leave behind. This developed out of an earlier pattern, with the realisation that she could throw away clothes associated with bad memories, for instance one jumper that reminded her of a particularly awful concert.

The full tattoo represents an extension of this material commitment to the past. Although she does not state the connection, it becomes clear that, while piercings are generally memories of events, tattoos are increasingly related to specific relationships. Her very first tattoo, which her mother agreed to as long as it was not visible, was a symbol of her twin. A critical tattoo was carried out with her lover, so that they both shared an identical tattoo. It was an image from Brazil, even though Charlotte had never visited the place at that time. She reports that she felt so secure and confident in what she was doing, that she fell asleep while being tattooed!

Charlotte is only tattooed when she knows exactly what she wants to do with that tattoo, rejecting alternative versions. For example, she is well aware that some people tattoo a cross or other memorabilia of a deceased friend or relative; but this is an anathema to her personal philosophy of the accumulation of happy memories only. Equally, she is adamant about the principle that, by relating each individual tattoo to the memory of a particular person, she keeps control of an art form which, left to itself, could run riot over her as a person. 'I did meet a guy who had a full, everywhere tattoo. And I said: "What do they mean?", and he said: "They started off meaning things and being points of my life like a story and then I just got back fillers." To me that symbolises a person who has given up, it really does, it doesn't matter anymore. I just get a block there or a little rhyme there . . . so he's just doing it because they have taken over him, rather than him controlling what should be? . . . I am so happy when I look at these as they symbolise a whole year of my life which was definitely the happiest time so far. I would never extend it.'

As part of her sense of control, she doesn't see pain as significant because, for her, the important thing is that she is subjecting herself to it. This is completely different from unintended pain, as when one has fallen over and broken one's arm. The pain in tattooing is a form of control rather than of relinquishing control. It sits alongside the way she wants to control her access to memory through these devices. One advantage of bodily decorations is that she can look at them any time and be reminded of who she is and what she has done. As she puts it, 'you can't just run home and get a photo'. She also wants to control the precise way the tattoo is created in order to facilitate the connection with one particular moment or decision in a relationship. While others will go back after months to have some part of their tattoo filled in, 'I refused to do it because I feel they were done at those points in my life. They mark that moment in time.' Ultimately she sees this laying down of memory as a resource she will be able to call on when times become difficult. 'Especially if you're upset, you just have to look there and it brings back such great memories.' They have already been important in dealing with temporary separations from her lover. This was why Charlotte took to our research immediately she sensed its intention. If anyone had already created for themselves a distinct project to construct a series of material cultures which could be organised as forms of attachment and separation, and which might remain supportive when it came to dealing with loss later on, then it was surely Charlotte.

HAUNTED

Those cartoon ghosts from the classic ghost stories now invariably come to us in the form of an apparition in a white cloth: the ghoul, scary but somehow also pure, colourless, now bereft of that which speaks to the substance of life. Stan's own life would be a great deal easier if his ghosts looked anything like that. But they don't. Stan's ghosts are full of colour, the bright cotton cloth of the women, the deep crimson speckles that spread from body parts flying through the air, the vivid colours of plastic buckets and bags in which these people had been carrying their possessions a moment before. And, for Stan, there are not just two or three such ghosts – a few white shroudings; there are dozens of them, many children, many elderly, some tall, mostly thin, mostly not recognisable now as anything much, so many fragments of bodies. These ghosts haunt with little purpose other than to pursue the individual who has removed them from the sentient world. If one is suppressed by Stan, so many others are ready to take their place; all equally innocent, poverty-stricken refugees, who now have only one place of residence: inside the head of the man they tried and judged a long time ago. They have waited many years for Stan to join them, and Stan has sensed – as they have sensed – they don't have much longer to wait.

Stan can only repeat to himself, to them and to the world the one phrase which was never particularly effective and by now has become almost emptied of any content through repetition. That he was only doing his job. It was a job, that's all it was, not even the one he would have chosen. Stan would have preferred to have been in the regular army, but he pretty much never managed to get what he had wanted from life. So for Stan it was a job. He was employed as a mercenary, a hired soldier, in this case protecting an arms dump in the forest of Colombia; that he feared, wrongly, might be under attack. Stan, just doing his job, triggered the explosion to ensure that these weapons did not fall into enemy hands. It was an explosion which left more than seventy refugees in no need of finding a home any more. Another part of them must surely reside with families, lovers, friends – that part of them that spoke to happiness, meals shared, watched sunsets, labouring together in fields. But Stan knew nothing of any of that. He knew them only as they died – some instantly and others through a prolonged wretched process: but each, in his or her own moment of terror, somehow found their way inside the head of the man who was responsible for this outrage. As for Stan, he is still alive, but only barely. Although we didn't know this until after we had met him several times, the day before one of these meetings he had just returned from hospital after yet another failed suicide attempt.

It is our thesis – that people sediment possessions, lay them down as foundations, material walls mortared with memory, strong supports that come into their own when times are difficult and the people who laid them down face experiences of loss. Having banked their possessions in the vaults of internal memory and external possession, they cash them in at times of need, at times of loss. In many of these portraits our thesis finds some support. But what happens to a person such as Stan, who when he looks deep down inside himself for this supportive structure, sees, not solid foundations, but vast gaps and depressions? When only nightmares, ghastly and unremitting, come from these depths? Every time one tries to build, or even just to find some bedrock upon which to build, the bricks and the stones simply slip back into that deep. Because nothing else that might have tried to occupy that space can possibly compete with this vastly more impressive presence, which insists that it is the only possible definition of one's own identity. Ghosts – not cartoon ghosts, but actual ghosts of those he has killed – are like black holes that suck the very possibility of substance from Stan's world. But they themselves have definition; unlike cartoons, they are only too clear. There are no colours bright enough to outshine them, no emotions strong enough to seal those feelings, no relationship built over years that could stand against Stan's one great monumental relationship to those who he has destroyed in that one moment.

Listening to Stan, it was no surprise to learn later on that he had attempted suicide several times – perhaps it was more surprising that he hadn't yet succeeded. After all, what did a string of failed suicides add to his treasure-chest of a past? A few more figures of the almost dead. And who would be the perpetrator? The very same man, trying yet again for one more, one final, death. Equally unheroic, equally a failure, equally a job not done properly. Hardly the stuff to start re-building one's life. Just more quicksand that sucked one back into depression, released and sucked one back again. Plenty of other people suffer from depression, attempt suicide. Often, for them, it is nightmares about what might happen: fears and fantasy. Compared to them, Stan is deeply authentic, he doesn't need to manufacture any of this. He is the real thing; the real Stan, now in his sixties. It isn't even that life is so deeply depressing. Increasingly, it is just deeply tiring.

Occasionally though, even Stan can see beyond this dense fog of depression, can go through some door opened by others and visit some other images of himself. We watched this happen, because we became one of those doors. It was probably a very long time since anyone had done what we were about to do. We requested and enlisted his help in our own quest, initially with no idea at all as to the possible significance of this. We couldn't know of the people he had killed, or whom he was trying to kill now; we have no way of knowing who a person is until the end of our encounters. We were just intent on listening, observing, following back down a road signposted by possessions we could see or hear about. It was a road which, for Stan, had been blocked for some time, but our enquiry opened it up, and he undertook this journey quite willingly. On that last occasion when he admitted he had just returned from another attempted suicide, we could experience his dramatic change. Within a couple of hours he seemed buoyed up, able to contemplate other Stans. Looking for a change not at the end but at the beginnings of the self. We even found some long forgotten photographs, tracking back to Stan at the age of eight. There were some images that looked quite idyllic, ornaments that seemed to hold a story. Perhaps we could resurrect a time before, an unsullied time. Perhaps we could become the conduit of some grand redemptive process.

But we are not Conrad or Dostoevsky, and this was not *Heart of Darkness* or *Crime and Punishment*. We could not help Stan find redemption. Nor are we analysts seeking to dislodge, like shamans, some impediment to freedom from being haunted by the past. All we did was to listen a bit. We mattered for a day or two, but not that much. Stan has had professionals on his case: psychiatrists working for years to help him, as he put it, 'submerging those things, holding them down'. In any case, Stan doesn't seem about to make his peace with the world, with God, with other people, or with himself. On the contrary, he faces the world bristling with bitter defensiveness. Stan knows that people call him violent, racist and crude, and for him this definition by opposition is all that's left to give him shape and form. He is not likely to change now. And if this means that there is some kind of hell he is going to, well, he has more experience in surviving those fires than most.

We could only sift the detritus strewn across the road we took back with Stan into his own origins. We didn't find that other past, the happiness, the sweet innocent family life. We didn't find the one thing that in almost every encounter gives some alternative base to build on: the significant relationships with persons or things. Those idyllic photos, all had some tragic flipside, hidden by smiles for the camera. Stan was nothing like George. Stan certainly had a life, but, if George's portrait was unremitting in its emptiness, Stan's was pretty unremitting in its content.

Usually one starts at least with the initial support implied by family photographs. There should have been Stan's mother, but she died when he was a child, and Stan, stricken with the same disease, spent much of his teenage years in hospital. There was Stan's father, but all Stan's memories of him were of violence and harshness; not just beatings, but the breaking and fracturing of limbs as he sought to withstand his father's temper. No qualifications, no skills. From this absence of family, Stan drifted into a world of petty criminals, quick money and flash reputations. Stan's first real education came with the gradual understanding of the extent and callousness of his own exploitation. He had tried to enlist, he had tried other jobs also. There were various twists and turns before he ended up with the one occupation which, forever afterwards, was scarred onto his flesh as 'merely a job'. Some of the earlier scars were more literal: he had taken a few bullets himself in his time as a mercenary. But it was becoming clear that there were deep scars on the inside long before the evident marks on the outside.

Nor was Stan able to tell that other tale, of redemption. The one with the good woman who stuck by him, or the pretty children whose unwavering love finally gave him the strength he needed to face down his own past. There had been no Hollywood scriptwriter on hand to help rewrite his story. Oh, there had been a wife all right, and not just one but several children. Stan had a sense that his life would depend on the friendships and relationships he could form. He had spent decades trying. But the friendships formed in a world of pimps and prostitutes were just set-ups for betrayal. He married a woman because he had got her pregnant, and her next pregnancy was courtesy of another man. Faced with such betrayal, he formed his own protective cynicism, his own sense that he needed to use people before they used him. It became more and more difficult to reach that basic trust that would allow relationships to deepen. Instead, he developed, relationships with other kinds of women: the Latins and the Indians he met in the jungles of South America – relationships of clear-cut dominance, which he found altogether more satisfactory than those he had experienced before, although they had their own limitations and transience.

In any case, all this was now long ago. It is well over a decade since he had any contact at all with any of his children. 'They are no longer part of my life. If any of them would knock on the door here now, I would tell them: "Look, please don't, you don't know me, I don't know you, and because I happen to be your father it doesn't mean to say that we have a relationship." To be honest about it, I'm too old and too tired. I'm not prepared to go through that kind of emotional crap any more. I don't need it. I don't need it. I don't need them bringing their baggage onto me. I guess that sounds horrible and selfish. I don't have any feelings about them at all really. They are there, end of story.' The children seem to have inherited something from Stan. In one story his son threw Stan through a window.

If Stan has lost it with respect to his wives and children, there isn't much hope he is going to make it in any other relationship; now that he is in his sixties, unattractive and unappealing in pretty much every way.

For one thing, Stan knows that to develop a relationship with someone else, he would have to create a better one with himself, and, though he has tried many times, he just keeps failing. He has plenty of stories about the low points. One came just before he moved into his present house. 'I was on benefits, I was the lowest of the low, I had no self-esteem, everything had gone completely, I had no credit, I had no bank. I felt like the plug had been pulled on my life, I felt like a nobody, written off so I couldn't. I was of no use to man, beast, society, whatever – I failed completely.' There had been the odd high point, like the one when he had a holiday in Spain, a really fun time, where nine of them ended up in the pool without a stitch of clothing; but then that was ruined by food-poisoning and then he took up smoking again, after he had so painfully managed to wean himself off it; and the sense of failure returned. When he shakes himself by the collar he can clean the house, sort his things out, care about his clothes, shoes and boots especially. But most of the time he and it are a tip. As he put it, mostly he couldn't give a shit if stuff was moved or dusted in a month.

So by now Stan has pretty much given up on what most people would regard as real relationships. Or, more to the point, real relationships have for a long time now given up on Stan. Today, in his sixties, he has returned to a place not very far from where he began. His first real independence from family had been in that world dominated by pornography and prostitutes, and, if there is no family to return to, the world never looks like running dry of these two resources. Having failed to find redemption in the objects of the past, we start our investigation of the objects of the present. As it happens, they are a genre of objects that have a particular significance in our work where a constant theme is the ambiguity between relationships with people and relationships with things. And one genre that seems to feed off this same ambiguity is pornography. Usually, especially since the rise of feminism, this is portrayed quite simply. Pornography consists in the reduction of women to mere objects for the purpose of male masturbation. But, in ethnographic observation, few things turn out to be simple, and few things turn out to accord with generalisations which come from taking a stance rather than making an observation. For Stan, one could almost argue the very opposite of this: pornography is about as far as he can go in the transformation of mere objects into sort of subjects.

If Stan is not going to find relationships directly, he has to find them vicariously, through some route or other. In his case it is definitely other. Stan has used pornography to find relationships with people through the length and breadth of the country. People who happen to share his particular obsession with reality TV babes, that is, with the various women who have appeared in the various reality TV series such as Celebrity Love Island and who, for one reason or another (and it is rarely just a question of looks), have attracted the prurient interest of at least some of the populace. At first, one might think pornography is the end point of this process – the turning of these subjects into objects. Certainly Stan communicates with others who get off on those particular scenes. This is not exactly unusual; one has only to look at the archive of a national newspaper like The *Sun*, or at the mass of weekly celebrity magazines, to know how much of a shared national fixation there is with those 'real-sex-on-TV' moments, when some contestant got her tits out, or there was some fondling under the sheets. Stan is one of maybe thousands who would video a whole twenty-four hours' worth in order to be able to isolate and get at some such particular moment.

So the starting point is pure pornography, the isolation of something, something that can take weeks of work undertaken with the patience of a fisherman. But in this case the ultimate catch is a flash of cunt. Yet from this starting point – this pure, isolated object, refined, preserved and treasured – the process seems to go into reverse. Because, having hewed a diamond from the crap around it, the object starts to be used to create actual subjects.

This process develops in two directions. Firstly, through the sharing of such images across the internet. On the internet Stan can find the appreciation of his connoisseurship. There is craft: the ability to manipulate computers, editing equipment, graphic technologies – all, in Stan's case, completely self-taught. Then you can transmit the results to others. Stan shows us many examples of the appreciative comments he has received from his internet friends, his fellow hobbyists, those who exchange like for like. From this common interest deeper conversations flow, exchanges about life, opinions, the problem of being flooded with too many immigrants, the way some women treat men, you know they walk past you 'like they have shit on their shoes'. There is something like friendship here. So Stan doesn't just catch his fish, he feeds on them.

There is a second process, which turns these objects back into subjects. The pure erotic entity becomes itself the foundation for a much deeper interest in the lives of the babes themselves. The genius of reality TV is that it lends itself to this process better than any prior programme. There is none of the usual ambiguity between actor and role, celebrity and real life. The whole point is that they were always real lives, what you saw is what you got, inside the Big Brother house or the Celebrity Love Island or outside in a London street. Thanks to reality TV, celebrities really did transmute, from having been the distant creations of the film industry to someone approximating the girl next door you spied at through a hole in the wall, and dreamt that you might, just once, catch her in the act of having sex. So Stan and his friends are not mere passive recipients of reality TV, they put themselves into the same situations as the contestants. Just like the other contestants, they learn more and more intimate details about these people who now share their lives. They become experts and they endlessly discuss the morality of each and every action. Who started the fight, whose turn it was to clear up. What's special about reality TV celebs is that they don't leave the set for the outside world. The outside world becomes included as part of the set. Now, wherever they go and whatever they do, they remain part of this vast network of discussion and appraisal.

Stan, as one might expect, has *attitude* in relation to what has become his babes. He celebrates the way they just don't give a toss. They don't take no crap. They argue when they feel like it, fight when they feel like it and get their kit off when they (and Stan and a million others) feel like it. Stan cares deeply about his babes and how they behave. Indeed, this is probably central to understanding his relationship to pornography. I don't know (frankly, I don't wish to know) Stan's sexual fantasies, but I imagine they are all about finding a means to turn these objects into his subjects. I imagine that he needs a means to encounter his object as a genuine person, so that, in his fantasy he can create a plausible encounter that leads to sex. He could have been her driver, he could have met her at that club she is known to visit. He could have talked to her for ages about music, since he knows exactly what she listens to. In fantasy, Stan has probably treated these TV babes with more respect than any actual woman he has spent any time with. So the sex becomes part of the story which is required in order to elicit the sex.

I certainly don't see anything redemptive about this. Equally, Stan doesn't expect anyone to see him in a redemptive light. He doesn't want any teary liberal to pretend he is who he isn't. His imaginations of any relationship with women are certainly clear with respect to the direction of power and control. It's not just fantasy, it is the way he treated the women he came across when he worked as a mercenary. When today he describes his ideal wife, she comes in the shape of a completely passive housewife, there to serve his needs. What he imagines (entirely incorrectly) to be the traditional Filipino or Asian woman. She would be totally loyal and he would in turn help her, as he describes it, to come out of the environment she had lived in. In his imagination, he has a similar relationship of power and control over the TV babes who now serve his sexual and other needs. What really upsets Stan is when one of his babes doesn't behave in the way he has come to expect of her. 'You know M has gone down a path that I can't handle and I don't like and this is why I have to shut it out.' He exerts whatever control he can. Prominent in his room are photographs of some of these reality TV babes, and they are hugely important to him. But when this particular character started turning away from his idea of how she should be, he threatened to put the photo into a drawer. As he phrased it, the photo was now 'doomed'. But then, as he started to feel better about himself and these relationships merely by virtue of the amount of time we were giving to listening to him talk about them, he relented, and by the end of our discussion he was willing to let the photograph stay just a while longer on the mantelpiece. I was tempted to make some sardonic comment to the effect that, no doubt, M was eternally grateful for Stan's magnanimity, but I bit my tongue instead.

Not that Stan would probably care much one way or the other. He has been on death's doorstep too many times, and always reached the same conclusion. These were not moments of final confession in which he realised what he could do for the world. They have precisely the opposite effect. Impending death 'throws everything about morals out of the window. You do what you do because you are the only person who is important in your life, and you are. I'm the only person who's important in my life.' The fact that so much of his time was spent in a shadowy world, in illegal activities, when he didn't even have a passport, is recalled today as his not having had an identity over those years. Perhaps this is why he finds himself, senses his own presence most fully and most easily, in his strongest assertions, in what he often refers to as his own 'bloody mindedness'. What he seeks as the evidence of his own continued existence in the world could only now be found fully affirmed, either through his own violence and opposition to others or through the attention of a good-looking woman. These have become the two possible passports that would restore his identity.

In the meantime, Stan knows full well the advantages of these internet-based relationships, both with the fantasy objects he obsesses about and with those other people who share his obsessions. In these relationships he doesn't have to give anything away. Using the internet, he can spend a good time with a bunch of twenty-year-olds (or younger) gossiping, sharing and fantasising on-line at no cost. Including loads of girls who, within his own mind, he can do what the hell he likes to. If this required lying and cheating, well, that at least was something Stan could do pretty well. Something close to a talent in life. Thanks to the reality TV babes and the internet, he has finally found the genre of relationships that work for him better than the real ones he used to have – but, in Stan's case, that may not be saying much.

PORTRAIT **10**

TALK TO THE DOG

Sometimes one feels that the key to understanding another person lies in those initial few seconds of meeting, in the way they open the front door. Some throw it wide open either to welcome or to confront you; some keep it on the latch until they have multiple reassurances. All of these responses presume a significance to the encounter, an intimation of help or harm, or, more commonly, just a desire not be involved or disturbed. In the case of Harry, there was that typically tentative, unwilling, gradual opening. Yet it was also clear that this was not to be taken as evidence of resentment or sense of affront at being disturbed. It was rather that the person in front of us simply assumed that this must be a mistake. That no one who was not just reading gas meters or a Jehovah's Witness could really want to come in and certainly, if it was the case that we wanted to speak and listen to someone, then it couldn't actually be Harry.

Harry simply knew that there was nothing interesting about him whatsoever, and therefore we would just be wasting our time. If there was some frustration, it was with the fact that we didn't seem immediately to understand this, to appreciate it, to have appraised somehow that Harry was the last person on earth we should have come to see. It seemed unreasonable that he would need to be bothered to establish in person his own lack of qualifications for being part of any kind of project at all. Not only was this made clear at the outset, but even after several meetings with Harry there was no real feeling that he had changed his views. However much we became excited, and showed our genuine interest and enthusiasm for him as a person, he felt that this was simply even more concrete evidence of our mistake. He couldn't possibly be the source of this interest. It was important to remain formal with Harry. He would have preferred us to have had a proper, fixed questionnaire instead of following him down every byway of conversation. He was reassured rather than disturbed by our little digital recorder, which at least signalled that this was proper work.

There was only one being for whom this was conspicuously not true, for whom Harry was unequivocally the most important person on the planet, the object of total devotion, love and interest, and that was Harry's dog Jeff. A feeling that was entirely reciprocated by Harry, who showed as much love and affection for this animal as most people could ever manage for another person. When, on our second attempt, Harry actually allowed us into his house, this was probably because the one thing he really didn't mind was that we may have come to meet his dog. Jeff is a large mottled brown and black elderly beast who quietly and slowly comes to the door to greet us. Jeff neither barks nor growls, from that moment until our time to leave. For all this, we somehow can't help feeling that, as far as Harry is concerned, we are only speaking to him in place of the true inhabitant of the house, the person who really matters here: the animal sitting patiently in the corner.

This impression is reinforced by the aesthetics of the living-room. At first it looks typical enough for an aging bachelor. The chimney breast is a dark glossy maroon and in its centre sits a clock. The surrounding walls are covered in a deeply lined textured, magnolia paper, stopped two-thirds up by a dado rail; the two are battened together and stained a dark red brown. A bright clean white paint finishes the top of the wall and the ceiling. The curved panel of windows at one end, common to these Victorian terraces, is covered in several layers. A central, light-coloured, wooden Venetian blind blocks out the main view of the street, to replace it with cracks between slats, met at each edge by white semi-opaque inner curtains, overlain by heavy cotton flannel maroon curtains draped in folds at the sides and tied. So far so normal; but, as one looks down rather than up, the room becomes progressively doggified. The carpet is a brown beige that matches precisely the outside of the dog's paws as they stand upon it. The furniture is either black or a darker brown, which are also Jeff's predominant colours. Everything seems to blend together, so that one is drawn to describe the room itself, and not just the dog, as mottled brown and black. Then there is the way the room is organised, dominated by what was once a large sofa – but this is very clearly not a sofa that any person has sat on for quite some time. This is where the dog sleeps and feels comfortable, and the patches and tears all speak to the comfort of the dog and the potential discomfort of any person who might try to appropriate the space. Then there are various objects which, one assumes, are there to be chewed or played with, or otherwise to furnish the room in accordance with doggie desires. Finally, lest there be any doubt whatever, there, on the shelf, is a montage which appears to show the dog on a sofa sitting next to Harry, with a balloon coming from the dog's head that states: 'This is the life: I have got them exactly where I want them.' Outside the house is Harry's car, which is no different from the living-room. This is a car out of some Disney cartoon, with the cartoon man acting as chauffeur and the dog travelling in style at the back. The seat has been removed and replaced with a rug, and there is the same set of tears and materials, so that one can imagine any number of mongrels and Labradors peering in and wagging their tails and thinking whatever the doggie thought is for – 'cosy'. In Jeff's case, an elderly dog who has occasional extensive trips to Scotland, this is undoubtedly, very much appreciated.

Thomas Hardy captures a certain English characteristic, or maybe one common to country people everywhere: the ability of two men to walk for hours in silence along a country lane with the sense that silence is somehow more sociable than conversation. One sees this sometimes in a pub: two older men, sitting nursing their drinks. It is as though each is aware that mere conversation, for the sake of it, for the sake of being polite, is a burden. It requires effort and in any case feels false and unnecessary. For two decent and taciturn men, it can be as though each is grateful to the other for the gift which is given in the mutual agreement that no such effort is required any more; that it is the proximity of this other like-minded person that matters, not some idle chit-chat. We never saw Harry except for extended conversation, but one soon felt that we were thereby missing another, perhaps more authentic, Harry: one

who does often spend a Saturday night at a pub with the same friend he
has been meeting at that pub on Saturday nights for many years; or the
Harry that occasionally went on long coach trips to away matches for
his local team. And I imagine that on those long journeys Harry would
sit in silence, a symbol of this ancient companionship of man.

I recall thinking once, during an extended stay in Helsinki, that
people in Finland might not be in the least bit boring, if it were not for
the fact that they seemed to be repetitively informing me of how boring
they were. In a similar vein, there were times when one could catch
Harry out, when he was to be found chatting with some of the younger
people in the street, but again and again he would find some way of
telling us that he was not sociable at all. The key to Harry's preservation
of pure unsociability is of course Jeff. Because Jeff has become the excuse
and the legitimacy for almost all Harry's social interactions. This is especially clear from the quite close relationship he maintained with his
difficult and usually drunk next-door neighbour, June, right until her
death, which occurred during our fieldwork on the street. Harry
described how he she used to come out of her door and ring his bell with
her stick. At this point you might think that these were two adults
intending to have a drink with each other. They might, but this wasn't
the point. The intention behind the action was that, with both doors
open, June's dog, Princess, would rush round and have a good drink out
of Jeff's bowl, and Jeff would simultaneously rush round and have a good
drink from Princess's bowl. The two dogs would then play together.
Nothing could have more firmly and affectionately bonded the two
humans.

Jeff takes on a similar role with respect to many others. When his other
next-door neighbours leave, they give Harry their new address. 'What
for?' says Harry with a meaningful look, before immediately answering
his own question. 'Because they want to see Jeff again.' His annual trip to
Scotland is described largely as Jeff's trip. Harry compares the vet there
with the local one in London. The Scottish vet is more laid back, easy-
going. He wouldn't have insisted on putting down Harry's previous dog,
something for which he has never really forgiven his local vet. He says
much less about the people he is visiting in Scotland.

Harry's sensitivity always seems to express itself most fully in his relationship to dogs. When June died, he considered whether he should take

care of Princess. But, after long and careful consideration, he rejected
the idea. It wasn't fair on the dog because she would be forever going
into the back garden, to look over the fence for June. They were so
close. She wouldn't ever have settled down; she would have pined for
June. It was better if she went somewhere far away. Jeff has an uncanny
ability to substitute for practically anything in Harry's life. So, when
Harry looks back at what he has lost, he tends to reduce it down to that
precise quality for which the dog compensates. Before his unwelcome
redundancy, the advantage of being in work was that it got him out of
the house early in the morning on a routine basis. But that's exactly what
Jeff does for him now. Actually, these days it is Harry who wakes Jeff up
early, rather than the other way around. One can imagine that Harry
would have loved to bring Jeff a cup of tea first thing, if only dogs drank
tea. Unfortunately Jeff cannot quite give Harry the sort of exercise he
was used to. Once there was an hour's brisk trot around the park. Now,
after twenty minutes, there is the risk that Jeff's legs may give way. In
response to this, Harry has no intention of compensating by taking
walks by himself. On the contrary, he notes that he has put on a stone
and half in weight. He knows perfectly well that this is unhealthy, but
somehow it brings him closer to the condition of Jeff. I almost feel that,
if Harry could possibly have arthritis in tandem with Jeff, he would.
Harry describes how, in the evenings, he will often fall asleep in front of
the television; but, of course, television seems to have just the same
effect on Jeff.

   Actually this torpidity is somewhat older and deeper. When Harry
reflects back on his life, he recognises that he is better characterised by
what he hasn't done than by what he has. Thirty years ago, he had
moved into this house with his parents, two older and two younger sisters. Today his parents are dead and all four sisters have moved on to
other places and other people. It was Harry who, for some years,
remained with his elderly mother, cleaning the house and looking after
her, when his sisters had left. And it is Harry who now remains home –
both Harry and Jeff would be offended if one suggested alone – but at
any rate without his family. Only just, the council tried to force him out
since the house was not in his name, but this was one fight that really
mattered to Harry, and eventually he won it. It was only the house that
mattered. His sisters cleared out all his parents' possessions, which for

him were just clutter. But that may be due to the one thing Harry did inherit from his father: a no-nonsense get-on-with-life attitude to the events that overtook one, an attitude that was supposed to be appropriate to a man.

So, when Harry looks back on all that he hasn't done and everywhere he hasn't been he describes himself as 'a lazy sod'. Yet it's clear that this isn't especially critical, because most commonly Harry would use the expression 'lazy sod' in relation to Jeff, and, when said about the dog, the expression is positively endearing. Harry doesn't just see himself in his dog, he has come to know himself more truly through his empathy with the animal. Being brought up in a house dominated by four sisters, there is an edge to the way Harry tends to talk about women in general rather than any one woman in particular. I wonder. If Harry had to choose his life again and was told he could have developed some deeper relationships with women, but only at the expense of missing out on the relationships he has had with his dogs, he would surely have picked what he undoubtedly regards as the more human of the two: the dogs.

The main regret Harry gives voice to now – now that it is obvious that Jeff is not going to be with him much longer – is that he never knew Jeff as a pup and thereby missed out on what could have been a more extended life together. His neighbour's daughter, a fortune teller, mentioned to Harry that he would yet meet a brown Labrador. No doubt she was well-meaning, but Harry was clearly very upset by this prediction and talks almost with anger at her presumption. One has the feeling that such talk is felt as a betrayal of Jeff; that Harry no more wants to talk in terms of Jeff's replacement than one would of replacing a wife or a child whose demise looks imminent. Nevertheless, for all that it can't and indeed shouldn't be said, I have the distinct feeling that this fortune teller saw something truthful in her crystal ball, and there will be one more brown Labrador in Harry's life.

Harry has had his own life of work and other activities. In *Fever Pitch*, Nick Hornby provides an affectionate portrait of a man supporting Arsenal during the times when it never seemed to win (I shared both those times and those particular frustrations). Harry is much more extreme. There is something about his self-deprecating dry sense of humour that fits precisely with his life-long support for his local non-league team. The kind of team that occupies the very lowest realm of the sporting food chain: the footballing plankton, for whom victory is a kind of betrayal of character. There is an endearing faithfulness to a team that always loses, the quality of the dogged. There is also the comfort of the glum, the company of the grumpy. The appreciation that glum and grumpy are not an absence, or a negative; they are two of the great refinements of civilisation. When carefully crafted, they become finely balanced so as not to veer into the maudlin, or the personal, or to lose their slight smirk and ironic twist. This is an art gradually matured over generations. Like the whisky that often accompanies them, there is no end to their perfecting.

For this reason it's very easy to take Harry, mistakenly, at his word. To see in him the uncultivated glum and grumpy, the misanthrope. It takes a while to see through to the art, the very dry humour of this downbeat view of life. It takes a while to see the affectionate, kindly side of this affinity with failure and siding with the underdog. After all, Harry has been invited back, in one case to the friend of a friend, for some thirty consistent years. And it's not charity. When he describes the team he has devoted his life to as 'rubbish', absolute rubbish; or when he talks of the Scottish Hogmanay custom of knocking on a door with a bottle of whisky and says 'if it's a tall dark stranger it is supposed to be good luck. I'm short, fat and grey' – then it's not hard to fathom that hiding behind Jeff there is Harry, and Harry in his own way is quality. Harry never missed a home game and actually rose to be an important official for the club – that is, if any official of such a team could be called important. Today he is getting a bit lax in his attendance. His main social outing is to his sister's, on Sundays, which, as always, is described more in terms of a day out for Jeff – 'He's a crafty one. Come back from sister's having had roast dinner and ice cream and now he's banging one paw on the ground at me saying, where's my normal dinner too?' Harry gets up and gives him a bit of dog food in a bowl.

Jeff is not the only other living creature in this house. Harry also keeps a fish tank, reasonably well stocked. This is something Harry takes quite seriously. He can converse at length about the habits of particular fish and the qualities of gravel, feed and water. His book collection is almost entirely concerned with fish. He seems to have no music whatsoever. There is some merit and some saving in properly knowing one's fish. As Harry noted, 'I spent £25 on plants a few weeks ago and that bugger there decimated them. They lasted a week.' This is a well-kept tank, it's clear that the water is regularly changed, the glass scraped down, the area around, hoovered and cleaned.

There is also a non-living creature here – in this case, particularly non-living. Something people miss about computers is their wonderful capacity to be reduced to practically nothing at all. A couple of little tasks or traits that stand in blissful repudiation of everything a computer can potentially do. Here is this machine, it can achieve unbelievable calculations, extraordinary virtual worlds, give access to vast archives of knowledge. But Harry's computer only ever gets to do two things. It plays patience, and it looks for information about keeping these fish in tanks. That's it. It does both pretty well. Its impeccable mechanical manners seem well suited to the endless card-turning of patience. It's been quite inventive with regard to fishy information, and Harry is now a regular at river.co.uk, 'where fish are family'. But the poor machine doesn't even start to compete with the dog.

The relationship between a person and their pet is hard to characterise with the respect it actually demands. It can be embarrassing enough to talk about the love between people, let alone about what we mean exactly when we talk about the love for an animal. When I was making an earlier study of shopping, I was intrigued by the way people used to be almost pleased if their cat or dog was a really fussy eater; only ever agreeing to some food difficult to obtain, such as boiled hearts, or food from tins that had to be opened in front of them (both actual examples). But then the contrast was evident between the animals who really seemed to appreciate all the hard work of shopping done especially for them and one's husband or children, who never seemed to notice what had been prepared for their dinner, however much work one put into it. When we reached the end of our acquaintance with Harry, I recalled one of the first things he noted; that Jeff never barked. At first it just seemed unusual or curious in a dog. But by then I couldn't help feeling that we had got to know one dog who basically never needed to bark.

PORTRAIT 11

TALES FROM THE PUBLICANS

One of the expectations that come with working on London households, and indeed urban lives in general, is that of the separation and fragmentation of people's experiences. So often work and family, hobbies and holidays seem to occupy quite unrelated segments of a person's time and identity. Sometimes, however, one meets people who live centripetal lives, where everything seems to be drawn inwards and integrated. In the case of Mary and Hugh, this was largely a result of their joint work as publicans. Being a publican was always so much more than simply having a job. The pub became the site at which everything in their lives seemed to have come together.

After forty years in England almost entirely based in pubs, Mary does voluntary work, cooking, talking with and looking after mainly elderly people. She is probably ideally suited to the task of listening to them, since through her years behind the bar she has mastered that special variety of informal listening and counselling role in response to the needs of the many regulars for whom the pub had become as much a home as the place to which they eventually returned. This ambiguity between pub and home was even more true for Mary and Hugh themselves. One result was their relative lack of long-term furnishings and material culture of their own. Managers of a pub are housed and furnished as part of the establishment, and so, when they lost their pub, they found themselves with much less than most people by way of their own possessions. As one glances around their flat, however, it is obvious that they have more than made up for lost time. There are many jokes about the flat having been turned into a gallery: with a couple more pictures they would never have to paint the walls, since you wouldn't be able to see any. This is a vast assemblage; hundreds of items that fill every nook and cranny of hall and living-room. Actually the other rooms are not so different; the bedroom has a pretty comprehensive display of toiletries and ornaments, as does the bathroom. There is something about this mass of stuff and its openness. It is impossible to regard it as mess, it seems instead the evident testimony to a very full life.

It turns out that, while it is on the whole Mary who tells us the tales, Hugh was the one who put up most of the ornaments and decorations; and these tell their own tales in their own way. Things are different from words; they rarely form narrative sequences, one followed by another, as words do. Instead they present themselves simultaneously, so that each may allude to its relation to several other objects and images if one can learn to read the whole. As one gets to know the provenance, content and meaning of each item and photo on these walls, it becomes clear that they cluster around certain key themes. But these are not discrete; rather, they are organised in such a way that they all contribute to the larger whole.

The objects that are directly reminiscent of what, for them, was the core of their lives, their work as publicans, cluster in one area of the hall. An old price list recalls days when light ale or cherry brandy cost what today would seem piffling prices. Two large blue tankard ashtrays, some glass decanters and silver cups also speak to that past. There is a certificate of hygiene, but also a certificate that relates to Mary's current voluntary work, celebrating her commitment to befriending older people in the community. While there are objects scattered around the flat which come either from Ireland in general or from their specific regions of birth, there is one part of the living-room which seems to be particularly preoccupied with Ireland. Featured items range from landscapes to portraits of leaders of the original struggle for Irish independence, De Valera and Michael Douglas and the later martyrs of the IRA. There is a shot of Mary and Hugh, posed with a cup from the winner of a Gaelic football competition. There is the beach where *Ryan's Daughter* was filmed, and some impressive cliffs. Also, a photo of the farmland where Hugh was born.

Another area of the living-room wall contains the main religious icons. Some of Jesus and Mary, but also Pope John Paul; images of St Patrick; a palm cross from Palm Sunday; and images from a religious trip to Portugal. There are candles in front of them, just ordinary domestic candles. Its not really a shrine in any formal sense, and Mary and Hugh would be unhappy to see these areas as in any sense a shrine to Ireland or a shrine to their work. But they would see it as entirely natural to devote a section of this flat – as they devote a section of their lives – to religion, and there is no doubt that the traditions of iconography, of shrines and of devotion are an important model for the way they relate, within their own domestic space, not just to religion but to all they have come to value over the years.

There are photographs everywhere, but on closer inspection those that relate to education, such as graduation photos of nephews and nieces, are mainly found around one section of a wall, while wedding pictures dominate another. A third area seems to collect together many of the items and photographs that have memorialising associations with those who have passed away. Again, these are not clearly separated off. The family, as present on the walls, is impressive in itself. Although they do not have children themselves, there is a host of photos of nieces and nephews, but also plenty of their own parents, grandparents and siblings. Wedding photos are particularly important, not simply because they represent happy occasions, but just as much because that is when large numbers of relatives can be photographed together. Time is suppressed here, as people might be present equally as children or elderly, in graduation pose or a confirmation, in mini-skirts and maxi-skirts, in black and white or colour, in Ireland or some far-flung holiday. A person can be represented here equally by any stage of their life. Furthermore, the pictures can answer all the questions posed to them. A nephew who wants to know what granny looked like when she was young, a sister who wants to remember who was present at a particular wedding can get their answer on the spot.

The very term 'migration' fails to capture the way this ability to retain an integrated life manages to transcend distances in space or time. For Hugh and Mary, the move to London, which was followed by a constant movement to-and-fro between London and Ireland, meant that in prac-tice theirs was more a case of bringing Ireland with them than one of leaving much behind. So many of their family members were in London that if they weren't making a trip back at any given time, then someone else was. An 'Irish Pub' was not, then, a commercial category; it was simply the natural form of a pub that they knew and retained. The con-stancy of accents, along with Catholic ritual, extended families and story-telling meant that, after a while, the Ireland they had known from their childhood and identified with was probably as easily found now in London as in the fast-developing young nation that seemed to be emerging across the water.

Yet a London pub also allows another kind of blending. A close friend may have been actually Polish or Spanish; but over the years, as part of the pub's community, the differences in their Catholicism simply became a mere curiosity. Differences largely submerged in the grand expressions of common humanity exchanged over some pints. Much of Europe and beyond could be absorbed into a pretty ecumeni-cal form of Irishness. More often, it wasn't so much religion as the family that became the extended idiom of incorporation. Working as publicans, it soon became apparent that, like it or not, one's family by blood and marriage, was soon further extended by those who had lost touch with their own relatives but seemed to have garnered some kind of claim of kinship through the fellowship of the pub itself. If this con-tradiction was not resolved in life, it was in death. One of the striking features of the walls of this living-room was the close integration of unrelated individuals, absorbed through memorialisation into this col-lective memory.

The fundamental sense of unity is founded in the couple themselves. So tight and taken for granted is this primary relationship of husband and wife that relationships are usually referred to as 'theirs' rather than 'his' or 'hers'. It is a unity that has become second nature through their joint managing of successive pubs and the periods of learning which of them was best suited to deal with which kind of difficult customer, or aspect of management, or stocktaking. Inside, the home replicated the gender divisions of work. For their generation men developed DIY as an acceptable masculine activity to be exchanged with female aesthetic choices, rather than just feeling awkward and superfluous to domestic life, as in the previous generation. So, although Hugh has put up almost everything around the walls, as Mary notes, there are more images of her family than of his.

One issue which arises constantly when Mary is talking about the room turns out to be what she sees as the negative result of the room's overall aesthetic: the way so many areas are devoted to particular aspects of their lives. The problem wouldn't normally arise; it was a by-product of our systematic interest in examining the flat as a whole, which effectively made everything of equal interest and importance. For Mary, this equalising is entirely unacceptable, and she is at pains to counter the effect. On several occasions she intervenes to ensure a distinction between what matters and what doesn't, what is of true emotional worth and represents the values of religion or a significant relationship, as opposed to mere ornament, jokes, decorative forms, the china donkey, the plate from Hong Kong – all that should be regarded in this light as insignificant. Actually, these ornaments were often placed by her rather than Hugh, and it's as though she doesn't want them to detract from the more important results of his work. She says: 'They mean nothing, just junk. I mean all this is just junk because I like junk. I just bought that somewhere because I liked it.' It's quite fun having Elvis Presley or Laurel and Hardy around, even to have a picture of the latter pretending to graduate, just to set off the actual graduation pictures. But the light-hearted should not displace the possibility of the heavy-hearted, the serious memorabilia of loved ones. It's not a strict division, the picture of the hen party is both fun and personal, some ornaments are significant gifts, but one should know the difference between silly and serious.

She is right to be worried. From our perspective, it does all matter. The juxtapositions of silly and serious help us to appreciate the larger, more comprehensive project represented by the room as a whole. Many of the ornaments have lost the connection with any specific memory of who gave them and when, but the sheer quantity of tea collections, glassware and the like is directly complementary to the *horror vacui* that leaves no part of the wall uncovered by photographs or sketches or something. The point is that it has been a full life, and a life as a publican is bound to have been a life with plenty of laughs and plenty of easy times, with things that don't matter too much and lighten the burdens, because, after all, why else do many people come into a pub in the first place? This is something that, we feel, can and should be appreciated in its own right. Contrary to Mary's fears, the skilled use of light touches merely adds to, rather than subtracts from, our appreciation of her humanity.

Furthermore it adds also to an understanding of the overall aesthetic. The concentrated themes are set against a background of other materials, which have no special area. Artificial flowers, pictures of puppies or beaches, a mass of ceramics and glass may be found anywhere around the room. Taken as a whole, the interior design of these rooms seems to echo this same aesthetic of a couple who have found ways to ensure that everything in their lives remains in conversation with everything else. They may have had particular times for church services, working-hours and family visits, but in practice all these blended in together: a funeral moved from church to pub, or a customer who was also a friend remained at a pub where opening and closing regulations could be honoured mainly in the breach. At first glance their flat doesn't look much like a pub, and the actual objects that come from those days are few. But at an underlying level the continuity is there, in their ability to integrate disparate worlds. The point about the pub was that this was the clear centre of their world founded in their own close relationship, and everything else – events, family, work – all circulated around this basic core. This is what they replicate within their home.

There is, however, one obvious difference between the pub and the flat. In the pub it was actual relationships, networks of people, who coalesced around this site, while in the flat it is mainly images of these people and symbols of their identity. But, as so often in our work, what could be taken as a simple distinction between persons and objects turns out to be much less clear in practice. Firstly, it is possible for the images in the room to be a spur to continued relationships. Rather like Malcolm with his emails, Mary notes at one point that, 'if I haven't phoned someone, I'll look at that wall and I'll say, oh I didn't phone so and so, I didn't phone this one – it's going to cost me a fortune!' So objects can face back to the subjects they represent. But the situation is more complicated when they relate to the dead.

At one point, Mary says: 'I don't like graveyards. My mother was like, don't be looking at me in graveyards, that's not me. I'm up here not down there. That's just my overcoat.' Although a Catholic, Mary is keen to diminish the importance of ritual itself, for instance sprinkling holy water on the grave or lighting candles for months after the death. She does some of these things but wants to distance herself from the formality of obligation in dealing with the dead. When she was talking about the holy water on the grave, there was a grimace and a kind of looking away. The way she mimicked the flicking of the fingers over the grave had a 'let's-get-it-over-with-as-quickly-as-possible' gesture. For her whole life she has kept dead and alive equally entwined within the extensive networks that emanated from pub and family, and it is their continued significance, not past significance, that commands her attention.

This was a craft that Hugh and Mary had practised over many years as publicans. Dealing with other people's loss was central to their work. Customers were constantly coming in to deal with death and divorce, betrayal, the loss of a job and other issues. They had no counsellors or analysts to help them, in some cases they had no friends or relatives. This woman behind the bar was all they had. 'I think the best thing is talking to them. If you just put it under the mat it's not good. You are better off saying to them, "you had some time together and you know you were happy and you will have memories as the pain goes away". All that, you know, because I have been through that myself, so I do know. But when you get to my time of life you are bound to have lost somebody, your parents anyway, and you kind of know how to treat people, to be kind to them, to be there for them. They would show you what their wives were like when they were young and their appearance. They become like family because we used to have lots of customers who were really regular customers and they became friends. Silly things like telling jokes and being daft, it was like a family thing.'

So, when Hugh and Mary construct their living-room, they do so with a lifetime's expertise at helping people deal with loss. Of knowing when to help people acknowledge and be explicit about loss and when to try and tempt them back into the world of jokes and banter. Mary has clear norms and expectations about how long one feels numb, when you can start to see the light again, when you start to recognise that the hurt is shared, and not only your own hurt. She talks of letting go as a process, of when it helps to listen to the music they loved and of when, after a while, it doesn't really help any more. You visit the grave every year, then every three years.

There has to be an economy of remembering in any case, a simplification into something one can evoke and recall in the long term. What we see in their flat is the end point of this trajectory. By now they have become the person memorialised in the magnifying glass they left them; the one who gave this gift for their first anniversary. On occasion, the person who took the photograph is the one being remembered, since the photo was put up when he died. But this simplification only occurs through a process. At first one is faced with the multi-faceted richness of a person whom one loved, when the music is part of the flesh, and one story simply opens up a host of other stories. Some just fade because they are not evoked, others are like that key track, one feels the need to listen to it again and again, as though to exhaust its potency, and only then to lay it to rest.

To see how this process finally leads to their living-room, it may be easier to look first at the way oral traditions work in this task. There are so many literary portrayals of Irish pub life in novels and plays in which the central role is taken by anecdote. Almost always a particular name triggers a little story, a tale – often funny or strange. Oh you know so and so, remember the time when he fell over the . . . and then . . . In effect this can lead to a situation when almost every time a person's name comes up in conversation it is with the sole purpose of recalling some such anecdote. You remember James or Mary, and the time when . . . Individuals are not so much reduced to ghosts as reduced to jokes. Furthermore, in many traditional pubs based around a group of regulars, a person doesn't actually have to die for this process to take its own path. A regular is often someone about whom there are three or four really good stories which simply cry out to be told to those who don't know them. The individual concerned might end up with a nickname originating in just one such incident. This is not regarded as dehumanising or demeaning, since mostly such tales tell of the simple everyday frailty of folk.

We didn't spend long enough with Mary and Hugh to hear many such stories. There were a few: the man who always swapped drinks in return for developing photos; or the one who lived his whole life in terror of *rigor mortis*. But we have been to enough pubs, and talked to enough older relatives or friends who lived in close traditional communities, to recognise a genre here. I have experienced much the same in bars in Trinidad and Jamaica, where I would hang out over several months during fieldwork. In this case, however, what triggered the story was not the mention of the name in a pub, but the glance at a photo or ornament in a living-room. If the photo itself is of a particular event such as a wedding or a holiday, which is also the substance of the story, then the connection is that much closer.

So, even when people are still alive, pub regulars are portrayed as becoming successively reduced to one or two images, one or two good stories. As they become older and frailer and less able to be the active presenters of their own selves, these images come to stand for them. As such, their final demise could make surprisingly little difference to their role in pub life. The process by which they had gradually been turned from subjects into objects was already well on its way. It doesn't mean a person cannot be rounded out again, two dimensions expanded back into three – at least for a while. But the process works, amongst other things, as a way people can deal with loss by finding in effect a new form of attachment, one that can last beyond the individuals themselves. Around the flat is a vast number of potential evocations of people and events, some alive, some long gone, some that can still trigger a story and some that only trigger that uncomfortable realisation that you have forgotten now whom they were connected to, as though the writing on the gravestone had faded into a blur, and all one knows is that it once served as a memorial.

This economy of loss and bereavement is essential to Mary. She has her own loved ones to recall in much greater measure as well as memories from half a dozen pubs. She will give these more distant dead their due, but only their due. For most of the day, she is far too busy helping in her voluntary work with the living, using the skills of serving and listening she has mastered from her trade, and seeing with some satisfaction the good they can still do in this world.

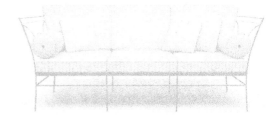

Portrait 12

MAKING A LIVING

As a study of loss, we anticipated discussion about how people had dealt with the long-term consequences of divorce. What we didn't anticipate was that, taken as a whole, this was almost entirely dominated by the way children had, over the long term, to deal with the divorce of their parents, even when they themselves were adults. In such cases it's almost as if the very word 'parents' is a problem. Parents are a collective entity, a pair. After a divorce, though, they stop being anything like a discrete unit one can relate to. One has to take sides, to start seeing them as a source of conflict more than as a resource. Sometimes the children would talk about the difficulty of having to, in effect, feel as if they had become the parents of their parents. In other cases it wasn't so much the divorce as the memory of constant rows and quarrels leading to the question whether you might not have been better off if they had divorced – especially when they claimed they were only staying together for you, the children. The effects were various, but in most cases divorce caused a long-lasting fragility, a need to find some other, alternative foundation to build on.

Donald didn't talk that much about his parents' divorce or about their constant rows, which happened mainly when he was between fourteen and nineteen. The impact and significance of these events surfaced in other ways: in the extent to which he talked about his relationship to his grandparents; in the fact that he simply refused to take things from his own home, his own childhood possessions, because it was his parents' home, because things from that place were sullied and spoiled through association with his parents. When his father died, his stepmother told him she had destroyed all his things, so there was no chance of a memento, which, given the poor state of his subsequent relationship to his father, he probably wouldn't have wanted anyway. But what really upset him was the destruction of the one thing he would have wanted to inherit above all: an object made especially for him by his grandfather.

'My granddad was the last manufacturer of a certain kind of hand-made tennis racket in the world. It doesn't mean a great deal to anybody else. When he died, the whole industry died. And when I was very young, he made me a racket and with my name on it and everything, perfectly hand-made. That was at my dad's. So sadly, that's disappeared, and it's something I'll never ever be able to get back. Um, you know, the good thing is that I've got the memory of my granddad, and indeed, when he died, they lifted up his workshop complete into a museum, so if I ever want to reminisce about him I can walk straight back into his workshop. I only ever used that one racket. I was never a great fan of tennis, neither was he, remarkably. It was that one thing that he specially made for me but sadly, my dad's second wife decided to skip it all.'

Donald's relationship with his grandparents was very close. Actually this was not his genetic grandfather, who had died in the war, but it was someone who always seemed ready to do whatever it was that Donald wanted as a child. Donald loved staying there at the weekends. Helping his gran with the cooking, picking the runner beans from the garden, while his granddad made jokes about worm pies. Donald does have a few inherited items from his granddad, a bag of silver sixpences and a set of cigarette cards from the twenties. But they are not particularly meaningful.

Instead, Donald inherited something else, something that he would regard as much deeper and much more valuable than a mere set of objects. Because this inheritance didn't stand for someone, it was a means to make something of himself. Donald inherited from his family his relationship to work, a relationship that he could and did constantly build on, and expand and make part of himself. His was a family that involved themselves deeply in what they did, and it didn't matter much if this was formal paid labour or the informal work of domestic life.

Whether as builders or in cooking, they threw themselves into the activity, and in large measure what they did was what they became.

For Donald, this is the key to his relationship both with his job and with his home. He has made a highly successful career working as a buyer for a string of companies in the area of home products. He loves his work and sees it as a craft. It's a pity, really, that the word 'craft' has become so conservative, mainly, curiously, as a result of the influence of radicals. It was figures such as William Morris who have bequeathed us a certain romantic notion of craft; for him it designated the activity of artisans, working with their hands so that design and texture, patience and artistry were forged in sensual, imaginative and creative relation to the material: wood, metal, stained glass and stone. Not many people today can afford to be involved in this kind of labour, and, in a way, its very painstaking nature betrayed the politics which William Morris hoped would be integral to it, since only the wealthy could ever afford to buy such hand-crafted forms.

The unintended but long-term result of this romantic repositioning of craft, through the arts and craft movement, is that today we find it extremely difficult to grant any of this same positive or romantic credence to the work most people actually have to do. When Donald describes his work, it is largely managerial. He has to consider a product range, he needs to understand balance sheets and turnover, and distribution through retail outlets, and supply chains and profitability. No one would consider a buyer for a retail chain as a craftsman. Yet I have no hesitation in using this term to describe what Donald is. A retail buyer has the capacity to become a craftsman, because he occupies a critical position, with responsibility to find the best possible fit between two complex processes: that represented in production and that in consumption. Retail buyers have to imagine the myriad worlds of customers, from a football-mad fryer of fish and chips to a schoolteacher devoted to Bach. They have to imagine these people in terms of how they would relate to wallpaper, to cushions, to sofas and to clocks. They have to imagine what continuities they wish to retain from the last season and what would satisfy their desire for change and distinction.

Then, having made those considerations, they have to turn and face in the opposite direction and consult with designers, factories and the vast edifice of capitalist manufacture and distribution. Somehow these two have to be fitted together, the potential of the work of design and production meshed with the taste and concern of the world of consumption. And a retail buyer will be held accountable for the degree to which they get this right, as reflected in those profits and losses, accounts and audits. For some people, perhaps for most people, this is merely a job. But I have no doubt that for Donald it is a craft. It requires skill, elegance, imagination, hard patient labour, experience, and then responsibility for action. If one listens carefully and patiently, one finds an incredible intricacy to this craft, comparable to those of medieval times. I can see the delicate tracery of a supply chain, the way bright colours of design have to be set into the matt background of order books; the warp and weft of negotiations over price and quantity; the pouring of product assemblage into the mould of window displays. It is not pottery making, it is not proletarian, but it is labour and there can be a joy of it, and Donald lives that joy.

Yet a retail buyer's job is precisely the kind of labour we hardly see at all. Retail workers that sell on the shop floor are there, in front of us in abundance; we know them well. In addition, we read and think about factories, manufacture, and aspects of work that seem tangible – people making things. By comparison, a retail buyer is practically invisible, even though they are the people who actually decide what will be stocked in those shops. They are the people we ought to thank when the stock appeals to us and blame when it doesn't. They are the lynchpins, the determinants of what actually exists out there, in the commercial world we encounter. Given the control that retail chains hold over manufacture these days, it is said that if the likes of Boots, Tesco and Marks and Spencer won't stock a product, there is hardly much point making it. So it is the retail buyer who ultimately determines what gets to be made and is thereby the arbiter of what we end up seeing around us. If there is one critical gatekeeper to these interior worlds that occupy much of this book, it is the retail buyer. It is typical of how little we remain in touch with the world of work these days, and of how little our formal education ever addresses that world, that for the most part we are completely unaware of their existence, let alone their significance.

With his experience, Donald appreciates the nuance of different styles and forms of business, their shades and textures. It certainly didn't occur to us that all of this could be found right there beneath our feet –

a map of his experience of, and relation to, work. When we first walked around his house, we barely noticed the range of rugs. We didn't appreciate that this was like the layering of an archaeological excavation, each giving evidence of a particular period of Donald's career, that there were Bronze Age rugs, Iron Age rugs and rugs of his occupational Palaeolithic. As we were walking over the blue and cream rug of his bedroom or the orange and green rug of his bathroom, we were walking on his catalogue era; the time when he had to choose products for a firm that sold almost its entire range through mail order. To be honest, there is no way I would have marked out the posh Harrods' rugs, or their cushions, which come from his period spent at this other, upper end of the business spectrum. But then I sometimes think I am qualified to work on home interiors, because of my almost complete absence of skill in appreciating taste in such matters. With such little confidence in my own taste, I can examine these objects more with a sense of awe than condescension. Typical was my response to another rug, grey and crisscrossed. Donald was working for a major firm, which hired its own named designers. In fact he had worked closely with this designer for some time, discussing in detail what was needed. In the event he came to feel that the final design owed a good deal more to him than to her. If anything, the other active partner was her stylist. Not that either of them would ever get any credit. The designer pocketed that along with their £120,000 annual fee. To me, however – to be honest – it seemed just a pretty ordinary rug. Still even I can just about periodise the sheepskin rug and the time it was trendy.

Donald has a keen eye for colour and ornament. He picks a Mark Rothko because the colours go with the walls and floor of a room, which strikes me as the only sensible reason for picking a Mark Rothko; but he also has some dazzling Buddhas and a fine collection of coloured glass which most likely came from his Harrods' period. Looking at this range of material starts to give clues as to why he might be so good at his job. Partly it is the range itself, from Harrods to the cheap catalogue. I imagine, though, that this has more to do with Douglas keeping his feet on the ground, so to speak, in terms of being sensitive to rugs which relate to the mass of ordinary consumers. I should think that someone too 'upmarket' in personal taste might find it difficult to retain also a skill in buying for the mainstream consumer. So the fact that Douglas' television is dominated by *Eastenders* and the music playing in his house is Coldplay seems to secure the right sort of cultural combination for this kind of work.

If retail buying is understood as a skill, then it must have a whole series of very particular facets and forms. For example, there should be some obvious differences between Donald's abilities, which suit home-ware departments as against, for example – someone more suited to choosing the stock for a fashionable clothing store. My guess is that, with homeware, it must be as important to retain a feeling for what might be termed anti-fashion as for fashion. As one can see from almost any of these homes in Stuart Street, very few people live with items of the moment. On the contrary, home may be sometimes almost a refuge from fashion, a place of domestic rest and comfort, which may retain something of that history of domestic comfort that comes from parents or, in his case, grandparents.

The successful home decoration that Donald creates for himself and for thousands of others is more like a jazz score, where, if one listens carefully, one can detect some tune that was popular fifty or a hundred years ago but is given some new personality and interest in the way it is interpreted today. The basic themes, the sofas, the cushions, the rugs, are the ingredients of living-rooms for decades, but they manage also to have contemporary flavours, which give interest to their recapitulation of much older tastes. Like a constant Renaissance, they need to be both classic and fresh. Donald doesn't do this with music, but if you want to see another source of what I take to be Donald's aesthetics as applied in his work, it may also be there in his relationship to recipes and cooking.

Donald has one more collection. It is of antique recipe books. There is the Elizabeth David *English Bread and Yeast Cookery* book, signed by the author and with a picture of a bag of flour on its front cover that looks like something out of the Opies' collection of historical brands. There is a Christmas cookbook and a 1,000 recipes cooking book in a fading yellow jacket. Some of these books he may never read, but there are plenty that Donald uses as reading material – as something of inter-est in itself – rather than because he intends making one of the recipes they contain. Some cookery books come from his mother, though Donald first became seriously interested in cookery from his gran, the source of other books. He was also fascinated by his grandfather's home-made drinks, the sloe gin and the cider. Later on, he would take recipes directly from his gran. He shows us one for Brown Devilled Chicken. Scanning the ingredients with their dry mustard, curry powder, Branston pickles and Worcester sauce, one can almost taste the continuity down the generations. To this, his mother contributed her love of baking and there is a whole leather-bound album of her hand-written recipes, including his aunt's best biscuits. Sometimes he replays these classics as they come down to him; at other times, when cooking, he adds the riffs and rhythms of his own invention.

So in choosing home furnishings Donald plays on the relation to present fashion, retro and classic. He develops a rhythm that can operate equally at work and during leisure, making his own temporal harmonies. You can hear this even in the way he talks about taking a bath. He has constructed for himself a little ritual for when he comes home from work. A bath that washes off not just the dirt of the day but the concerns and worries of the day. To accompany his bath he plays music – almost always, music from the period before he was in full-time employment and the divorce. As he puts it, 'I do think music is a strong connector. Um, God yeah, it just takes you back to a time when, you know, I suppose life was easy when you were a kid; you didn't have to worry about anything, you didn't have to pay your mortgage or your rent. All you have to think about is going to school, getting money off your mum to go and buy whatever you want, and generally chilling out. God I'd love to be a child again.' If anything disturbs him, it is when this periodisation of the world is upset. For example, he recently saw a televised concert of the Eurythmics and was genuinely disturbed by the image of an aged Annie Lennox; not old, but simply not of the appropriate look that he associated with listening to the music. It disturbed his ability to employ their music as an accessory to his bath, as a representation of this pre-work period of leisure. The concert was an enforced harmonisation of past and present that had become an intrusive dissonance.

Donald is in good company; whether it is my own favourite period of design, the arts and crafts movement, or the Renaissance itself, it is curious how rarely the arts try to invent themselves *sui generis*. Each movement was playing imaginatively with newly discovered pasts, whether classic or gothic. I feel sure there is a similar play with the tension of past and present that enables Donald to do his job well. Perhaps it stems initially from the way he has had to be selective in his relationship to his own past, crafting his life partly through rejecting many aspects of his parental relationships and substituting for them his relationship with his grandparents. The art of commercially successful modernity has, for a long time now, been that of gentle acceptance, of packing the innovative into the familiar, and of reassuring people that to gain the new is not thereby necessarily to lose the familiar; this is the comfort of a popular sofa, with its combination of classically scrolled arms, modernist touches, but deep upholstery. Donald has mastered this art, which has become the source equally of his making a life and making a living.

McDONALDS' TRULY HAPPY MEALS

When Marina casts her eyes downwards, she sees a vision of the most beautiful creatures on this earth or any other: her own children. Unfortunately, if she chooses instead to glance upwards at the preceding generations, she has visions of her worst experiences and most painful moments, in the form of her own parents. One of Marina's self-given missions in life was to disrupt the continuity of the generations, to ensure that what had come down to her stopped with her; the sins of the parents would not visit the generations beyond. Indeed, along with what is very possibly a large swathe of her own generation, Marina saw her model of parenting as being based much more on the repudiation than the reproduction of her own parents. What she owed to her parents was a masterclass in how not to be a parent.

These were sensitive issues. It was possible to tell when, one day, her ten-year-old had come back from school accusing her of bullying him. Of course, she knew perfectly well that all this meant was that they had a class on the topic of bullying that day at school. Since he was certainly not being bullied at school, she had become the only object he could fit to this new idea of possible victimhood. But, even though she could see that these words were entirely innocuous and inconsequential, they still hurt deeply. They couldn't but touch upon the most bruised part of Marina's psyche: the treatment of children by their parents.

In many ways this period of her life, devoted to her own children – the sheer pleasure of motherhood and the sheer labour of it – had only made her own parents more incomprehensible. While other people's parents fly back to be with their pregnant daughters, her parents had always chosen to leave the country at those times. While other parents tried to build confidence in their daughters, hers had made it clear that her choices made them sick. Where other parents faced the world with some measure of truth, her parents represented everything that she found deceitful. To her they seemed to present a façade of icy politeness and refusal to discuss anything. Their manner seemed to imply that what couldn't be mentioned couldn't thereby exist in the word. Silence as a talisman against reality. As it happens, she was at least speaking to them again. For five years, silence was all there had been between them.

Her task in life had been to turn this negative impression into something positive. Given her own treatment, she couldn't prevent it from becoming her primary reference point. But she could challenge the way it might have channelled her through life. So what it meant to her today was that she knew with absolute clarity almost everything she did not want to become. Her mind's eye was full of the models of that she would never want to be. She would recast herself like a bronze sculpture, its features filling with precision the voids of this mould – a mould made from parental absences and failures. On the basis of this systematic negation she had crafted, nurtured and recorded a world forged in the crucible of her own origins. The testing-ground of this defining act of repudiation was bound to be her relationship with her own three children. Apart from that morning, and that horrid little comment about bullying, she had always been able to take enormous satisfaction from the world she has created for herself. Even to the casual visitor, these three children couldn't have seemed sweeter. They radiated out all the love and care that had been infused in them by their parents. As Marina had hoped and intended, they, at least, seemed to be growing into precisely the inverted image of their grandparents.

And, as is often the case with good casting, this love and care was the more intense because it was formed under pressure. Marina didn't have an easy time, indeed she never had. She was involved in highly stressful and demanding work, with all the fragility of freelancing. A specialist in household security systems, she had launched out on her own and, although things were building up reasonably well, this was a not a job that allowed one much relaxation. Yet on the first day we met she was busy making costumes for the school play on top of everything else. The play was based on Dickens and her costumes were inspired by a book of photographs of Victorian London. And because it was associated with her children, she worked on the sewing lovingly and painstakingly, taking far more hours than she could really afford. She was poring over the picture of one little boy in the photograph and reflecting on the differences in fortune between him and her own child. She felt it was a mark of her respect to both of them to try and get these clothes right.

Of course, this may be an illusion or projection but we felt that this passion for her children reflected back Marina's own beauty. Aged forty, she has always been extremely good-looking – looks that had served her very well, and sometimes very badly, in the extremely male-oriented profession of security systems. But it was as though a certain kind of motherly beauty had evolved from the earlier girlish good looks. She still stands out from any crowd. This beauty was inwardly rather than outwardly cultivated. With her hair half-blonde and half-grey and her entirely casual and unpretentious clothes, it was clear that any such beauty would have to be understood as natural rather than constructed. It was, again, a mirror image, that kind of beauty that one sees cast back into a face which knows how to convey love.

The repudiation of one's own parents is not something that is often accomplished simply in the abstract. Objects may play a core role in this task. In some cases, as with her furniture, objects were the bones of contention; in other cases, such as the children's collectables, they were the means of escape. Marina's parents were from a colonial family based in South–East Asia. These were families who did not expect to be directly involved in much child care. It was what their 'native' nannies did on their behalf. The values they tried to inculcate were very much Victorian. If Marina learnt anything as a child, it was that one said lavatory and not toilet. As it happens, her father lost his money in a financial crisis, so when they settled in London not only did they experience the difficult transition from the (then anachronistic) colonial tradition to London's swinging sixties, but they had lost the means to retain those class pretensions which might have helped them to keep their noses above the *hoi polloi* of this cosmopolitan city. Marina saw class consciousness as simply despising all those lower than oneself and resenting all those with more money than oneself. What was the point?

Marina could never identify with her parents' values, their returns to Asia or their interests in pure-bred stock, whether horses or dogs. Most of all, she rejected her parents' appreciation of what they saw as genuine old furniture. The kind of big old chests-of-drawers where the drawer inevitably gets stuck as you try to pull it out and the clothes are still inside. She certainly didn't want the old baby-walker, which she felt was rusting and would give her children blood poisoning. Her mother was aghast when Marina moved into a modern house, but then what could she expect of a daughter who was training in engineering and had been a tomboy practically from birth? But the real insult to her mother was when 'I went and bought my child's chest of drawers from IKEA, and I bought it from IKEA because it was easy to open the drawers, you know. And it was wood, and I could build it myself and it was £200, not one for £600 that didn't work and smelt and probably had worms.' Her mother had big old wardrobes, Marina had fitted wardrobes. Marina understood that part of her mother's bitterness was precisely that she was no longer able to afford for herself the kind of antique furniture her daughter now didn't even want. Her mother used to put items of furniture into Marina's house and then become angry when they were not used, when they were put into the garage, or finally given away. Buying IKEA was 'as if I had spat in her face'. This was one of the factors which eventually led to her rift with her parents, when they didn't speak for five years.

What she repudiates extends beyond her parents, as she realises that they really may have inherited the former sins of the generations. She notes, for example, how her father clearly failed to bond with his own parents. She attributes this partly to the absence of her grandfather, who was at war during a critical time in her father's childhood. But that, in her eyes, does not absolve her father of the fact – she discovered only recently – that he didn't even know where and when his own mother was born. She was shocked, but it helped her to explain the subsequent lack in their relationship to her. This was why it was important to make the break from her parents so absolute. If this coldness and distance could pass through generations, like a genetic disorder, she needed to take full measures to ensure that she did not pass it on to her own beloved children. She needed some inoculation against this disease. And she found it in a most unlikely form: the McDonalds' Happy Meal.

For six years, Marina took her three children, every week, to McDonalds to eat a Happy Meal and keep the toys produced in series that came free with the meals. If they were going on holiday, she tried to make sure she went to the McDonalds at the airport, so as not to miss out on any toys from the series. She is lyrical in her praise of the toys and the place. She says: 'I just think they are incredibly well made, such beautiful things and they're free, you get them with the meal . . . They are mass-produced to an exceptionally high standard.' For years she collected these series. As was intended by the producers, toys also matched the films watched by her children. So she has the whole Toy Story series and the Bug's Life series. They have subsequently been mixed with many other similar figures in the children's playboxes. But these she often disparages as lower in quality, those super hero figures supposed to be realistic but their legs fall off – and she sometimes looks for opportunities to give the other toys away and restore something of the purity of the original McDonalds' collection. Though she finds it difficult, she admits that there are all sorts of reasons why she feels she ought to keep a toy, such as the fact that they were a gift from a childminder. She talks lyrically, too, of the McDonalds' Snoopy collection; each of the thirty representing a different nationality, and how much the children learnt as a result; how they would look up the toys in the relevant books. And it's not just in the form of education that she sees them as an investment in her children's future. Over a long period she collected two of each toy and stored every second one in a cupboard, which now contains a large and systematic set of the toys: she hopes that one day they will be valuable as 'collector's items'. She keeps them in the original packets: 'they will be their inheritance'.

Even now when the children are older, the toys are brought out each summer and the children renew their creative play, still constructing scenarios based on the toys – although even she has to admit, with regret, that the two older children are now somewhat beyond this stage. She is quite mournful that the youngest child hasn't had his fair share of this Happy Meal period, because the other two grew beyond him. Watching them play with these toys has remained one of her greatest delights. She also sees this ritual play as the form by which her children developed and stored their own memories of childhood. She says: 'If you have objects it triggers so much more, it triggers the moment that you bought the object . . . and it triggers the visual . . . and I think a lot of children do remember things visually. And so when you ask me what was the toy when that fight happened at McDonald's, I would have to get them to tell me.'

She also waxes lyrical about McDonalds itself: their baby-changing facilities, the way they encouraged breastfeeding, the reliability of their food, which she also claims is healthier than alternatives. 'The beefburger is always going to be something of a certain quality. I've eaten them in Germany, France. There's going to be a certain standard, a certain reliability about it . . . I don't think my children are going to get food poisoning.' She relates how she got to know the personnel; that nice Indian man who would sometimes give them extra toys, left behind by other children as he was clearing away. As they grew older, she encouraged the children to go up and pay for their meals themselves to make them feel more grown-up. The restaurants are seen as sympathetic to the interest in collecting; so, if you had two of the same, you could take one back and swap it for another. She has a few criticisms, for instance about the difficulty of getting fruit instead of chips for her daughter when the restaurant promised this as an alternative.

This was fast food, but not a fast meal: 'We used to sit in McDonalds for an extra half hour, playing with the toys and doing all the stickers. And it was fantastic because they were happy and I was happy . . . I could go to McDonalds with three children and spend at least an hour, if not an hour and a half, and they all ate and I had a snack and we got these toys. What more could you ask for? It's not a lot of money for that.' They developed little rituals. Firstly, they had to eat the meal itself before they got to play with the toys; then they would put the stickers on; and then follow instructions for tearing the box along the dotted lines, to make something out of the box whenever this was one of the features that came with it. All this helped to extend the stay. During those six years, she would also have her children's birthday parties at McDonalds, with perhaps twenty children, all collecting their Happy Meals. As she is telling us this, we are watching the children play with a toy race-track in which the chips go round chasing the burger.

She is well aware of the virtual class war which erupts around these issues of taste. Her middle-class friends try to persuade her that McDonalds' hamburgers are largely composed of animal brains. But she, in turn, disparages the way they try to take their children to unsuitable restaurants: 'I mean they're just little monkeys really, you can't enjoy a meal with children of that age, they throw everything on the floor.' It's partly her training in natural science that gives her confidence in her passionate defence of plastic as a marvellous material, with a remarkable resistance to deterioration, and which allows her to pronounce on the high quality of the McDonalds' toys, despite the fact that everyone around her would dismiss them. 'I mean somebody will bring out some disgusting tin from Victorian times and wax lyric about that, and it just doesn't appeal to me.'

Marina needed something beyond the furniture to extend her aesthetic repudiation of her parents into the creative development of her own children. The furniture works well enough in the negative separation from her parents, but she also had the need for something that would create a positive bond with her children. As so often in determining what becomes significant, there were several factors which came together in making McDonalds this focal point to her life. It's not just her middle-class friends in general who wouldn't set foot in McDonalds. Above all, her parents wouldn't be seen dead in there; and this is the fact which – like the IKEA furniture – enabled this place to satisfy her first task, that of repudiation. But there was much more to it. The six years of Happy Meals were sandwiched between the time she stopped speaking to her parents and the more recent unemployment of her husband (an extensive period, now thankfully over). This meant that she was so busy working, she never had enough time to spend with her children. Simply the time involved in looking after the home while coping with the pressures of her work, meant that taking her kids to McDonalds and enjoying the half-hour of play with the new toys was for her almost the only moment of pure indulged-in motherhood, away from competing domestic or occupational tasks.

These Happy Meals provided the occasions when her children learnt to develop their imagination, collect systematically, to care about and help create perfect moments of family life. If Marina's memory is unequivocally positive, it is because these were the moments when she forgot about other concerns or demands, and when the negative repudiation of her parents had become totally absorbed into the positive identification with herself as a parent. To use a phrase from Jean-Paul Sartre, in a context he would probably have entirely detested, McDonalds' Happy Meals became an aesthetic totalisation of her existence.

PORTRAIT 14

THE EXHIBITIONIST

The older English reticence with regard to the public presentation of sex seems to have more or less disappeared. Mainstream television from *Sex in the City* to *Big Brother*, has put sex not just into the background, but also the foreground of our vision. It's hard to pass a day in London without confronting images or hearing lyrics which vie with each other in coming close to actual depiction. But that is the public domain; when it comes to the private world of everyday conversation and people's discussion of themselves, sex is still usually hedged a bit, through jokes, irony or reference to others rather than oneself. It is still very rare to find private individuals who seem to employ the same foregrounding of the subject as one finds on television. At least it's hard to think of other people on this street who would have ever dreamt of making their own sexual encounters the direct subject for the decoration of their home. The clear exception is Aidan, whose flat is just as exhibitionist as he is. As we are taken on a tour and introduced to the wall decorations, these are not the usual landscapes, cats or generic modernism, not the plates, holiday souvenirs or posters. Here instead are some knickers he once swapped for his underpants, when both were suitably moist; also, a prize for guessing the bra size of a batch of strippers who appear in a photo next to it. Then there is part of a bungee jump contraption, which had been used as a kind of sex harness.

Within a very short time, Aidan has made it clear that he has tried every (in)conceivable sexual position, every narcotic substance and a good range of alternative music. It is hard not to feel voyeuristic, even awed, by the descriptions of what lies at the far reaches of his roads to freedom; Aidan's journey down the broad path to sex, drugs, and rock and roll. His journey started in the post-Punk period, when everyone was going 'fucking mental', because the Indie music was so brilliant and new. That led to those times when he worked at a bar and was paid over-time in cocaine. Then, while others just dreamt about what might lie ahead, while in various states of stupor, Aidan went on. He went so far that he actually did hit Texas in the company of a porn star and saw the wildest of the West. He ranged from Australia to South Africa, in search of the ecstatic. By the time he returned he was a devotee of excess. Other wall decorations include a letter of outrage from a concerned important citizen whose property he had burned with his cigarette ends; letters from the lawyers when someone threatened to sue him for another mis-demeanour.

When we consider the number of times he has tempted fate, but skipped away before he could be gored on its horns, Aidan's agility impresses. He really had become the stuff of all those pop lyrics he was brought up on. Basically screw them and be this. Sex is, possibly, not the easiest thing to portray in full trophy-style on the walls of a house, but Aidan has the imagination for that challenge. The drugs are perhaps even more difficult, and are largely alluded to in a patchwork of high modernist art pieces, high as much as modernist.

To take this road to sex, drugs and rock and roll as far as Aidan, demands qualities which are not as common as we might like to think; not just the consistency of purpose but also a bravado, probably sup-ported by his particularly extrovert character, so that the presence of more or less any audience is likely to ensure he follows though with his declared intentions. Most of us have a pretty clear image of what must lie at the end of this road – the gravestones of its vanguard. Eventually, if one goes far enough, we expect to join the likes of Jimmy Hendrix, Kurt Cobain and Janis Joplin, the shooting stars that burned brightest, but then burnt out. It emerges that Aidan also reached that end point of the road; but, unlike these others, he came back with his trophies. In his own words, 'the worst time was in . . . I took so many drugs in a very

little space of time. I ended up in a hooker's apartment. I'd won a bet
with someone and the bet was that I'd get some girl to walk to my room
and the girl came to my room. It was insane, we did so many drugs:
pouring out like a gram of coke and making two lines out of it. Basically
I ended up on her bed, sweat pouring down me, my heart going incredibly fast and it was one of those moments where you have the summons
and you go – right I'm not going to have my parents deal with me on a
drugs OD in a hooker's apartment – I just can't let that happen! How I
got out of that I don't know, I just did.'

Aidan didn't just reach that point. He also brought to it an element
of existentialism that defined freedom through the choice of how the
road would end. At one point he talks about an elderly relative: 'she was
suffering from cancer, not badly, but she thought, "fuck it, I've had
enough". And she ran herself a bath, took a couple of brandies, took a –
it's like an opiate – I don't know what it is, but it is pill form, but she had
it from like 40 years ago from a doctor. There was a line in a song which
goes: "When you lie in the bath looking at the ceiling, you start to laugh
as your face goes underwater". She left me 1,200 quid.' But Aidan never
had whatever quality it is: madness, greatness, weirdness, despair, fate or
some imperative we cannot understand because we don't possess it but
that fascinates us about the victims of that road. Even in the midst of a
delirious profusion of drug-induced experience, it was evident that
Aidan himself could see little reason to sacrifice his own life to such an
abstract logic of freedom in death.

The reason lies perhaps in Aidan's relationship to the third of this tri-
umvirate of modern freedoms: rock and roll. Aidan was no rock star; he
was never part of a band. On the contrary he gradually formed a scheme
in his head to use rock and roll not as an extension of, but rather as a
counter-weight to, the excesses of the sex and drugs. As Aidan became
aware of the contradictions of this life on the free road, he saw that, in
order to escape its fate, one needed to retain some sort of grounding,
some means of attachment to something in this world that prevented
one from floating off into the ether. Aidan could both sense and understand the basic contradiction to the ideal of a self-chosen life: that the
main threat to absolute freedom is emptiness. As noted by most of the
founders of social science, pure freedom without attachment and commitment can soon make everything seem equally superficial, and even

the most extreme hedonism can eventually become bland when the individual becomes blasé. When one reaches the point where a drug is just another drug and any sexual experience is just another variety of sex, one has lost discernment and stepped into the final section of this road: a landscape of featureless wilderness, the site of the rock-star suicide. So Aidan felt the need for a deep and committed attachment, the need to use the music to ground himself rather than to lose himself. But at the same time he wanted to do this in a way which was not a betrayal of the road itself. He kept faith with his commitment to the path he had chosen. Which meant that it was vital that he retained his freedom to make the choice for himself, and to choose nothing imposed on him by the external world, but something he could give himself to in the same spirit as everything else he had done in life. Something that spoke to his commitment to the pop lyrical experiences of sex, drugs and rock and roll, but that could be both meaningful and ironic in itself.

Aidan researched his choice. He had read extensively about the music scene, the genealogies of the little Indie bands, some of whom became the lasting icons of modern life. Apart from his confidence, one of the things he took from his parents and his quite posh upbringing and education was that, on the whole, he knew a good deal about what he was doing. So, when Aidan was good and ready, he determined which band he would attach himself to, so as not to float off into indifference. Nothing too obvious or too secure; there always had to be risk involved; but Aidan was confident in the depth of his own knowledge and judgement. He had so often predicted the next wave, surfed ahead of the field. He could see a small swell in the distance, a relatively new band; that had the gift, something quirky but English. Such bands were gestated in art schools and post-punk youth cultures. Clever little digs at contemporary mores and a style that could banter with the pretensions of one class and the authenticity of another. Often a bit of ethnic, some gender ambiguity, lyrics sufficiently obfuscating to intrigue. The musical style was central. The unexpected juxtapositions and quotations from classics, set in new frames. Riffs that were vaguely reminiscent of something in soul – or was it jazz? There was a pattern, that David Bowie glam, but more jokey, or that particular English louche that led to Franz Ferdinand. There are hundreds of such bands and new musics. Done well, it was heady and attractive and led the field; done badly, it puked.

So Aidan spotted a promising swell, and launched forth on what, he felt pretty sure, would be the next big thing. Or, even if they never became that well known, they would at least have cool and style and an authenticity as art. As always with Aidan, once that road was chosen, there was no half measure. Aidan embraced the fledgling band with passion and total commitment. This was for life. More than that, it was for art. 'I always thought they were far more different to anyone else, they were doing something far more unique and interesting.' His home gradually became a shrine to the band. Yes, really a shrine. Every wall surface, every storage space is full of the band's paraphernalia. All the artwork that contributed to their CD cover has found its way to Aidan's flat. The band leader's paintings, his sketches, his ideas and concepts, his lyrics, his accessories, anything that seemed touched by his art is here. Many of the pieces from his original collection of band memorabilia were burnt in a fire in a previous flat. So now he keeps the twisted charred forms, which resulted in a kind of artwork in itself. Looking for still greater commitment he has tattooed the title of one of their CDs on one side of his body, and that of a single on the other.

A band as an art form represents one form of relationship. It works partly because Aidan can abstract it as a sort of pure commitment, unsullied and made explicit in the way it occupies his flat. Equally interesting is the way Aidan's existential aesthetic plays out in his relationship to the street itself. Again, Aidan seems to take his commitment to what others would see as extremes. He probably rivals us in his paean to the street as a conveyor of the richness of contemporary London. For him the street is, just as for us, in essence a random place – he just happens to live there; but – again, as for us – it is also the most interesting place in the world, because he shares our unbridled enthusiasm for the street as a microcosm of humanity's extraordinary capacity for being. This is his and my modern romanticism: idealising not some utopian street but embracing the actual street, this tumultuous mix of quirky and mundane, achievement and tragedy, strange passions and empty banality that makes up a London street. I share this wide-eyed awe of what is generally dismissed as boringly familiar. Aidan knows as well as I do that it includes isolation, depression and bewilderment. But his and my modern romanticism refuses to gainsay what people nevertheless accomplish in the otherwise unpromising conditions of the almost random juxtaposition of unrelated peoples.

Aidan's response parallels our commitment to participation. He celebrates the pub, where he is a regular, going in four or five times a week when he has the money. He celebrates the characters and anecdotes, and the good times that come with being a regular. He is fascinated by the eccentricities of other individuals along the street. While others worry about the street's wide boys and putative gangs, he befriends them all, and trades banter and respect with kids whom other people cross the street to avoid. He also knows much more than we ever will about the parties that went on for days and the hedonistic excesses which sound out the high notes of urban rhythm. He, of course, contributes to all of this as one of the liveliest characters in the street; and, as a rampant exhibitionist, he helps to 'make' both the pub and the party. His genuine attachment to the street is grounded in his love for his own flat, which is small and pokey but now of course also an extraordinary museum dedicated to his favourite band (not to mention the sex). The contradictions of this commitment are most evident, though, in the fact that, at the time we met him, he wasn't actually living in the flat. He was skint and couldn't afford the rent, and so had rented it out to a friend. In order to get inside and see his possessions, we, and Aidan himself, had first to obtain permission from the present incumbent.

This for Aidan is also highly appropriate because his aesthetic creates an ambivalence to possessions themselves. When we first met him in the pub he was on his way to a friend, with the intention of giving away one of his prized possessions; the number plate from the car that took him on his Wild West experience. He puts it simply and clearly: 'The things I value most I tend to give away.' Knowing how possessions could detract from freedom, he accentuates the extreme nature of his collecting and giving. He hopes that the continued extremism of his gestures will ensure that he transcends the merely utilitarian or mundane relationship to things. I have no idea if he ever read Bataille, but one can hear the same desperate rejection of mere functionalism in the violence of this sacrificial act. So, when he collects memorabilia from his band, he treats them as fragments of a spiritual totality, from the shavings on the studio floor to the half-squeezed paint-tube tossed to the floor by the band's leader. The other strategy is to give things away, in the grandest or most spontaneous of gestures. He could never simply take something to an auction and have it valued. It would have to be just got rid of, as though it were nothing, perhaps to someone he had one fantastic night with and whom he will never see again – and who has no idea why the object has value in the first place. There must be an art to possessing and dispossessing. One that exposes the absurdities that domestic façades seek to hide.

It is hard not to try and impose the clichés and moralities of some TV script upon this story. To assume that soon we are going to expose some cracks, through which we can see sadness, disappointment, or even despair. That it would be almost comforting to hear that Aidan was on anti-depressants. But Aidan has read these scripts too, and he is clever enough to make sure the depressions are momentary and the elations are extended. He knows that people will assume that there has to be some deeply exposed underbelly. But he would much rather that we view him for what he largely is – a beacon that takes its energy and light from his extreme experiences, and shines it onto an otherwise largely unappreciated mundane world. So we cannot take refuge in the false logic of an inherent nemesis that inserts Aidan into standard morality tales. I suspect that Aidan is not that predictable, and deals with his problems to the degree he needs to and no more. But I don't know this. There could be another world that lies beneath, that conforms to such expectations. Because this was someone whom we only knew to the small extent that he chose to show us his life as an exhibition.

Still, going round these possessions will inevitably prompt some regrets; if not about the past, then certainly about the present. Aidan is not old by any standards except his own. It infuriates him that he can no longer drink himself into a stupor – one of the most essential rituals of everyday life – and then come back fresh the next morning. Nowadays it can take him two days to get back into shape. His girlfriend is fifteen years younger than he is. He still feels there is more to him than she would get from anyone else, but he knows that the fire of present adventure doesn't blaze with the same incandescence as the past. What's worse is that it is hard even to conceive of a future that could match this past. When things have been that good, the expectations they impose become a burden. If life starts looking predictable, he needs something that will put chance and fate back in control, to ensure there are twists and turns to make the drive sufficiently exciting to be worth continuing. He knows he can't just return to the past roads; there is no better sex, no other drugs.

The one clear failure is the band itself. They just never fulfilled their promise. They are still around, and Aidan would still swear that they are as good as it gets. But even he has to admit it's galling that so few people ever came to recognise their abilities, and he almost has to apologise for his devotion to them, to explain who they are. Truth be told, he would rather have tattooed, well, not Chelsea or Arsenal, but maybe Bolton or Wigan rather than non-league Hendon. To at least have others around who could share the exhilaration and know what he is talking about. There are a few such people, but it's more like a reminiscence of past promise. That's close to sad, and Aidan has no desire to be close to sad. He puts the blame, not on the band itself, but on the music scene, which today is just crap. But even there he is cautious. He hears himself sounding like the old git who harps on about how much better things used to be. Aidan quickly turns around – screw that! He would much rather expound on his new enthusiasm, something that perhaps gives him another road, one he hasn't yet explored but which looks genuinely promising.

If it's no longer going to be sex, drugs and rock and roll, then Aidan has decided it's going to be the world of international gambling. This has considerable appeal. It's immediately associated with the larger-than-life characters who are his peers: a game of life that leaps up ladders and careers down snakes at the fall of the dice. The glamour of casinos, half tawdry past, half new-money vulgarity, seems ideal for re-shaping as modern art: the next cool, that he has spotted before the others. This could give him the buzz he craves, and it is an older scene which will not leave him feeling the weight of years. Remember those films with Paul Newman; he never got old. Aidan can imagine a month or two of dispensing ridiculous amounts of money, gifted by luck in vast extravagant gestures, which soon plunge him back into the challenge of being unable to afford the rent and having to sleep in someone else's kitchen while he regroups. The imagined possibilities are enough in themselves to push him forward. A moment of depression and hesitancy was quite enough. He just wants to carry on being 'there' when 'it' happens, whatever it turns out to be.

If one looks closely into the logic of Aidan's aesthetic, one can see how it is that he manages to retain this degree of positive optimism. Why, maybe he is neither as manic nor as secretly depressive as almost everyone, half-envious and half-appalled by his antics, would expect him to be. The secret seems to lie in this distinct form of modern romanticism; its rejection of the utopian and its acceptance of the quotidian. It means that Aidan doesn't have to pretend to something other than his actual past and attachments. For example, Aidan is pretty cool about his parents and his education. At his level of confidence and experience, he doesn't feel the need either to repudiate or to re-constitute them. He doesn't feel the need to pretend to have roots. Nothing needs to have been exotically ethnic or authentically working class. As far as he is concerned, his parents were pretty ordinary and decent. He may well have inherited something of this collecting drive from their sedate collections of pottery and plants. They, too, had their record collections.

Aidan is open to, and appreciative of, how much his own confidence and knowledge is owed to the labour of his parents. He knows how hard his father worked to put him through a good private school; but also the poignancy of that generation's form of masculinity, so that they could never quite say things that were as close or intimate as they felt. None of this is hidden away. As one looks around the walls, mixed in with sex trophies, there is a momento from Aidan's gran, references to his school and his family, the place in England were he was brought up. Though used in irony, there are also religious icons, Pentecostal exhortations about Jesus. There are items of clothing he is attached to, having worn them for many years, and which, like all his clothes, were second-hand when he got them. Not all his paintings are associated with the band. Some of them may be regarded by others as pretty rubbish, but one was from an artist who actually has become something of a name. This is the great advantage of a modern romantic of the street, who is neither just philosopher nor artist. Aidan has never had to repress the ordinary in order to feel extraordinary. On the contrary, he celebrates it.

Aidan's romantic commitment to personal freedom also contained its own moral logic. He never wanted his freedom at the expense of others, never felt he exploited the women he slept with but always hoped that they would enjoy as he enjoyed. He understood the reciprocities of meaningful sex, but also of mad silly sex. There have also been a number of relationships to people he cared about, and these had to occupy a different niche in his life. His relationship to objects, the grand gestures of his collecting and giving away, of things burning down and spontaneous moving on, those were his life. If women, or indeed men, wanted to ride the fast road with him as companions, that was fine. But some of the women he has cared for were different. Like his current girlfriend. He discourages her from following him into this new gambling phase. He feels no problem about losing his shirt, but she shouldn't take such risks with the little she earns at her work. The photos that remain with him from these past relationships are the one set of items he chooses not to show us, and indeed it's the one set of possessions he insists that his present girlfriend does not see. They are held in storage, along with love letters and special postcards. Because these alone are there not simply as testimony to his road to freedom. They are not trophies and cannot be given away in grand gestures. They are those external forms that give shape to the heart. Things that you know must be there some place, because, even on first meeting Aidan, you can tell that, of the two kinds of contemporary existentialists, he is with those who do give a fuck, even if he sometimes shares the road with the nihilists who don't.

Portrait 15

RE-BIRTH

Anna was explaining to us how they started going onto eBay's specialist section devoted to vintage Fisher Price toys. The intriguing point was that this was not a search for toys as vintage in the sense of antiques. Rather, it was an attempt to locate and buy more or less the exact same toys that Anna, and indeed Louise, had played with when they were children themselves. Their child, Florian, now has the same Fisher Price garage, the same Fisher Price doll's house and the same Fisher Price record player, with its little plastic discs that play nursery rhymes. It wasn't exclusively Fisher Price. There were other toys from their own childhood that were being born again. One was a big Tonka truck. Not quite as indestructible as they remembered from adverts of their own childhood, but still impressively robust. Another major find for the forthcoming birthday was one of those fishing games, the one with little magnets suspended from each line and mini plastic fish with metal rings waiting to be caught. On this occasion it wasn't an eBay find; it was from that other store, which has such a retro quality as the palace of treats for generations of middle-class Londoners, Hamleys of Regent Street.

There are many more toys they are looking forward to revisiting through Florian, and the only problem is that they are going to have to wait until he is old enough to desire them and to play with them. His legs aren't yet long enough for the pedal car they are after. As Anna puts it, 'there were lots of things with wheels that I would really really have wanted when I was little and didn't have . . . or that other people had, so I rarely laid my hands on them . . . but they held such excitement for me that I would just love him to have them'. Given that Florian was only turning three at the time of our encounters, they were going to have to wait even longer for equally eagerly anticipated sharing and re-reading of certain of their favourite books. There was the *Iron Man* by Ted Hughes and loads of others, still waiting their turn at one of Anna's sister's or her parents' house. But Anna admitted she was already looking up still others on Amazon.

The obvious interpretation of this reaching back for the 'authentic' toys of one's own times is that it represents a desire to re-create for one's child one's own childhood. I was drawn to this interpretation because it fitted well with an academic paper I had published a few years ago, which was in part based on my studies of mother/infant relations during shopping, but also (to be truthful) on my own experience as a parent. In certain respects, Anna's and Louise's relationship to parenting reflected back on my own. The time when my two children were born seemed in retrospect the high point of an obsession about trying to do everything in the most natural way possible. My wife and I spent weeks learning about natural childbirth, then breastfeeding. My wife had given birth to both our children without painkillers and never once used a bottle, let alone a dummy. Many parents around us were still more obsessive, avoiding anything with E-numbers or sugar or a host of other substances whose ingestion was supposed to ruin the child.

In general, parenting seems to have relaxed a little in recent years and become less obsessed with these ideals of purity and nature. But Anna and Louise retained something of this overwhelming fear not to do the wrong thing by one's child. Louise talks at some length about her passion to ensure that she was totally protective of Florian while he was still inside her. During pregnancy she was extremely careful about what foods she ate in order to try and be the ideal nurturing mother, eating fish such as mackerel which, she had read somewhere, would provide him with the best hormones. Then she matched this by an equal fear of what others might throw at him in the playground or in some other way harm him, once he existed as an independent being outside of that protective bubble of her own body. This anticipation of harm and cultivation of good continues all the way through to their present concerns. While we were working in the area, Anna and Louise sold their house and moved out of the Stuart Street area. This was prompted, in particular, by a really poor Ofsted (school inspectorate) report delivered on the school for the Stuart Street catchment area. So they decided to move to a leafy middle-class suburb where they could be sure they would be living in the catchment area of a good school, although they spoke of this with some embarrassment. It was as though the neighbourhood had become the larger womb, and they would do whatever they could to secure the environment within that outer flesh in which their infant now had to live.

In a previous publication – 'How infants grow mothers in North London' (*Theory, Culture and Society*, 14.4 (1997): 67–88), I wrote about the way academics have focused on how the infant develops a gradual sense of itself as an independent being through a series of stages of separation from the mother – a theory most fully developed by psychoanalysts such as Melanie Klein. But it seemed to me that three beings were born simultaneously: the infant but also the parents, and in particular the mother. The mother, at first, was entirely bonded to the infant, and saw the infant, in effect, as her re-birth in a much purer, more natural state. It was as though she had a second chance – to live her life again, through the infant, but this time to avoid being sullied by the world, as had inevitably occurred in her own life. I saw this projection of a perfect version of oneself in the pure infant as a form of narcissism. Over time, however, the mother had to learn that the infant was not a pure extension of herself, that she, too, was a separate being and had to pass through various stages of separation in order to let go of this more narcissistic aspect of parenting. I examined the way shopping and consumer culture becomes an integral part of this process. The implication was that while psychoanalysts write about a series of stages it is thought infants go through, in many respects it is us, the parents, who are experiencing them. It is the parents who have to grow up gradually and leave behind an initial image of pure idealised good and bad projected onto their infant, leading eventually to a maturity that accepts the inevitable contradictions embodied in their own children.

At this level of generalisation, it was obviously, in some respects a simplistic theory, and of course there are many different ways these relationships develop over time. Listening more carefully to Anna and

Louise suggests that, as a route to understanding their vintage Fisher
Price toys, things may not be so straightforward. On another occasion
Louise talked about receiving some boxes with objects from her own
past, such as toys and diaries, that her parents had sent her. For quite
some time she could not bring herself to open them. As she put it, 'I
think possessions play an important role emotionally in how they belong
to a certain time and it's almost like digging up the past and maybe that's
why you don't pay much attention to your childhood and your family
when you are in your twenties, because that's the break-out time and
that's maybe when you return to it later.' Also, there was a kind of super-
stitious fear, that what lay inside was some kind of Pandora's box that
would release all sorts of demons from her past to plague her present.
Louise didn't like to tempt fate. In much the same way, she couldn't
bring herself to buy anything for Florian before the birth itself.

Eventually, however, she allowed herself to look through these childhood remnants accompanied by Florian. While she may not have written an academic paper on the topic, she had her own awareness of this
potential narcissism between mother and infant. She says: 'He looked
at things and the books didn't interest him at all. And I didn't want to
do that thing that you see people do when they say, "Oh you must have
this, I had this when I was little", because half of it wasn't very interesting to him and he doesn't like dolls very much at all and there were
a few dolls in there.' I suspect that, if Florian had been a daughter,
my theory of narcissism would have provided a closer fit. But Louise
is quite sensitive to the fact that Florian is a boy and that, perhaps
especially in a case where there are two mothers, she needs to curb her
desire to project herself onto him and to allow his own preferences, especially gender preferences, to develop. Indeed, she recounts
to us a genetic theory which explains why boys don't respond well to
dolls.

While these toys are intended for Florian, the eBay activity is experienced more in terms of the relationship between Anna and Louise.
They are a very close couple, who have lived together for many years.
They heartily enjoyed the pre-parenting period, with its music and parties, and in turn were totally committed to becoming parents. As two
women, becoming parents required a considerable amount of planning
and negotiation, particularly in determining the right biological father

– things quite apart from those encountered by a heterosexual couple. They launched themselves into their new roles with strong expectations and much, much discussion. So, rather naturally with the focus upon the new infant, comes also another opportunity to develop their relationship as a couple.

As one listens to their conversation flowing back and forth between descriptions of their own respective childhoods and that of Florian, another possible interpretation develops. Ideally, such a close couple would have liked to have shared that original childhood, their own. All those times before they met become a source of regret for the unshared origins of their lives. They never knew each other as children, but today it's as though they have a new opportunity to repair that gap in their relationship. To some degree, they are not only sharing their parenting of Florian, but also using this as an opportunity to share at least an element of what they missed out on as children: each other. Their ability to do this is much enhanced by direct reference to the familiar objects and images from that time. This is just what vintage Fisher Price toys can do for them, more effectively than almost anything else. Through Florian, they too can play together with these – now shared – toys. And, frankly, for many parents, including myself, most of the playing that takes place with such special toys is done by parents.

At one point I suggested this interpretation to Anna, whose own occupation involves working with children and thinking about their relationship with their parents. Of course, she couldn't know if this was truly the case, if I was right in my musings. This is not the sort of surmising that can be reduced to some clear cause and effect, right or wrong interpretation. All she could do was to respond positively to the suggestion, as it gave her another perspective on her own actions that seemed to make sense. This was often the way in our conversations. While the interpretations presented in these portraits often emerged in writing, on those occasions when they first arose in our original conversations with the people on the street, we often discussed them, floated ideas to see if they rang true. This exchange helped to show our genuine interest, and illustrate how we hoped to use the material we were accumulating through listening to them and observing them. It explained our presence to people. Even a tentative interpretation was rather more concrete that simply saying we want to write a PhD thesis or publish an article about you. Almost invariably, they found that they, too, started seeing themselves reflected in the looking glass of their own possessions that we held up before them. They would almost always remark on the possible insights that these provided, insights they might never have thought of, or at least never have made explicit. But then they had no reason to; that was our job.

Sometimes they were very clear that our observation could not possibly apply to them and we were mistaken. Of course, that of itself didn't necessarily make us agree that we were wrong. As in any relationship – and our interpretations are often not so different from those one makes about personal relationships – there is the occasional vehement denial which gives rise to the feeling 'they doth protest too much', and that this approach may be worth exploring further. But, either way, what was striking was that most people were fascinated by the mere possibility of such discussion. They might refute our suggestions, but where they agreed they might add detail. Anna could recall the imaginative play that centred on toy-kitchen equipment, shared with her own siblings and with her father. Since Louise could recall a similar positive relationship to these same toys, this formed their main present to Florian on his third birthday.

The most powerful influences, then, came from things that were shared between them. This was not something that started with them becoming parents. There were plenty of precedents from the time when they first came together as a couple. They both had very extensive music collections, which are now completely integrated as a single collection, with particular emphasis on shared tastes. For example, they found they were both interested in seventies Reggae such as Burning Spear, and saw this as saying something about the success of their relationship, though they could never have said quite what. For Anna, this emphasis on sharing goes back further. She was, and remains, close to her siblings, who were near in age. She doesn't often need very smart clothes; so, when she does, she still borrows them from her sister. Recently Anna and her sister shared a birthday party which consisted mainly of replaying this shared musical background, especially loads of Boy George.

At the same time, since this was a triangle of relationships, Anna and Louise also had differences in their backgrounds leading to differences in their relationship to Florian. Clothes have become one of the most

explicit media for exploring these differences. Both parents start with
the more direct transference of desire. Anna had always loved buying
clothes: 'I do have a major shopping thing.' But there have been substantial costs involved in having a child. They couldn't afford to buy
both good clothes for themselves and for Florian. So Anna, like many
middle-class mothers, describes quite an extreme shift in the object of
shopping. 'So that's been one of the shocks. That I have had to close that
bit down and give expression to Florian through his clothes or to me
through his clothes.' Just as earlier she wanted to give Florian the
wheeled toys she herself wasn't allowed to have, so here she wants to
cleanse herself of her bad clothing experiences as a child: 'I have memories of clothes that I just hated. I have memories of having to wear
green crimpoline trousers about 1973, and it was all kind of straight and
tight. We had some dresses that had got too short for us, green crimpoline little patterns teamed up with green crimpoline trousers that were
really uncomfortable, and we had to wear them at some office party and
I remember spitting on them, throwing them on the floor. And so that's
the thing about them needing to be comfortable.' Of course, one suspects that, when Florian is a bit older he will more than likely rebel
against having to be 'comfortable' and pick some kind of tight, difficult,
synthetic clothing his parents would abhor.

For Louise, there was a different – and in several ways still more complex – form of projection in her relationship with Florian. While Anna
was continuing in full-time employment, Louise, as the biological
mother, had given up a highly successful career, which had more or less
defined her life until then. She had started in a low-paid job at the very
base of the hierarchy of her chosen profession; so low that her father had
been furious with her for wasting her public school and Cambridge
University education, and they had not spoken for years afterwards. This
made Louise even more determined to prove what she could make of
herself. Over the next decade and a half, she rose through the ranks and
ultimately became a senior figure in the firm, responsible for some of the
most lucrative, prestigious and important deals. It did not end well, however. She was confident that her firm would allow some compromise
for child care, and that she would be able to work part-time at some
stage after settling in as a parent. However, she was horrified to find that,
even after fourteen years, they would not agree to a single hour less than

the full week's commitment. So there was not much of a prospect of return.

The early stage of mothering was also something of a shock, for all her mental and physical preparation. It started with the nightmare of the thirty-six-hour birth itself. After that came the sheer tiredness and tedium: claustrophobic times inside the house, staring at the four walls while feeding her infant at one end and cleaning him up at the other; the fear that she would sink into a life of day-time television. Well, more than a fear, she started watching anything from golf to soaps. 'It's almost – that's the first time in my life that I had watched something in my life disappear as it was actually happening. Usually I've looked back on it afterwards and thought, "Ah it's a shame that I'm not at college anymore, I miss my friends", and looked back on it. But now I can actually see it happening while it was happening.' Nothing in her previous life has been so 'seismic' as that simultaneity of leaving her job, the trauma of birth and waking up to find herself a mother. It is likely that she had some form of post-natal depression with that feeling that she simply wasn't a valuable person any more, that she was reduced to doing nothing except looking after this baby.

So the effect of transferring her interest in clothing onto Florian had greater repercussions on her than on Anna. As with Anna, there was a real curbing on buying clothes for herself. She readily admits that she used to spend a fortune on clothes, and it was clearly enormously important to her to look good at work, at the office. Anna could use clothing as a kind of re-birth, to avoid her bad experiences and to gain for Florian the good ones she missed out on as a child. But for Louise the dearth of good clothing for herself reflected, not on her past, but on her present. It was almost as though her body expressed that lack of worth that she felt initially about herself as a mother. Because what a woman becomes, with pregnancy and breastfeeding, is basically summed up in that one word, that one absolute anathema to one's struggle to create oneself and one's self-respect: *fat*. Louise had hoped this was something that would disappear within three months of the birth, but it didn't. She recalls: 'It was horrible losing that person, because I was quite fit and active and did feel really slobby and disgusting for ages, and having to wear those maternity clothes even though I wasn't pregnant any more. It's horrible, it was really nasty.'

For this reason, clothes have a vital role to play in her re-construction. Louise has become a person who needs to re-cycle back to an earlier self, and her clothes are an obvious route to this recovery. Of necessity, in these circumstances, Louise's rehabilitation cannot happen through the acquisition of new clothes. It also has to be the recovery of the person she once had been. 'The ones that really excited me were the, um . . ., they were quite interesting because they were quite an expensive pair of trousers that I got in New York, when I was working, and they were three quarter length, really nice. And I tried them on last year and they didn't fit and I just thought – that's great, I'm just going to stay fat now. But this year I put them on about three weeks ago and they did fit. And I did feel absolutely ridiculously so pleased. I don't know why, because it's only a pair of trousers. It wouldn't have mattered if they had been new trousers. I don't think I would have been so excited. But it was because I could match them to a time when I could wear them.'

Louise has even thought through the different potential of different forms of clothing to help her through this process of rehabilitation. She is now looking forward eagerly to bags. She had some pretty cool bags in the past, but, between pushchairs and running after toddlers, where bags just get in the way or have to be stuffed with yucky kid's stuff, she knows she is going to have to wait a little longer to return to bags. Shoes might have given her some continuity and support, since her feet never really became swollen; but again, as she is running around the parks and playgrounds, somehow they haven't worked either. Now, however, thanks to her trousers she can see light at the end of a bad-clothing tunnel. She knows that this represents a recovery, but not simply a return to her old self.

So, to understand those vintage Fisher Price toys, we have to see all the angles in this triangle of Louise, Florian and Anna. It would be easy to dismiss these particular toys as some irrational projection of one person onto their own child, or as a futile gesture towards the past. Yet actually it represents just another imaginative way in which a couple sought to exploit a possibility offered by the relationship formed with their child equally between themselves. It wasn't as if these toys were especially important. This eBay phase didn't even last that long as a period of toy purchasing. As far as Florian was concerned, it was the same as most toys; some of them, such as the record player, he took no real interest in, while others, such as the play garage, were a great success. But the toys certainly worked in terms of the relationship between Anna and Louise. Even the mere fact that eBay can offer quite an exhilarating form of shopping one can do from home, when looking after an infant, worked for Louise; especially the bidding aspect, which returned her to something of the excitement of her previous employment – in a small way.

Material things are often like that. They have a certain humility. They don't jump up and down and confront you as critical symbols of yourself or your relationships. They don't theorise themselves or abstract themselves. Often one only really pays attention to them when they don't work, or look awkward or out of place. Normally they just serve, in their relatively humble way, as forms through which relationships are expressed and developed; the simple technology through which – with some play, some passion, some muddling through – we come to accept and occasionally celebrate our various relationships. Even Florian is now getting in on the act. He obviously hasn't used the word possession, but the idea of 'mine' is emerging. He responds to everything by saying 'Florian's' these days. Perhaps he has realised that, for now, this is pretty close to the truth. But, ironically, the more he insists upon possession, that everything is Florian's, the more he will release his parents from their narcissistic bond and confront them with the independent existence, first, of his will, and then, by opposition, theirs.

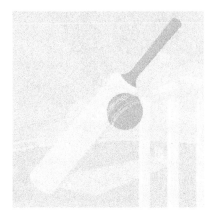

PORTRAIT **16**

STRENGTH OF CHARACTER

Although our fieldwork was based on Stuart Street, it also included a series of much smaller streets, mainly cul-de-sacs, that led directly off Stuart Street itself. Obviously there were exceptions, but in general it seemed that there was a dearth of neighbourly relations along Stuart Street. Most people didn't even seem to know their neighbours, and there was very little social interaction based around the street itself. This was not a place one could imagine holding street parties. Even long-term residents could only talk about local society and neighbourliness as something historical, not a feature of contemporary life. By contrast, people living in these cul-de-sacs, with only a dozen or so premises, tended to know most of the other people living there and had some sort of interaction with them. Furthermore, they thought of the area they lived in as relatively friendly and sociable. At one point Charles, who lives in one such cul-de-sac, suggested that they don't bother having a resident's association because they know each other so well. It would be hard to imagine a stronger contrast with Stuart Street as a whole – where the idea of a residents' association seems impossible, since most people have no feeling of being residents of any particular place.

In the case of Charles, however, this is the kind of thing he may well have taken into account when buying his property. Because Charles cares a very great deal both about neighbourliness and about property. Of all our hundred households, he is the most committed to both these things. He runs the local Neighbourhood Watch, he certainly knows everyone in his side-street, talks to people there with some frequency and exchanges many Christmas cards with people he knows simply because they live close to him. If a meeting has been organised in order to consider some local issue, from speed bumps to policing, it is more than likely that it was Charles who organised it. It was Charles who gave evidence in support of the local pub when some people, regarded by many as NIMBYs ('not in my back yard'), tried to limit its opening hours, if not to close it down. The NIMBYs in question then included Charles in their campaign of attack. Mind you, the NIMBYs in question had a young child to keep from being woken up and Charles does not, and Charles is the kind of person who would want us to be scrupulously fair in our reporting.

I imagine that the term Neighbourhood Watch is more often honoured in the breach. People vaguely hope that a little sticker will act as some deterrent, but in most cases, even when one's neighbour's house alarm has been sounding off for twenty minutes, to inform the police of this is far too 'intrusive'. But Charles does a good deal more than just watch. This is the man seen chasing off burglars from other people's houses in the street, alone and armed with only a baseball bat, on more than one occasion. On television crime programmes there are loads of people like Charles, but on the average London street . . . you must be joking.

Charles would see nothing at all contradictory about his caring both about people and about property. Even to suggest that he invests in both would be regarded as a compliment rather than a sneer. Charles certainly wants the value of his properties to increase, but if this is achieved through putting in new sports facilities, upgrading the road, creating schemes to counter local unemployment so that the area becomes a more desirable place to live, then that is the way Charles would want to see property values rise, and he is active in pursuing all these goals. For him, value and values are part of the same semantic stretch. In complete contrast to those who fear that the value of their properties will be lowered by association with others, such as new immigrants, Charles wants the welfare of anyone and everyone in the neighbourhood to be increased through their association. Charles is one of the very, very rare gentlemen in gentrification.

So Charles can tell us a great deal about this street. He knows when various sections were built; he knows how much each type of home would currently sell for, and how that has shifted over the last decade. He knows which ones are Housing Trusts, which have been purchased as investments by property companies, which have been broken into shared flats, and which are privately owned. It's something we have been trying to work out from outside appearances; but generally we can't and he can. He finds it sometimes in the care and attention given to the way they have done up the outside, sometimes in the type of car parked outside. Even the front door is more of a clue than we have realised. But then Charles has met some of the key landlords in the area, he has accompanied police and councillors on walks to discuss the street. He knows who owns the pub and how it is run. He can even describe the different kind of clientele who tend to hang out there on different days of the week. When he hears that Fiona is planning to move into the street as part of our research, he immediately offers to help with finding her suitable accommodation.

Charles is not one of those who can be pigeonholed merely by reference to his public-school education. He is well aware of the inhumanity and insensitivity that can be associated with a certain kind of toff. But then Charles did not go to a typical public school. From Dickens and many other authors we have inherited the image of the private school which was austere and ascetic as a means of suppressing the individual and inculcating a mean-spirited ethos of punishment. Such schools had their metal-framed beds, with horse-hair mattresses and their traditions of caning. When my own mother died, I was sent, at the age of six, to a boarding school; the first thing I was shown was the bamboo grove, where they grew the canes used for punishment. Unlike Charles, I have no fond memories of school whatsoever.

Nevertheless, through Charles, one can start to envisage an entirely different relationship to boarding school. This was a school that built character through austerity – character and the altruism that were intended to create courage on the battlefield, based not on the stupidity of mindless sacrifice but on a thoughtful ethical sense of service to humanity. They understood that installing courage was not enough, in the light of a British history which now saw those slaughtered on the Somme as wasted lives, and those who fought to overthrow Hitler as martyrs to our freedom from fascism. This seemed to be a school that tried to include some measure of critical judgement as an aspect of, rather than in opposition to, courage.

Charles' brand of public school also had an austerity which came from Welsh roots. In its disciplines, its games and its orders, it forged a bond between men who, in another age, would indeed have signed up together. Some did join up. It's no surprise to learn that Charles has schoolfriends who have subsequently won awards for bravery in the fire service, or were fighting with the SAS. But most drifted to ordinary streets scattered throughout the country and reserved their soldiering for the likes of Neighbourhood Watch. The school also inculcated a certain ethos: that version of liberalism that takes no issue with dreadlocks and spliffs, or the black hats of Hasidic Jews, because, if anything, it sees in them a fellow commitment to communities of individuals – better still, eccentric individuals. What is despised in this ethos is the selfishness of the 'merely me'. The heart of what Charles retains as his personal legacy from these spartan Welsh roots is the mutual commitment of firm friends to firm friends. Charles remains happiest in the companionship of perhaps the best friends he will ever make. He was in touch with around thirty men living within London who had been to this school, and, until relatively recently, Charles reckoned that he would see one or other of them, if not every day, then every two or three days. This seemed completely implausible at first, until all the other details that affirmed the sheer intensity of these bonds gradually emerged. Of course, those who went to university or into the army had mates from those places too, but nothing ever created quite the same intensity of attachment, something more like a bonding of blood, like the distant memory of a shared womb. Charles would like to have children partly in order to send them to such a boarding school.

When we first met Charles, he had a partner, whom we never met, and Charles had assumed that this would lead to marriage. Later on this relationship broke up, and it became very difficult not to interpret what Charles had told us initially about the material qualities of that relationship, other than in the light of its subsequent ending. Because while this was clearly a couple in name – and for all we knew a couple in many successful intimate ways – in terms of the material culture we were studying they seemed decidedly an unlikely couple. When Charles' partner came to live with him, it was the occasion for doing up the house, as commonly happens; but it seemed that Charles was doing all the doing up. As is often the case when couples live together, there were suddenly two of many things. But Charles' partner really wanted to keep her stuff, and it was of course Charles who, with good grace, filled an entire charity lorry with his surplus things, even those he cared about. But then Charles was not brought up to respect sentiment. When he left his parental home, his bedroom was turned into a guest-room and his own childhood things given away, something that would have seemed to him simply the right and proper thing. Similarly, the objects left behind when Charles had broken up from previous relationships were either re-designated as useful, in which case they were kept, or discarded. Or so he seemed to be implying at that time.

Typically, one can watch couples developing their relationship vicar-iously, through the gradual merger of all sorts of items in the house: books, CD collections, pictures on walls. The things, and not just the people, start to take up residence with each other, getting to know each other and sometimes eventually becoming indistinguishable from each other – to a degree which has subsequently made divorce lawyers sig-nificant profits. In this house, however, the material culture was remain-ing resolutely aloof; things were barely on speaking terms. This was developing as a his-and-hers house. His office, her office; his books, her books; his ornaments, her ornaments. There were gifts given by her to him that belong to him, and gifts given by him to her that belong to her. I guess one doesn't expect her to have assimilated his videos of rugby matches, or that he would have integrated her collection of cosmetics. Perhaps it's fair enough, too, that she would hate to see him using her laptop, and he would hate to see her using his PC. But when it comes to his office functioning as his separate dressing-room, and her office as hers? This seemed to be taking personal autonomy surprisingly far for a couple who had agreed to live together. At the time, however, Charles took all this as the most natural thing in the world – even an affirmation of the supposed attraction resulting from the difference and comple-mentarity between genders:

> She's come in and rearranged my house, that's basically it. And she's imposed her will on my house, that's how it goes. Just because she's a

woman, that's what happens. I mean every time a woman moves into a bloke's flat or house they rearrange their house for them, it's a normal thing, it's just how it happens, you know. Well, it's not that it's rearranged, it's sort of they move in with their stuff. There isn't enough room for two of each, and therefore your stuff has got to go. That's what's happened here. Because women are just much more dominant and much more – you know. When a woman gets to thirty plus, mid-thirties they get their way. It's as simple as that and we have to sort of doff the cap . . .

It's a bit like living with Lady Penelope and being Parker the driver, you know. But that's happened to all my friends, and especially ones that own the property first, and their wives or fiancées move in. It's exactly the same thing. All their stuff has to go, all their treasured items have to go. And the women move in, move their kit in and then they say, 'right, you've got to have that colour, we're painting this colour, that one, the other'. And that's how it is. You've got to have a little shed somewhere, or my little room downstairs where you can shut the door and just have a little peace and quiet on my own and just have my few things around me. It's like that's the compromise, it's the only compromise you have.

There are couples who work best through the cultivation of autonomy. I knew two very appealing academics, one of whom lived in Cambridge and the other in Hawaii, who reckoned that autonomy was the saving of their marriage. As this book will hopefully show, material culture is very rarely simply the vicarious sign of a relationship. The play between persons and things is much deeper than that, it has much more to do with actually constituting the people themselves rather than just standing for them. So this separation of things need not have been the sign of a lack of commitment. But I couldn't help feeling that, for all his Welsh public school, Charles retained a wellspring of sharing and sentiment that another woman would have seen and embraced. He loves a good wedding and I would guess that, given the opportunity, Charles would probably be ridiculously romantic. He is now in his late thirties, and this may be something that will happen in his forties or sixties. Or, as is the case of some others in Stuart Street, maybe not at all. But I think it will happen.

Charles' official attitude remains this kind of slightly bemused live-and-let-live response to the world, whether applied to women or to the local institutions of council and police that he has to deal with in relation to his work in property. At one level, none of it made sense and it was all some kind of absurd game, whether personal relationships or local bureaucracy. But if you could just take things as you found them, learn the rules, think of it as another sport or board game, then it wasn't too hard to live with it. In many ways the intricacies of local council bureaucracy, and even the intricacies of women, were a source of slightly distanced fascination.

In the event, when the relationship broke up, Charles looked forward rather than back. It did seem, in retrospect, that Charles had actually taken a more sentimental, or at least protective, attitude to some of his possessions than he had initially implied. Some of his things had actually gone to the lofts of friends rather than charity shops, and these came back. Some could be purchased again, and he did so. In particular, some paintings he had done himself, specifically, to go with the room, but which had been ousted by his partner's preferences, had survived pretty well in a friend's lock-up. That they were subsequently joined by some chairs, a lamp and various other furnishings helped confirm our suspicion that Charles had indeed a few more regrets and attachments to his belongings. But one could hardly blame him for something he probably needed to deny to himself at that time. The general lack of integration of things had become something of a blessing. As far as material culture went it must have been an easy parting. The photo albums were about the only problematic joint legacy of their two and half years together and these they simply copied. At this point he could also admit to a few possessions that had survived from previous relationships. As long as they showed no overt sign of their symbolic connections, they had thereby survived the determination of each 'ex' to root out and exterminate any sign she could detect of her predecessors. As an example of this determination, even when he removed the photos of himself and a previous girlfriend from their frame, his current girlfriend guessed that the sequined frame was not something he would have bought; so it had to go. But there was nothing evidently girly about this leather cushion or that light. Nothing to hint that these things actually had some history behind them. So these items remained behind. Funnily enough, he says now that it is the women, the wives of his friends, who are telling him what we, of course, could never have said . . . that there were signs that things wouldn't work out . . . especially in their relationship to things.

Charles was helped through the transition period when one of his schoolfriends moved in for a while during a temporary separation from his own wife. Charles is fully aware that the intensity of the bond retained between these men is of itself an issue for all of them in their subsequent relationship with women. For a while, he and his mate could sit there, the odd couple, and wonder about women from Venus or whatever planet they are now supposed to have come from. Then Charles did something a mite predictable, albeit no less efficacious for that. He bought himself a car – and not just any old car; fast, American, sporty, though not what he thinks could be regarded as naff or Chav. It does have £2,000 spent on the suspension, but it makes no demands for the bedroom to be painted in pink.

Charles imagines that one reason why he is capable of this easy detachment from things lies in the spartan conditions of his school, the very lack of possessions, together with the fact that this led to intense personal bonding, friendships unmediated by things. Objects should therefore be superfluous to relationships. At school, activities, not things, were seen as appropriate to bonding; drinking together, or playing sports. Objects were much less appropriate, more a female way of doing things. So Charles remains neutral about attaching sentiment to things, even the paintings he did for the walls. When we approach the topic too directly, he plays the functional defence, that doing the painting himself cost him only fifty quid each, whereas otherwise he might have had to pay three hundred to buy something suitable.

I am surprised, though, that he hasn't seen a rather different model for his relationships to things coming out of his work. Charles has an unusual understanding of the importance of homes and properties, but he didn't immediately translate this into insights about the role of these smaller possessions, although by now he sees that both little and big things can contribute in important ways to people's welfare. What is becoming more difficult after all those years of almost daily contact is to keep up the same intensity of relationships with his friends from school. Most of them now have marital, parental and other commitments, pressures of work, the extra burden of the second or third child. They still revere friendship, but they are just too knackered.

So, even if the spirit of the fellowship remains, it is hard in practice to bring people together. Where there were once thirty of these school-friends living within a few miles of each other, now about half remain and of those, only half again are around to meet up more regularly. Charles still wants to be there, to lend a hand, say, when his friends move house. But today he has to wonder whether it's OK to phone when the kids are resting or the wife is taking a nap, or they are busy finishing the spare room on their own. The school ideals are much harder to sustain. It's become more a sort of Knights of the Round Nappy-Changing Tables and the Fellowships of the Napkin Rings. Many of the wives have formed their own friendships based on a solidarity – a common realisation that they needed to find some collective response to this intense attachment that pre-dates them.

The wives may fear exclusion by reason of the strength of the bond that existed, and was retained, by these schoolmates. But they may well have appreciated that this represented at least an ability to create attachment and bonding. After all, it was not Charles who was averse to integrating his possessions with his partner. but rather the other way round. By far the most cherished possession in Charles' house is his collection of wedding and funeral invitation cards. Charles finds both events incredibly moving. Two of the funerals he has attended are of friends he knew from school. The anniversaries of their deaths mark two of the key times when he and his friends meet to drink and celebrate the lives rather than only mourn the deaths of their departed friends. Inevitably, memories have become an increasingly powerful part of their bonding. But he also loves weddings; part of the way Charles practises attachment – to people, to neighbourhoods, to potential partners, to friends. He celebrates weddings with real feeling. I could see him as a character in *Four Weddings and a Funeral*, where, under the brilliance of comedy, there is that almost embarrassed sense of these events as occasions for real feeling. In the case of Charles this forms part of something quite rare on the street: a genuine sense of responsibility for, and care for, the abstract ideal of community. Charles is a figure one rarely meets these days: a citizen.

PORTRAIT 17

HEROIN

Dave speaks in a strong working-class London accent, South London rather than cockney, and a voice that begs to be listened to for much more than its content. It is a voice which appropriates all the traditional hardness of that accent; a tough, no-nonsense strength that doesn't give a toss for the law, but has its own morality built from history and community, and an edge of potential violence, if push comes to shove. At the same time it is a voice with tremulous undertones, almost unheard but definitely present, which open up an extremely vulnerable underbelly, partly built of that same historical sense of lack of respect and hurt – but here one also detects a highly personal quality of fear and self-concern. I distinctly remember that, before we knew anything at all about Dave and had only arranged to visit him, there was something about that voice which said so much, although one couldn't articulate it: it was only after Dave had told his story that one knew how much of that story was already present in the voice itself.

Dave's story seemed to come from Dante's *Inferno*. Nothing about the journey ahead was clear at first. But at each stage a phrase or reference told us that we were about to step down further, descending into yet another level of his personal hell. These were phrases that you wouldn't just hear, they seemed more like alerts: 'PAY ATTENTION – DANGER OR REVELATION AHEAD'; phrases such as 'they say I am sick', 'heroin is such a . . .' 'depression', 'alcoholism', 'when in court'. There is clearly a ritualised element to the story; it has been told so many times. Dave spends much of his current energy on helping others towards various forms of rehabilitation, and it is likely that telling his story is a major part of that co-counselling. The process itself requires structure and support, which he obtains from familiarities and repetitions in the narrative itself, though it still contains hints of uncertainties and continued fears. It can only be told in certain ways to certain audiences. Although we are sitting together and addressing him, he can never bring himself to address Fiona directly. By contrast, there are periodic references to 'Dan'. Questions, assurances that Dan knows what he means, that he's had some parallel experience, that empathy may be sought and found there. Dan the interlocutor is being constructed as part of the narrative itself; my task is to work out what the proper response should be, to adapt to the role I am being asked to play: when to nod, when to offer an analogous experience, when to say 'I know what you mean'. Fiona, by contrast, knows that this is the time for her to sit quietly, unnoticed in her chair, listen but never to comment. For her to claim to be part of this world would be to diminish it.

As in so many interviews, there is a tension between the narrative of self-storying, which Dave has rehearsed many times and which when told naturally would pay but scant reference to the dimension of objects, and our attempts to lead the story back to the role of objects and the evidence that would allow us to assess their significance. But once this is done, once materiality is brought into focus and not hidden by a curtain of words, it seems here, as so often elsewhere, to have a substantial presence. Things now appear to be an integral element, without which the story would have been absurdly incomplete. Material things in general have a strange and little understood humility. After all, objects are concrete, upfront, evident to the eye. Yet they work generally as background, as that which frames behaviour and atmosphere, and they do this job best when they are not noticed. You compliment the painting; you are not supposed to notice the frame. You tell a woman she is beautiful, not only that her make-up is brilliant. You comment that the room has atmosphere, but you don't just discuss the wallpaper. Objects are artful; they hide their power to determine the way you feel. Our job is to confront and expose this crafty life of things.

This is not necessarily a difficult thing to do. True, left to his own devices Dave would have ignored things *per se*. But once he smells the mystery of the chase he has no difficulty in taking part. In a way, we have saved the encounter from being just one more recitation. Here is new meat. It is soon clear that things – objects – are immensely significant to him; and, being ordinary, unthreatening and mundane, there is no reason not to dwell on them. He is soon enlisted to our cause, amateur archaeologist digging for their deeper significance and, despite the horrors of the story, he starts to enjoy this excavation and to share the sense of discovery that we cannot hide either.

From our point of view, faced as we are with a human being so transparently wrecked in various ways and so fragile, it seems impossible not to objectify him, not to think of him, analogously, in terms of some object. Focusing on things helps to keep us from merely descending into a mutual depression of reflected trauma. After a while, the image of a ship came inexorably to mind. The hull of this ship was the house, but the hull needed ballast and balance to stay afloat. In the storm-tossed waters of this personal history, the ship bears many signs of its previous periods of wreckage, when it has foundered on rocks and has been overturned by powerful currents and undercurrents. Yet so far it has always managed to find repair and keep afloat, although with each misfortune it has become increasingly dependent upon its own material structure to maintain this essential balance.

As Dave showed us round and we explored the deep interiors, it became evident that he and his house were supported with ballast, as are so many ships, by the goods transported on their journey. One side of this ballast consisted of photo albums and the other side of CD albums. Indeed, perhaps one of the reasons why the image took root was that this was exactly how Dave presented himself to us. While telling his tale, he sat the entire time in a corner chair. To his right was a glass-fronted set of drawers filled to capacity with CDs; to the left was an old set of pine drawers he would occasionally rummage in to find the photo albums he needed when he wanted us to visualise his story as it poured forth. In both cases, it was the sheer weight of these material resources that seemed to keep Dave from floating off in this haze of drink, heroin and depression. Their weight lay in their specificity. Each CD album comprised a multitude of tracks, each photo album was full of images, and every track and every image was grounded in a particular memory and time.

The clue was in the very first things he told us. He started his account with his problems over time itself; problems of finding ways to keep it and not lose it. He said he wanted to tell us his story, but time was too elusive; he simply couldn't remember when different things had happened. The only memory which always seemed to help him to tie time down was the birth and aging of his children. For eighteen years their presence, their solidity, the clear evidence of their growth put other things into temporal perspective, gave them a context, a place, more of a position in his mind. The room in which we sat was overwhelmingly dominated by some very large portrait photos of his children.

Yet, as we progressed, it became clear that the children themselves were not the only resource; there were other ways in which his own personal time could be grounded, and these lay in the albums. But in no instance was this straightforward. Take the photo albums. The early photos could and should work this way; he could and should be able to locate himself. At one moment he latched onto his memory of a piece of furniture in the house he had been brought up in. It wasn't even a proper piece of furniture. It was a box intended to have plant pots arrayed along it, a box with holes for them to fit into. In talking about it he was seized with the desire to find the photo that recorded this image, and indeed he found it. But there was something about these photos that was very disturbing. They were black and white; but black and white seemed out of synch with his attempt to control his narrative. They were simply too old, too much of a rupture from the sequence of photos as a whole: too old to represent him, because he is not that old; too old to convey him to others – which is what photos are supposed to do. That was one of the problems of people today – they were too young, people like Fiona. They wouldn't recognise black and white photos in relation to the living. These photos wouldn't display his own vibrancy even as a child, his wildness, the core to his authenticity. They lacked the definition and specificity of colour. Dan was OK, Dan would understand – given Dan's age, which for the sake of convenience he took to approximate his own; but never Fiona. Black and white was wrong. It was inauthentic, anachronistic, untrue to what he had hoped they would convey.

The CDs had their own problems, their own vulnerability; because music was essential to memory. He could specify each individual track, where he had heard it, how he had himself tracked it down. The details and the exactitude were fascinating in their own right. Clearly, he had always insisted upon precisely locating what often was relatively obscure material but of importance to him – because music was his expertise, his resource. He had worked in the industry and knew about stuff other people wouldn't know. In music he was somebody, somebody who knew stuff, and his lack of reading and writing didn't matter so much, it wasn't so painful. But the very obscurity of these albums made them hard to replace. This mattered. He needed these hooks to reel in his own critical memories, which were lying scattered around the ocean floor. But people borrowed these CDs. Worse still, when he was in need of a fix he could sell anything and everything. With heroin, all specificity was lost, reduced to what could be exchanged for a pittance – but a pittance which could find his fix. All that had mattered once was reduced to the only thing that mattered now.

This is why some of the other groundings of his own self-esteem, however valuable to his narrative, had to be removed for their own safety. Especially the trophies. He had always collected trophies. The first were the symbols of prestige and status: tokens of what he had successfully nicked from others and displayed in his room, as a child, as trophies of his daring. Presided over by the hub cap of a Rolls Royce, his early pride and joy. Later on there were his own sporting and musical achievements. Trophies mattered; they reflected his worth back to him; and they mattered most when he needed such mirrors. Mirrors that would tell him the truth about what he had been and therefore still was, or perhaps could be again. Mirrors that were not shattered like those deceitful truths, the silvered glass mirrors which only sent back to him the image of a shattered man. But the time when he needed his trophies most was the very time when he was most likely to disregard them and to lose them, under the imperative of drink or drugs. So all the trophies had had to go to his mother's house for safekeeping. As, of course – although this hardly bore thinking about – had his children, his most precious and vulnerable mirror of all. Gone, too, were the women in his life – the people he needed most but who, in their turn, needed the security of distance, of having their own place to escape to when things got so rough that they were at risk of getting caught in the maelstrom of hurt, violence and sheer desperate necessity of addiction. Nothing was more important than these other people – people you could love and be loved by. But they couldn't be there, it was too dangerous. They could only come to show support, and leave again. So we were discovering what other people might have missed: that there were other things in Dave's life, things which seemed of little importance, but ultimately may have been critical to his survival. The old photo albums and old obscure CDs. They were of so little potential value to others that they survived, the two ballasts on either side of the hull; fixed because they couldn't bring a fix; worth so much because they were worthless. Only – to us they seemed weighty: the true source of stability that could re-right the fallen.

In Dave's case, objects didn't have an easy time of it; they almost lost him. But then, for Dave, nothing had been easy. His parents divorced early, his mother couldn't handle the situation, his first step-mother was only seventeen. The woman who ended up looking after him grew so close that his father became afraid of losing him and took him away from her, making him stay with another relative. Both his father and mother remarried. Dave was given precious little by the world, and what he valued was what he nicked, because he was good at nicking and this became the first evidence of his ability to make something of himself. But nothing he would steal could equal what life seemed to steal from him. He just about made his way through adolescence; he was quite proud of his ability to cope. Then, just as things were settling, he became the father of a child – but a child with disabilities beyond anything he could have imagined, and certainly beyond anything Dave the lad could possibly have coped with – nor the mother either.

Quite possibly it was these vulnerabilities and the weight of respon-sibilities that opened the door to the biggest thief of all – the heroin. For a while, it seemed that this dark shadow would enter the house every night and leave with something else. There was no stopping it; it could slide under locked doors, open casement windows and leave with Dave's possessions. Things reached such a state that the room we were sitting in was quite empty. Empty to the extent that even the carpet and furni-ture had gone; only the shell of the fireplace and the walls remained.

When it came to nicking stuff, even Dave was no match for heroin; he just didn't possess the same relentless greed, the insatiable heartlessness of the drug, which, having removed all rival substances, sought his blood, his veins and always found them. With many of his friends, heroin emptied them out from the inside until there wasn't much left even to bury or burn.

I am convinced, however, that it was things that saved Dave, and one thing above all: the house itself – the one stroke of luck that cut through the stranglehold of drugs and drink. He was only supposed to be in the house on a temporary basis, but somehow the council screwed things up so he found himself there for quite a while and on this account he managed to get a tenancy. After that, however bad things were, the house was there as a refuge, the hull that kept him afloat; sometimes emptied down to its creaky caulked planks, but at least there; and, when things were not so bad, he would rummage around and find the remaining foundations upon which he rebuilt memory and some sort of narrative of his life that could shore him up and provide a spine around which he could fit his errant parts.

The foundations were pretty insubstantial at times. More substantial support was provided by the memories of what he had done, and there had been times when things were good. Dave never expected to amount to much; without reading or writing, jobs were scarce. But he was strong, he could move stuff about, he could fight, and he could be good company. In the wildness of the music business there were places for people like Dave. So music and memory developed in tandem. Music, for Dave, had extraordinary precision; it also spoke with great feeling to moments in his life. Maybe that precision was what countered the drugs' tendency to replace the actual with the disembodied. As he listened again to a specific track from a CD, he could feel again that blonde's arm on the dance floor tugging him to her body; he could recall that joke he had told or the round he had bought when he first heard that particular track. It was a habit of his, when he heard something he liked, sitting in a hotel room, at a party. He would find out who was playing, go up to the DJ, ask the hotel manager. It was just something he had to know. Music could reclaim space better than anything, filling every crack and corner. Dave knows how much he relies on his collection and its integrity. 'I am into it, and like if something goes missing, like I lose my nut and think – I gotta go and replace it.' The vinyl eventually dissolved into the drug; but he was able to buy back much of it now in the form of CDs.

Photos supplement the music, working in a different way. In them, Dave can re-colonise other spaces – New York, Ibiza, Manchester. Above all, they document the most painful and most precious thing of all: the growth of his children. They are there, in album after album. And today they have also come back into the open. The sheer size of those on the walls could in some way make up for all that time when they couldn't have a presence in the house. By contrast, there is just one other major photograph – a presence who could, and did, remain when the children couldn't. A dog, and the kind of dog that could look after itself, a pit-bull. There are no pictures of Dave on the wall, but I suspect the dog's photo does the job. This is a dog that will protect Dave's girlfriend when she is out on the street without Dave. It will curl up and be kind to his children when they are staying in the house. It could remain and protect the house itself. The dog could stand for Dave, his avatar of what he could be, embodying that sort of caring, protective violence which other people simply couldn't comprehend, just as he couldn't comprehend why anyone would want to destroy such a creature as his dog. 'If you want loyalty buy a dog. Right, Dan?'

If Dave is best reflected back onto himself though his dog, for other people he has become something of a living picture. Dave tells his story, but by now he also knows that he is himself testimony to the possibility of survival. He now helps others, tells them to be strong, that they can climb out of depression, that the high walls that surround them on every side have small fault lines which can support a hand or foot if you are only willing to make that climb. As he did. Not everyone listens, and many simply can't make the escape. Most of his friends are dead from the drug. But some have come up, and in some cases he knows his example mattered. It's not that he is much good with death, illness or depression as such. He tries to keep his distance from those demons. But Dave knows how to make people laugh, and, if you want to make a crack in those dark high walls you can cling onto, there is no tool as suitable or powerful as a good strong laugh. For our part, we see another support that up to now was absent from his story, as from most people's stories. Certainly we recognise, as he does, the role of his dog and the role of his relatives. But our story is about the comfort of things, and we, too, feel a drive to tell anyone who cares to listen that there are other people out there like Dave, who one day could benefit if those helping to support and counsel them were alerted to the power of these other help-mates, quiet, unseen and modest: possessions.

PORTRAIT **18**

SHI

In a book called *The Propensity of Things*, the French sociologist Jullien has written extensively about the Chinese concept of Shi that seems to comprehend the quality that I see in Pauline. Shi is central both to the art of war and to art itself. It is captured in the dynamic twists and turns of that quintessential symbol of China, ancient and modern: the sinuous dragon. Shi is all about foresight, the careful determination of strategy and subterfuge: ultimately there is no point even having a battle, since the consequences have already been determined by the superior craft of that general who more fully commands the skills of Shi.

Pauline strikes me as a master of Shi. She is slim, with small waist and hips, a disciplined figure, kept entirely under control – as is made very clear by her tight jeans and a navy-blue, open-necked top, held in with a belt. She has perfected the art of semi-smart in the manner which is well taught at universities such as Bristol or Durham rather than Oxbridge – a more intelligent and effective mode than Kensington or Chelsea. To appreciate Pauline, one needs to pay attention to her sixteen pairs of sneakers. An extensive range, but not an expansive range, since most of them are quite similar to each other. Pauline has disciplined her clothing as she has disciplined her body. She has a repertoire of clothes which, she knows from experience, work well for her in particular. Wearing a pair of sneakers, she is confident that she will get things right as these sneakers offer a suitable complement to her other clothes. But Pauline is someone who wants to get things absolutely right, and for this purpose she needs to select from within that preferred genre, precisely the right pair out of these sixteen pairs – the sneakers entirely appropriate for the occasion. Pauline's job depends on matching people exactly to their task. It helps if she begins with herself.

This careful control over her place in the environment creates much more than just an ensemble. It is equally evident in her interaction with us. Pauline doesn't so much discuss as assimilate and consider. Some people are so delighted to have a willing listener that they gush. I can't imagine that Pauline would ever gush. She is circumspect in what she says, respectful, actually very interested, but also appreciative that what she is participating in might provide a different perspective on the things in her life. This might one day be useful; but, for now, it should be merely stored, considered, given time and contemplation before she decides whether it is valuable or useless. For now, she will be as helpful as she can be within the limits of circumspection. She may say something substantial in reply to a question, or she may just return the enquiry with a non-committal 'mmmmm', in a tone that suggests she has properly considered the point but, for now, we should move on to the next.

Ideally, the art of Shi consists in doing nothing much at all. If one has calculated, planned and positioned, action itself should barely be necessary. In some cases, when Pauline contemplates the forces that might have laid waste to their house, she can afford a wry smile, since these forces are so completely ungainly and misdirected that very little is required to keep them at bay. One of Rupert's grandfathers was a big game hunter. In their country home there are enough stuffed heads and antlers to re-populate a small natural history museum. Fortunately, in Pauline's small discrete house it is quite clear that a herd of dead wild animals will find little room. Perhaps one token gazelle; but surely no one could expect more. Rupert's mother is far more insistent that her collection should indeed pass on to Rupert. But fortunately her possessions are not one iota less anachronistic than his grandfather's. Rupert's mother's pride and joy is a collection of Blackamoors – those colonial wooden statues of the stereotypical negro; utterly ghastly and offensive, but seeking protection under the shield of irony (or, these days, under the equally ugly armature which calls itself post-modern irony). As part of a sophisticated couple in multi-cultural modern London, Pauline doesn't need to say a word in order to convey that 'not-over-my-dead-body' support for Rupert against the ravages of his mother and her army of Blackamoors.

But the Blackamoors are only the worst; there were plenty of other monstrosities. Pauline's mother-in-law had decided that the time had come to downsize radically her own home. The silver lining of her own distress would be that this thereby liberated these gifts for her children. As it happens, Pauline can, in the spirit of Shi, enlist Rupert's own ambivalence about his relationship to his mother. In fact Rupert's true point of ancestral identification is with his grandfather on his father's side, the chemist. As a chemist himself, Rupert feels this inheritance to be rather like a mutant gene, since all the other relatives are firmly on the side of the arts. One of his mother's most unforgivable acts was to sell off the fine collection of chemistry books, which Rupert would have loved to inherit, rather than all those 'antiques' that she wished now to pass on through his line. On these matters there is complete agreement between Rupert and Pauline. As he comments to us while contemplating these unwelcome potential intruders, 'Well, you need a rather sort of grand sort of large sort of house to have that sort of thing, without it dominating the whole thing.'

So Rupert, without thinking of it particularly this way, has done his bit to salvage a male line from this domineering female aesthetic. He may not possess the books he would have treasured from his grandfather, but he does have the latter's old medicine chest and a collection of beer mugs. These are things that matter to Rupert, since they are 'locked into the family, sort of tales or fables attached to them'. He has a chest of drawers from his father too, but most of all there is a bowl, the one object which, for Rupert, somehow captures his relationship with his father. This was the bowl in which his father used to place the money for Rupert to pay for his school bus. They had a little ritual whereby his father fished for the right change so that Rupert wouldn't need to worry about it. There is something about that bowl. It seemed to capture the essence of that older English male tradition in which the direct expression of care and concern, of love and affection was considered unmanly and inappropriate. Rather such expression needed to be indirect and mediated by an object. Rupert's father didn't give him the money directly, just as there were things he couldn't say directly to him. Now, a generation on, the bowl is allowed to develop the patina of sentimentality, to become one of Rupert's most treasured possessions. Rupert found ways to prise what he wanted from his mother without exposing his preferences, his own small gesture to Shi. His father's army uniform was practically on its way to Oxfam, when Rupert rescued it from his mother. It was all he had from his father after his death. The one thing Rupert's father had bequeathed to him in life were plants from the garden, which became his passion in retirement; but at that time Rupert had been interested neither in gardening nor in inheritance, and the plants had all died.

Finally, Pauline had to deal with the things Rupert himself retained from his own childhood and from his pre-Pauline days: all those books and the paraphernalia associated with war games. It wasn't that she didn't appreciate them. They bore witness to a certain kind of boyish charm and emergent manly interest in things, which was a large part of Rupert's attraction. This is exactly what she would have wished for him to be doing as a child. But the time comes for the putting away of childish things, perhaps in storage for some future child. Pauline knew that, in the meantime, there should be no hint that the adult had not yet fully emerged from the chrysalis. So the war games materials seem destined to move only from attic to attic. By contrast, his father's history books are ideal for promotion to the sitting-room: they are fully adult. On the whole, Rupert has little expectation of securing his own presence in this material world. His family always seemed to have a strong matriarchal bias; both his mother and grandmother held sway. Also his older siblings were always competing not just for attention but also over these material presences, so that Rupert would always find his photograph on the grandparents' table pushed to the back, while his older brother's came once again to the fore. Later on, the same brother received the stuffed leopard. The old house is still there. Rupert hopes that one day, when he has children, they will return to this or some other country house – a proper place to bring them up.

For now, Rupert's things remain largely in storage, mainly in a garage attached to the country house. It was impossible to reconcile his own interest in collecting, what he would have to admit was actually more a hoarding, with his appreciation that things in a house such as the present one should be rather minimalist. Given that both his mother and his father tended to hoard things, he couldn't hope to escape this trait. One way or another, Pauline, the sinuous and sensual dragon, has shifted Rupert into the proper rhythm of their shared space. Rupert has plenty of experience in acquiescing to the stronger opinions of women in such matters. In any case, Pauline was in this flat before Rupert joined her, so it seemed natural that her things should have retained their initial claim to occupation.

In her turn, Pauline has had to deal with the inheritance of things from her own line, mainly from her father, when he moved out of his flat in order to emigrate. She fully acknowledges that most of what she has is sentimental more than functional; or both, like those paintings on the walls which were collected by her father and grandfather. Overall, though, there wasn't that much; Pauline's sister was quite upset by the amount of things their father sold or got rid of rather than passing them on. Pauline took some of his things partly because he emigrated at a time when she was beginning to regret that she hadn't kept things from her own childhood. She hadn't yet seen them in the light of potential retrospective interest. Now, with the prospect of having children herself one day, she sees around her nothing of her own childhood. But Pauline, unlike Rupert, is not a hoarder and remains concerned with the overall aesthetics and the need to keep control over the accumulation of things. For a car-boot sale she carefully sorted through what she could part with, including her granny's china. She knew her granny loved this china, she knew she loved her granny, but she also knew she was never going to love this flowery granny-style china. Some things she gave to charity shops; but she feels that Stuart Street isn't the kind of area to have the charity shops that would appreciate, and get a proper price for, possessions of the quality of those she has to give away.

Pauline is too intelligent to think in terms of a narrow pragmatism; she understands the spectrum of value and values that pertain to things. She just needed to find ways of incorporating these values without overburdening the home she was creating. An example is the inheritance from her mother, which she sees largely in terms of food and cooking. She has plenty of kitchen-ware, but mainly according to needs: plates, cutlery, saucepans and bowls from her mother. On the other hand, she has a vast collection of recipes, even though she has no ambition to cook any of them herself. But recipes are relatively undemanding in terms of space. One book of cuttings can effectively compress so much of her mother's labour and ambition, interleaved with the recipes that her mother loved to dictate over the phone. This is the sort of thing one could afford to hoard: recipes that will never be cooked. Also, something one could afford to inherit. Pauline finds herself doing the same thing – cutting recipes out of Sunday supplements, but cutting rather than cooking. If anything, it is her father's Indian recipes that she probably uses more in her actual cooking.

And this is the point of Shi, as I see it in Pauline. The analogy is not meant to be at all disparaging. My image of a Chinese dragon-general is not at all militaristic in the narrow Western sense. It is full of intelligence, colour, emotion and sensuous energy. Yet, as Shi, all of these things have to be negotiated through the twists and turns, up and down motion through which it travels. No Chinese dragon was ever stupid enough to move in a straight line. Pauline, the good general, acknowledges the strength of all the forces with which she must contend, and, since these are mainly made up of family pressures, they are emotional depth-charges which threaten to blow up in her face. All over her house are mines which may have to be negotiated carefully at every step. But one way or another she manages to keep them at bay – to ambush a gift before it is actually given, to find an alternative storage space so that an unwanted item doesn't have to invade the home, gently to assert the needs of the whole over some incompatible part; to marshal her very disparate forces, from recipes to medicine chests, to modern light fittings, and out of this create a tight, elegant and appropriate place for them to dwell within.

One of the battles which has been fought and won is that of the relationship *to* things and the relationship *between* things. A professional interior decorator or designer is going to be primarily concerned with the relationship *between* things. The ideal is that designs should in some sense *go* with each other. Obviously, this doesn't mean that everything has to be blue; one can use contrast, be quirky, have one room modernist and the next Edwardian; but the choice is based on an aesthetics in which each and every thing has to acknowledge its appropriate contribution to the overall effect. By contrast, the personal relationship *to* things is often a fortuitous result of accumulation: things inherited from one's parents, souvenirs from holidays, gifts from a lover or a brother. There is no reason at all why such things should bear any relation to each other in aesthetic terms. As a result, most living-rooms include this additional cause of conflict – the degree to which the personal relation *to* things will disrupt the aesthetic relation *between* things. This is often an ongoing battle in its own right. So there are the newly purchased items, sofas and cushions that match, a kitchen with plenty of aluminium and white. But within these are personal things, an inherited chair, various ceramic bowls, and there is no feeling that these are disruptive; rather, there is an overall reconciliation between the different sources and different genres. This makes for rooms that are not in any way special – they clearly aren't intended to be – but rather a space that works well enough. Rooms that show no scars from the battles fought to this end, unless of course that is what you are looking for.

During the year and a half of our fieldwork, however, the inherent dynamism of the room as a process, rather than as a thing, emerged. Not all the conflicting pressures had been reconciled when we first met. Rupert and Pauline both did some of their work at home and both felt that the space available was insufficient. But, more than that, the kitchen needed modernising, and as a result they suffered from what the anthropologist McCracken once called the Diderot effect. The idea comes from an observation made by the philosopher Diderot, when he was presented with a fine new robe. The problem was that, up until then, everything he owned seemed satisfactory. But now, compared to that fine new robe, everything else suddenly felt shabby. In the case of Pauline and Rupert, the new kitchen altered the balance of this relationship *between* things and *to* things. Since it was new, it contained more aesthetic harmony within itself. There was a more evident stylistic integrity to the objects that it contained. As a result, some of the personal, inherited objects seemed to detract from the harmony of the interior design and no longer looked as comfortable as before. So, having done up the kitchen, it was clear that the living-room too would have to be repainted and reconsidered.

There was one more disruption, to which I must shamefacedly admit. Pauline knew enough about Shi to have won her battles silently, without any explicit consideration of what the selection of material culture might mean in terms of these past struggles between relationships and relatives. When we had come to visit, we certainly had no intention of disrupting her order. But by constantly asking questions about where things came from, we covered the furniture with words and implications that could not easily be vacuum-cleaned from the surfaces. The imbalance between what had been retained from Pauline's inheritance and those from Rupert's past became evident, and, once evident, no longer acceptable. Actually it turned out that they had had a major row after our first visit. Rupert pointed out that there was almost nothing of him present in the furnishings, that it was all hers. Worse still, we had made evident a link between his history of suppression by a dominant matriarchal family and the incipient creation of something analogous in his own partnership with Pauline. This was undoubtedly our fault. However, between our visits, the balance had been adjusted. Not too much, though. Pauline and Rupert are a couple who feel that it is entirely appropriate to think of interior decoration as something that should interest a female and yet bore a male. But there is now definitely more explicit consultation, and they are starting to buy more objects together, as a couple; such as a painting they bought together on a holiday in Italy. She is having some of his pictures from New Zealand framed for inclusion on the wall, to displace some of her own inherited paintings.

But then this is inherent in Shi and the path of the dragon. A dragon can never stay still. Time moves on, the forces that act on the world change, and so too must the strategy that is formulated through intelligent contemplation to restore the appropriate balance. With sufficient foresight, all battles can be avoided. There is an ancient wisdom in knowing what is at stake in what seem tiny details, trivial and mundane issues of what hangs where, and the place of photos on mantelpieces. Through such wisdom, the embittered inheritance of the generations can be laid to rest, potential conflicts avoided and harmony returned to the world – for a while at least.

BRAZIL 2 ENGLAND 2

These days, most of the newspaper coverage on current immigration into Britain focuses upon refugees and asylum seekers, and therefore tends to highlight conditions of persecution or countries of origin such as Zaire, which have no particular link to Britain itself. The opposite condition was captured brilliantly by V. S. Naipaul in his book *The Enigma of Arrival* which conveys the feeling of migrants from the Caribbean that they were not just coming to Britain but coming home to the place whose history, geography and culture they had learnt about at school much more than those of the island they lived in. It is only in contemplating the farming areas around Stonehenge that Naipaul comes to terms with England – an England itself in constant change, rather than that still, ancient pillar of his own identity for which he had come in search.

Jorge is, however, a good deal more typical of those migrants found in Stuart Street than of either these two extremes. Judged from Stuart Street, where less than a quarter of the population was born in London, migration today is more fluid and much harder to define. Most people first came to London not as intentional migrants but either out of a spirit of curiosity extending a holiday or through a stint of temporary work, as an *au pair* or a labourer. If they have stayed, it is either because they have found a significant relationship, or because they are having too much fun.

Or, surprisingly often, there may be continuing reasons not to go back, for instance an unresolved quarrel at home or the fact that they haven't yet saved the money with which they promised to return. In one case, migration resulted from the experience of coming out as gay; in another, from the unresolved breaking up of a relationship which the migrant refuses to go back and confront. Many of the people that we meet don't know if they are migrants or not, because they may still return home. In most cases it depends on what will happen to the relationships they have formed, or to the work they have found here in London. They simply have no idea whether they will end up living here or might just continue to move on.

Classifying people as migrants in any case begs the question of how they see what we presume to be national identity. I have only paid one short visit to Brazil, and, each time I hear about it, it seems harder to reconcile the different images of that country. While there, I met an anthropological colleague who has been carrying out surveys of what people eat on a daily basis. She reports an extraordinary degree of homogeneity, irrespective of region and class, ethnicity and education. Almost everyone, on any given day, is eating white rice, beans and meat, such as chicken or pork. I presume there are other things, such as football, which hold the country in an equally tight embrace. By contrast, watching films from Brazil has always conveyed the impression that there are two entirely distinct Brazils: the *favela* or slums, depicted in their most extreme form in films such as *City of God*, as opposed to an affluent middle class parading on the beaches and clubs of Rio. Then there is also the regional heterogeneity of Brazil, the Mediterranean style of the South, which appears very different from the Caribbean atmosphere of Salvador and Bahia. In anthropology, one could be reading one day about Amazonian Indians and their kinship systems, the next day about a syncretistic religion which combines Catholicism with the Africanised rituals of Candomblé. So what does it mean to say that Jorge comes from Brazil?

The problem with all these images, indeed with all such generalisations about migrants, is that they never quite touch the personal, the way people feel about who they are and what matters to them – things which often have little to do with any formal distinctions of identity. To be honest, I never really liked the word 'identity' anyway. With Jorge, all these abstract, political, contentious or academic discussions quickly fade away. In Jorge one not only encounters the complexity of a person, but also the realisation that this complexity is not a problem looking for a resolution. It is much more a continual process, a life. It is too easy to regard Jorge as a Brazilian who has settled in England. But Jorge is just Jorge. As we left his house after our first visit, Fiona and I realised with some shame that our discussion with him had been too forced, too directed by this assumption of identity – looking for what he had brought with him from that place to this place. Rather than allowing Jorge to take command of his own story. In the present portrait I am reverting again to these issues, but largely in order to illustrate their limitations and constraints.

For example, there was that confusion about Christmas. Christmas is a festival where many people feel the only way to properly celebrate is to return to the specific local and traditional customs they were brought up with. Home is the only place where they celebrate a 'real' Christmas. So when Jorge made it clear that what he really missed at Christmas was the smell and taste of *panettone*, I simply assumed that I was just ignorant of how Brazilians celebrate Christmas. But actually this was because one side of Jorge's family is originally from Italy. Jorge's mother usually sends him a small *panettone*, well wrapped. It takes twenty days to arrive and, to be honest, it doesn't quite taste and smell as a freshly baked *panettone*. But it certainly tastes of a mother's love, and it is still very gratefully received by Jorge. In addition, he will buy one from a local Italian shop.

Then there is the question of which part of Brazil Jorge is from. In fact, he was brought up in Sao Paulo, one of the world's most cosmopolitan cities, which probably shares more with New York and London than it does with much of Brazil. It's quite likely that, given the amount of time I have lived in Trinidad and my affection for the novels of Jorge Amado, which are set in Bahia, I would feel rather more at home in Bahia than Jorge would. On the other hand, my anthropological colleague from Brazil would no doubt feel vindicated in her research if she learned that, when Jorge sometimes puts on a special Brazilian meal for friends, he cooks . . . white rice, black beans and stewed pork. This is also the occasion when he plays music from the CDs sent by his sister, and effectively entertains his guests by personally performing – and embodying – the man who comes from Brazil.

It is, however, about the only time he does play music that would be regarded as typically Brazilian. For more of the time he prefers to play the music he listened to in his own childhood in Sao Paulo – that is, Duran Duran and Queen. From very early on, he found that the pop music he enjoyed most was not Brazilian, nor that from the US, but from England. One of his main incentives in coming to London in the first place was the chance to see the bands with which he had grown up. He has not been disappointed, and his musical tastes continue to evolve in the same vein. His favourite band when we met him was Coldplay. When he was growing up in Sao Paulo, he had not the slightest difficulty in becoming as English in his musical tastes as he was Brazilian in his food. Television had been one of the main routes to his mastery of English – which is such that, today, English is close to becoming his main language. As with most bilingual speakers, however, there are always going to be occasions when some Portuguese word is particularly apt and there is simply nothing in English that properly captures the nuance; when you just can't help hoping that, if you just say the Portuguese word, someone will 'catch the drift' even if they won't understand all the substance.

There again, just because Jorge developed a fondness for a particular genre, it didn't mean that he was especially attached to the place it happened to come from. Jorge's other real obsession, from early in his youth, was with paraphernalia associated first with Bob Marley and then, after a short time, the Beatles. He had posters, books, vinyl, badges and figurines. As he became increasingly serious in his collecting, he located items from the 1970s and 1960s, some considered rare and valuable. Bob Marley didn't make him want to visit Jamaica. But his attachment to the image of the London of the swinging sixties through to the innovative eighties was sufficient to create, not just the desire to come, but also its realisation. In London the original passion behind his collection remains undiminished. We calculated that, given his circumstances – in which paid work has been intermittent at best – his continued buying of items from specialist collectors represents a huge commitment of his modest income. These days he is in the company of specialist collectors, the source of several local friendships. And, as is often the case with collectors, he now knows all sorts of esoteric facts about which companies made which facsimiles, and the techniques of printing and vinyl production of the time. It's not exactly a secret, or private, collection. The bathroom has a whole cabinet piled high with these carefully sorted layers of plastic folders, each with their respective forms of leaflets or posters. There are many more objects, stored in his bedroom and the loft, but he will dig out a particular recording or image if he wants to make a point, or simply because he hasn't seen or heard something for a while.

Not long ago, Jorge was faced with what for him was a hard and difficult decision, but one about which he felt that, ultimately, he had little by way of choice. He sold fifteen years' worth of his collections in order to help pay for his sister's wedding in Brazil. Thanks to the falling price of modern communications, he remains constantly in touch with his family. He knows just how much trouble he would be in if he failed to phone his mother every Monday. Things are a bit more relaxed with his sister, and, given the internet connection, rather less expensive. He usually emails or chats on MSN once a fortnight, and this way he can also see pictures of any nieces and nephews and share something of his sister's joy and pride in every tiny detail of their development, which she keeps him in touch with through this constant stream of up-to-date pictures.

That is probably the one thing that shocks Jorge about the English people he has come to know: how little they seem to remain in contact with their own families. Also, how they seem to leave home so young and to live on their own. He claims that people stay in their family home in Brazil much longer because it is so expensive to be independent, even though he is probably well aware that London is still more expensive. Still, if he can no longer live in his family home, something of his family can become part of his home, and, when you look around Jorge's home, this is evidently the case. The most obvious signs are the dense arrays of photographs, stuck with magnets onto the fridge, and also found on the small bedside cabinet. Jorge does not share the Catholic devotion of his sister – well, he makes fish on Good Friday but he doesn't really go to church much. Nevertheless, he can still be charmed by the wooden carving of a typical Brazilian priest he has on his mantelpiece. Fortunately, on Jorge's shelves priests and saints seem on friendly terms with the odd Paul McCartney and other figures. There are plenty of secular ornaments from Brazil. They range from a carved scorpion to a miniature

Brazilian flag. Most of them were given to him on one of the three visits he has made back to Brazil in the eight years since he moved to London. Perhaps it is because he comes from Sao Paulo rather than Rio, but I can't see any hint of that other quintessential visual image of Brazil favoured in London: Carnival.

More than any store-purchased ornaments, Jorge values home-made objects, since making things oneself has been at the core of his family tradition. Jorge is particularly fond of an ornament made by his sister. It is a tiny porcelain figure of a child, with bunched red hair and a bubble gum protruding from her mouth. But this child also has wings and sits on a white and pink bordered setting that looks as if it were made of icing. The figure functions as a stopper for a jar intended for keeping sweets. He also has some small paintings, ornaments and drawings made by friends. Every year up until now, he has made by hand every one of the fifty-five Christmas cards he has sent back to family and friends in Brazil. But then, until recently his work has been intermittent – much of the time non-existent – leaving him much more reliant on his partner's income than he would have wished, but with plenty of time to make cards. Now he has a good job with a decent income, but also an extremely hard-working one, with long hours, from which he often comes home at unsocial times of the night, quite exhausted. So this year he just felt unable to give the time and mental energy to crafting these cards, and made do with a collection of images from the Victoria and Albert; images he was impressed by, although they could never match the personal touch of hand-made equivalents. This has been one of his key regrets of the last few months. Again, he notes disparagingly that in England hardly anyone seems to make anything.

As it happens, his partner's brother has a Brazilian girlfriend, it seems as if everyone is assuming that they would get on exceptionally well and have loads in common simply because they are both from Brazil. Actually, though, there is a fifteen-year age gap, her passion in life is skateboarding (something he hasn't the slightest interest in) and she comes from Rio, an altogether different city – to his mind, rather less naturally European than Sao Paulo. So he feels nothing in common with her at all and sees no reason why he should. After all, here in London the distinctions of class, region and interest hardly lead to any particular expectation that one person from England shares much more than language with any other; and, given those Geordie and Liverpool accents, some Londoners might feel closer to Jorge in language than to migrants from the regions. On the other hand, he suddenly felt very English when he saw the complete confusion on the face of a Brazilian friend to whom he had just given a DVD of Ali G as a present.

The reason Jorge came from Brazil was personal rather than economic or political. This deeper understanding of him shows why our first encounter was forced. For reasons that had to do with academic projection and not with Jorge himself, we were too interested in what it meant to him to come from Brazil and to live in London. Over the course of the next year and a half, we were to come to know, and become very fond of, an altogether different and more authentic Jorge. This Jorge was much more about his relationship to his partner, his ambivalence about architecture and home decoration, issues to do with how to manage a difficult, time-consuming job as well as a home life. It's not that this excluded his relation to Brazil, because Jorge was always more involved with his family than most of the English-born occupants of the street, whose family lived only in another part of London, rather than another part of the world. The situation had its frustrations, as we sensed during the first meeting. Later on, for example, we found that he had come to know his partner's family pretty well, while his partner had met his family just once in Sao Paulo and, given their lack of English, it wasn't really much of a meeting. But then these asymmetries in terms of family and partners are common, probably typical, even if you all come from the same town. The point is that Jorge doesn't come just from Brazil. Jorge comes from the Beatles, from rice, beans and pork, from Duran Duran, from a closely knit family and from an Italian Christmas with *panettone*. So it seems that while a draw between Brazil and England might be an unlikely score these days – given the way England played in the 2006 World Cup – as an expression of Jorge in London, it's a fair summary.

PORTRAIT 20

A THOUSAND PLACES TO SEE BEFORE
YOU DIE

It is common to associate both the possession and appreciation of free-dom with the young, especially the adolescent. Yet this has never been a particularly persuasive idea. The problem for the young is that they seem under such an obligation to feel free. Often they seem trapped in a performance of freedom that, paradoxically, becomes directed largely towards satisfying this obligation. By contrast, of all the households on the street, the sense of freedom is perhaps most palpable in the presence of Peggy and Cyril, a couple in their seventies with several great-grand-children. Theirs is a freedom that manifests a confidence built on the love and the support each derives from the other. But it comes most of all from a mature understanding that freedom requires various resources, emotional and material, which allow people to go from aspiration to ful-filment. The knowledge and experience freedom requires to achieve its potential richness and depth are things the young rarely possess. This couple make their choices with eyes wide open, quite appropriately since, despite their age, Peggy and Cyril have eyes that are neither rheumy nor glazed, but sparkling, joyful and greedy to see more – to see as much as possible, while they retain this clarity of vision. If one still insists on this association between freedom and youth, then one would have to con-clude that, whatever their formal age, Peggy and Cyril are young. But in fact they are young in a way that only the elderly could be.

Their youth comes across most clearly in their attitude to time. They have a remarkably unsentimental relationship to the past. They have a satisfactory and well ordered relationship to the present. But, most of all, their eyes are firmly fixed on the future. They belong to a special, select, society, which literally cruises into the twilight. Since they became a couple, they have never gone away on a cruise less than twice a year. They are devotees of Saga, the organisation which facilitates holidays for the retired. In their bathroom, the shower curtain is designed to look like the side of an ocean-liner with portholes all the way along, while the bookcase in the hall is full of books with titles such as *Ocean Cruising 2004*. With experience comes skill and they pride themselves on their ability to find the cheapest car hire in Malta or the right restaurant in Durban.

They don't have to enquire who else will be on a cruise, because they inevitably meet acquaintances they have come to know from previous cruises. Their actual family is quite limited, but they talk of their many 'adopted' children, in the sense of people they have met on cruises whom they have taken under their wing. They are sufficiently well-off rather than wealthy, but they are quite clear that they do not intend to leave a penny to their children, who are all well settled in their own right. They also have ways of extending their resources. For example, Cyril retains a flat in the centre of London, where he lived before he met Peggy. The main purpose of this flat is to serve as a *pied-à-terre* for friends whom they have met abroad. At the time we met them, there were bookings for friends from South Africa, Australia and Canada. In return they have easy access to places to stay if they wish to go to these countries, the US or some other destination. The extent of this cruise-based network is evident from the 230 Christmas cards they sent out last year, culled from an even larger number the previous year. Using these resources, they can develop their ambition, which is nothing less than to see the world. One of their constant reference books is *A Thousand Places to See before You Die* and they literally cross off destinations once they have visited them. Apart from travels to family in the US, they very rarely go to the same place twice. But the world is a big place, and a thousand is a daunting number. They feel strongly that 'when you get to our age there is less time to do everything we want to'.

To live up to this orientation towards the future, they have to keep a clear control of the present. Fortunately, order is something that Cyril does rather well. A pioneer in what was later to become the IT sector, he had plenty of experience in ordering company matters while still working. He was already using computers in 1969. Today he brings the same skills to his private life. His laptop is a repository of data that keeps them in administrative trim. This is where incoming Christmas cards are logged and outgoing Christmas cards generated. Indeed, such recording is about all they can do with the cards they receive, since they are never at home during the Christmas period. So that once logged, the cards are bundled up and taken to a card-recycling box at the local Tesco. Similarly, the computer is the place where the affairs of Cyril's flat are sorted: who is staying there when, and what requires to be done. The same is true for his collection of Wedgwood plates. Cyril is not content just to collect these plates; he has a huge amount of background information on their production, significance and associated scholarship. The computer is also the place where he can order and store his digitised ordnance survey maps, which are part of another keen interest: London and all its byways. These organisational skills are also essential for managing the couple's financial security, which above all allows them to view the world as the locus of endless possibilities. For example, Cyril surfs for information on favourable exchange rates and ways of most effectively paying for their trips abroad.

Cyril provides order in many ways. Even his flat is now seen as a kind of overflow for their possessions, somewhere possessions can be kept in order, so as to prevent their joint apartment from becoming disordered by the sheer quantity of their things. But there is also a sense of order in their relationship with each other. The mere fact that he is skilled at maintaining order through the use of his laptop is seen as an appropriate male endeavour, analogous to his labour in building many of the cupboards in the house. Peggy is not expected to master such masculine pursuits. Her collection of Halcyon Days enamelled trinket boxes, which take up several shelves in their living-room, also aims to be comprehensive, but it is essentially ornamental rather than an excuse for delving into historical details. Peggy and Cyril now view themselves as appropriately complementary in their skills and interests; appropriate, that is, to the kind of male and the kind of female each appreciates in the other. And this, too, forms part of the satisfactory order which is the present.

The same attitude helps to preserve their unsentimental view of the past. This is quite explicit. At one point Peggy says: 'We don't live in the past, do we?' To which Cyril responds 'Or, to put it another way – do we live in the past? . . . No!' It's not that they neglect their children or grandchildren. As they put it, spending five weeks a year in the US with the grandchildren probably means that they see them more than a good many grandparents would. But they see no particular purpose in accumulating things which are intended to dwell upon the past. They admit, for example, that they rarely look at photos. They took twenty-seven rolls of film on their cruise around the world ten years ago, but have never looked at a single image since. Photographs become of interest when they can be used in the present, something which is more feasible now thanks to digital photography. As a result, photography can now be assimilated as an integral part of Cyril's computer skills. He now spends quite some time ordering the photos, using software to alter and improve them. He even demonstrates these skills by printing out improved family pictures and gifting them to relatives. Indeed, he had considered creating their own Christmas cards that year. This was less from an attachment to the photographs themselves and more because Cyril suddenly discovered that photographs could become an instrument and mode to develop his love of ordering and creating through the computer. Given their freedom from the past, they see no particular reason to bring back souvenirs from their cruises, although they do buy family presents. As for themselves, 'if we do bring back anything, it would be that we went round a very nice kitchen shop and saw a gadget that you can't live without, better than we have got. We might possibly buy that.' In short, they do little that is intended to facilitate memory itself, or anything that implies an orientation to the past as opposed to the future.

A similar attitude applies to the collections. Cyril notes of Peggy that 'she has got every figure in this particular series except for the first one . . . and we have made enquiries, in fact we're on a list to buy one if it ever comes on the market . . . but you know, we're going to be looking at several hundred pounds, something like that . . . for one box'. But, even here, when we suggest that this final piece would provide a sense of completeness, he responds with a twinkle: 'If you wanted to get rid of the lot as a complete collection, that would put more value to it.' He adds that this would certainly pay for a cruise or two – a remark he has made before with respect to a potential sale of his own Wedgwood plates. Having collections also makes it fairly easy to buy presents for each other; and this is the kind of relationship where easing the chore of selecting presents is a token of how much, not how little, they care for each other. At first we thought that, perhaps, the objects could be forgone as sentimental references to the past, because it was their conversation that took on the task of remembering. But, as we came to know them better it was clear that this was wrong; that they simply didn't need to have recourse to nostalgia, whether verbal or in object form.

They are not the only older couple of means on this street, although, as in London more generally here too, poverty is commonly associated with age. They are more conspicuous in the coming together of desire and the financial wherewithal to fulfil those desires. But it is other, more subtle, resources that enabled them to fuel this 'life begins at sixty' lifestyle. There is the experience of rupture that has accompanied their actual past. Peggy, for example, has lived now with Cyril in this house for twelve years, but doesn't think she previously ever lived in any one place for more than seven years. She never really had a chance to stabilise her past. As she recalls, 'we moved out to Canada in 1947; I went out with my parents and so lost all the things I had earlier than that. When my parents came back, I had nothing left of my childhood.' Her former husband worked in Syria, and she lived in various countries before returning to the UK some twenty years ago.

For Cyril, the instability and rupture had as much to do with relationships as with place. His past life included a marriage which ended in divorce. 'My wife had to find herself . . . I don't know what it means, but off she went . . . Amicably enough.' Cyril was one of the very few people who seemed genuinely not to know exactly who got what in the divorce settlement, and Peggy is quite friendly with his ex-wife. Nevertheless, there is a profound sense that Peggy and Cyril are soulmates, on the basis of a deep appreciation that they have finally found the right partner and that it was certainly not too late to celebrate the possibilities of love and support. Their experience of rupture has not only helped them to appreciate their present stability, but has also given them the habit of getting out and doing things: something that had once been forced upon them, now renewed and invigorated by positive desire.

With some of the households in Stuart Street, one feels that the very first attachments were critical in influencing what people subsequently became. Often these were relationships with parents. Many branches of psychology tend to stress the quality of these first attachments as determining the rest of life. Peggy and Cyril are a salutary reminder that this need not always be the case. For most of her life Peggy had sought stability because she was beset by rupture. If she had never met Cyril, we would have met a very different Peggy. We would probably never even have guessed that there was this other side to her. The really critical relationship for Peggy was not something that happened to her at six, but something that happened at sixty. It was only when she met Cyril that she could jettison so many of the defensive aspects to her character which she had needed up to that point and would probably have defined her at that time. Then, in her sixties, the experience of mobility and change no longer had to be a burden but became an asset, something to combine with Cyril's love of finding out about the world and to be jointly launched, in the form of cruising.

This becomes clear through careful examination of her relationship to objects and collecting. As well as to the collection of boxes, earlier on in her previous marriage Peggy has been devoted to another collection, which involved a charm bracelet. This started when she was living in Kenya and her then husband bought a bracelet with four charms. From these followed a tradition which ended up with a bracelet replete with forty-five charms. Each charm had a very particular story attached; some related to private jokes between them, others to little gimmicks, for instance a goose with golden eggs inside. Recently Peggy gave the charm bracelet to her daughter-in-law, but she noted that she had also given charm bracelets to quite a few of the grandchildren, and this seems to have become something of a tradition that she has established.

The point is that, today, Peggy is resolutely unsentimental about objects that pertain to memory. It's something she says many times, that she simply doesn't particularly associate objects with memory. When she talked of giving this bracelet away, her gesture was couched in terms of her age. But from the way she talks about the bracelet with its multitude of associated stories, it seems clear that had her life gone in a different direction, Peggy might well have become much more like many of the older participants in our study, whose relationship with such objects of memory is indeed sentimental. If she were now without a partner, lonely, with a real need for support from memories of better times, of laughs and love that had come into her life over the decades, then her relationship to possessing such things, and to collecting and passing them on to the next generation, would probably have been much less pragmatic and unsentimental. Then her collections could have helped her to look back rather than forward. The possibility of completing the box collection might well have become a sort of life project, with considerable importance in its own right. She does have pictures from the past, including several of Cyprus, which could have meant a great deal to her and which she can provide considerable comment on. She will also talk wistfully of the Bisto (a brand of gravy) kids and of the smell of Bisto as an evocation of her childhood in Canada.

But things did change and at the age of sixty she found an ideal partner and does not require that kind of support. After living in this house for twelve years, her new life not only feels secure, assisted by Cyril's skills in ordering and consolidating their world, but also provides a form of security compatible with a constant sense of excitement and adventure. At this point the earlier memories are rarely shared (the charm bracelet is unusual in that respect) – 'Because Cyril was never in any of the places I was, if I'm with my daughter it's a different matter.' So she might now consider who was around she could still chat to about such things; but this is about the only use she would make of the past. As for her time with Cyril, this doesn't require the accumulation of souvenirs because things are simply too good as an experience of the moment, and their orientation is towards the future they are building together.

In short, Peggy is unsentimental today because she can afford to be. Today, she and Cyril are people of action. They rarely watch television, and, even more surprising for older people, the radio is mainly limited to times of ironing and other chores. For one thing, there is nothing conservative about this couple's attitude to change; Cyril's adoption of digital photography was one of the most complete and rapid that we encountered. The key to their lives today is that they have no time to contemplate the past; but just about time to live the future.

PORTRAIT **21**

ROSEBUD

For decades, Orson Welles' masterpiece *Citizen Kane* topped the polls for the best film ever made. The narrative of that film is dominated by the search for Rosebud, the last word ever spoken by the great man. The characters never discover the secret of Rosebud, which is revealed to us to have been the name of the snow-board that Kane used as a child. The film's portrayal of Kane's life represents one of the foundational myths of American ideology and, to some extent, British also: the myth of materialism, which implies that in the modern world we have become so oriented to developing our relationship to objects, especially commodities, that we have lost the ability to forge relationships with people. In the case of Kane, we see his ability to garner unprecedented wealth and luxury based on his media empire. But this was achieved at the cost of any sustained and fulfilling relationship to the people around him, so that in the end he leaves the world with the memory of the one thing that he could look back on as a meaningful relationship, an object whose memory supported him in his isolation: a childhood toy.

Dominic is no Citizen Kane. He is not wealthy and I doubt he ever will be, partly because he is unusually satisfied with the level of economic success he has already achieved. He is even talking about taking some sort of mid-life break from work to be spent trekking around the world as a kind of late gap-year. But, while I would be very glad to be wrong, I can't help imagining for Dominic a death-bed scene somewhat reminiscent of *Citizen Kane*. In the case of Dominic, the place of Rosebud would be taken by the pottery figure of an owl. I don't know if this owl has a name. It's not a particularly impressive owl; I doubt it was expensive. Aesthetically, it's pretty ordinary. It was made by a Belgian pottery workshop, in a style typical of contemporary folk arts and crafts, that is, slightly more up-market than mass-produced souvenirs. It is not intended to be realistic, since there are bright green, blue, yellow and orange patches which signify modern craft's continued allegiances to modern art. While as much abstract as realist in style, it is clearly an owl, with those large eyes and what would be characteristic ears – except that one of them has been broken at some stage.

It is not a particularly visible owl. It stands among other ornaments on the mantelpiece, along with brass candlesticks and bowls – very much the sort of ornaments and souvenirs one expects to see these days on mantelpieces, although this one doesn't happen to have the typical invitation cards, vase of flowers and clock that are found on most. The owl only stands out from the rest through the filtering effects of Dominic's own narrative and an understanding of how he sees this room. When you first enter the flat, it seems crowded with possessions: bookcases, ornaments on the walls and windowsills. But then Dominic explains that the flat is just a temporary let and belongs to someone else, as do ninety per cent of the things in it. Dominic himself has really very few possessions, given his age and income, and in any case does not see himself as staying long enough to want to make major changes. So, rather as one views a play against a theatrical backdrop, one needs to find a way for most things to fade into a fuzzy background and allow his possessions to come visually into focus. Only then can one see the room as his room. I try to do this as I listen to him, but even then the owl does not really fly out of its own accord.

Only later, when I am at home reading the transcript of his interview do I feel the poignancy attached to the position of this owl and its ability to represent Dominic. It is simply that everything else he possesses has, in his own mind, an aura of transience, leaving only this one single object to stand for the connected thread that is his being. The owl is the only object which actually comes from the past, from his own point of origin, the only thing which conceptually, along with his own body, has a sort of 'made in Belgium' stamp forever attached to it. It is also the only object that, in his mind, is destined to remain with him, accompanying him into the future. I hope he never loses this owl, because I fear a time will come when, just as for *Citizen Kane* and Rosebud, there will be only one relationship which has remained faithful to Dominic and that stands as the material presence of the man. One of the poignant moments of *Citizen Kane* is when we see Rosebud being burnt, unacknowledged and unmourned, along with countless other possessions. Archaeologists are much beholden to the ancient custom of burial goods, where certain prized possessions were placed with the dead. Sometimes I wish this custom could be continued. I think that one ought to be able to place this owl with this man one day, when he is no more than dead flesh or ashes. Not for an afterlife but because the idea might be a comfort to him.

By starting this book with the two portraits, entitled 'Empty' and 'Full', I intended to challenge the myth of materialism, as represented by *Citizen Kane*. All my academic studies have shown that the people who successfully forge meaningful relationships to things are often the same as those who forge meaningful relationships with people, while those who fail at one usually also fail at the other, because the two are much more akin and entwined than is commonly appreciated. Sometimes, however, we can meet a Citizen Kane, a figure for whom the really significant object is the one which represents the viable material relationship that stood in the stead of viable social relationships.

Another figure in this room presents a contrast with the owl: a Balinese sculpture of a monkey. A familiar enough souvenir, at least for anyone who has ever witnessed the extraordinary dances of that island – whether the night-long celebrations of Ramayana, or a short version of the *Kecak* dance for tourists. This particular figure, nearly a metre high, with gilt edging, is rather more commanding than the owl. Dominic reveals its importance to him as a gift that came with a relationship he once had in Bali: a gift from a lover. The only time Dominic ever mentions such a relationship. Yet the more one comes to talk with him and to know him, the clearer it becomes that the imposing dancing figure will never be a match for the owl. The owl's ability to encompass emptiness and absence is much stronger than the monkey's evocation of the presence of another person. The fact that this was a holiday romance, possibly intense and memorable, but also fleeting, makes the larger monkey ultimately less substantial then the little owl. In my imagination, it is appropriate for it to be an owl that helps me to see into that absence. An owl speaks to me of the wisdom of the night, the bird's clear vision through what would be, to others, an empty dark landscape. An owl would see the particular kind of truth for which I am searching.

Dominic is one of the very few people on this street who simply does not want to talk about his relationships. Most people seem reluctant at first, but after a while it turns out to be the main thing they do want to talk about. We have various ways to make people feel secure and come to an appreciation that we are genuinely interested in listening to such conversations; but none of these worked for Dominic. And we always made it clear that we were entirely comfortable with people not talking about any topic or part of their life that they might prefer to keep private and discreet. Still, there is enough in what Dominic does talk about, and in his expressions and general opinions on life, to make it evident that this is not just an issue of what he does or does not want to reveal. There is enough to suggest that relationships are a problematic and unfulfilled part of Dominic's life.

So I am drawn again to the owl; it is this figure that I want to understand. To try and suggest reasons why here is one individual who has almost no sustained relationships either of the social or the material kind, despite the fact that, unlike, say, Harry or George, he is constantly surrounded by others. When asked about his aesthetic preferences, Dominic is quite clear: he prefers minimalism. As often when people use this term, what is implied is not so much the positive aesthetics of a branch of modernism, but rather a preference for absence and a detachment from things in general. There is also a tragic aspect to this minimalism since it also refers to his failures to establish desired relationships. Tragedy implies that the failures that are experienced as highly personal and individual are also to be understood in the light of much larger forces of history, economy and populations. The tragic aspects of Dominic's personal history derives from the meeting between this Belgian background and a certain kind of Englishness as he encountered it in London.

Dominic starts from a condition of poverty. A house with only an outside toilet and no electricity. Historically, many such families would send their children out to exploit economic niches as they emerged, with

opportunities for employment. In his case, he found work with the seasonal tourist industry, which provided labour in catering and other such
activities for the summer months. For Dominic, to work at the English
seaside was a natural extension of the more traditional work at the
Belgian coastline, and it established him with skills in the catering industry. From the coast, he worked his way inland to London, and through
his hard work and the thrift ingrained by his family, after ten years of
seasonal work he was able to accumulate sufficient capital to open a
place for himself. Eventually this led to the establishment of his wine bar
near Richmond, which has sustained him for more than a decade now.

For many years, then, Dominic had moved about as employment
possibilities opened up and, in particular had travelled frequently
between England and Belgium. This created an expectation of continual mobility, in which possessions were largely a burden. The few things
he kept from his life at home were subject to attrition and, in consequence, this single possession, the owl, established its position as the
sole representative of his life in Belgium from quite early on. Like
Dominic himself, it was destined to be an individual by default; but,
once it possessed this particular significance, it became the one object
which always travelled with him and thereby managed to keep up with
his restless movements between sites and circumstances.

The owl and the Balinese monkey were not the only things that could
evoke his past, but others were more problematic. Clothes could take on
such a role; some of them were gifts, or connected him in other ways
with particular persons or events. Clothes had an advantage. At any
given time Dominic could put to the front of his wardrobe those associations with the past that he wished to evoke and leave at the back those
he preferred to avoid for some period. In contrast, photographs, once
placed on the wall, confronted him too starkly with very specific images
of people and in that sense removed his own sense of agency, his freedom to determine, according to his own whim, what images he would
like to conjure within his own mind. This desire to control the image he
holds of others may have been problematic when he engaged in relationships, for other people inevitably fail to remain faithful to the
images of them we wish to conjure up.

Dominic's point of origin and initial involvement in largely seasonal forms of employment were most likely the first cause behind the

restlessness one perceived in him. This flat is at least the fourteenth place he has lived in. But eventually he did try to ground himself in a commitment, to put down new roots, in Britain, through the cultivation of his business – the wine bar. He has formed a lasting interest in British and Irish culture; he reads Oscar Wilde and Graham Greene. He still goes to English classes, now to perfect his intonation, since it is important to him to feel he has fully mastered the discourse of his chosen place of residence. He is also completely fed up with jokes made in the wine bar at his expense when people find out the source of his accent: invariably, jokes about Hercule Poirot and the 'little grey cells'.

The tragedy for Dominic, however, was that the route, which he had intended in part, not necessarily consciously, to negate the restlessness of his origins, was particularly unsuited to this function. What he discovered – and it took him some years to fully appreciate it – was the relentless superficiality of English culture as it presents itself in a place such as a trendy wine bar. Dominic had assumed that a wine bar would be a place of conviviality, for sure, but also that this would then be the grounding for the development of more meaningful relationships and concerns for people, including himself. Many other migrants, for example Jorge, didn't necessarily intend to stay in London, but they formed an important relationship which kept them here. With Dominic it was the other way around. First came the commitment to stay in London and, with that, the desire for a relationship that would follow from this initial decision. Today, however, Dominic speaks at some length and with a degree of bitterness about the English, based on his years of experience and quite careful and considered observation of wine bar behaviour. Many of these observations are reminiscent of those recently described by the anthropologist Kate Fox in her book *Watching the English*, which has an extensive section on pub behaviour. She is more empathetic, but then she is more English.

At one point Dominic says:

What I hear from these people, that I see from these people, from the last few years is this. If I switch on the TV, if I listen to what the people say in the wine bar and if I listen to Big Brother, it's the same conversation, it's the same expressions, they use the same sentences. It's fright-

ening. I feel like people don't live. They play. I really wonder if when
people are by themselves whether they just play all the time.

The people who frequent his wine bar today are mainly financially well
off, first supported by their parents, often now working in banking or
the media, mainly renting rather than owning property. In the wine bar
they do not meet new people. They come with the same people and they
leave with the same people.

> You can see straight away 'please leave me alone.' They will be polite,
> but especially British people – they are very 'nice to meet you' but that's
> it . . . Also the amount of alcohol that people consume here, it's unbe-
> lievable . . . they get pissed from Friday night to Sunday evening.

So, although friendly, the wine bar turned out to be not at all the opportunity to create roots through relationships. At one point, Dominic
notes that 'people don't see it as a place to make friends or this kind of
thing. You are not making relationships.' Instead, there are the endless,
repetitive, irritating jokes about Belgium and being Belgian, which after
ten years are almost unbearable, even though the thirst for ever more
alcohol is financially very rewarding. The English are masterful at the
surface play of banter, but for years Dominic just couldn't believe there
was nothing behind this, nothing deeper. Today, however, this is
increasingly what he does believe.

These observations are as much a reflection upon Dominic as upon
the clientele of the wine bar. It reflects his disillusionment with this
workplace, but also the sheer length of time he has worked there and the
sense of his own time ebbing away. One of the most frightening aspects
of his work is the feeling that the customers are getting younger every
year. He claims that this is actually the case, but it could well be merely
relative to himself. It is also a reflection of the fact that his initial hopes
of building up long-term relationships with regulars who would become
his friends were dashed by the sheer transience of the place. There
remains not one single representative of the regular customers he initially built up. They have all moved on. In his memory, those first customers were more interesting, more down to earth, less superficial – but,
above all, less young. When he just started out he could join in much

more fully, be the life and soul, help the customers feel they were having a good time, and in turn feel that he was at least popular – an asset. Now he leaves this bonhomie more to the younger members of staff. He just can't be bothered, or maybe he can't do it any more. In the end he would almost rather the English were not so superficially friendly, that there were fewer smiles and greetings – something which now just strikes him as somehow fundamentally dishonest.

There are, undoubtedly, many other factors to account for Dominic's feelings today. But there is enough in what he does reveal at least to place that clear opposition in his room, between the Balinese monkey and the owl, along a tragic trajectory. An origin in poverty, then seasonality, which made it difficult to settle; to be repaired through a commitment to England, as his country of residence; but then, fortuitously, he encountered the English at the place of their most relentless superficiality – the wine bar: in retrospect, that was a really poor throw of the dice. It is not so surprising that he is planning to take a gap year, a return to the rest of the world.

I think once more about the little owl. There is an aura of wisdom that seems integral even to the most superficial representation of an owl. And this owl has been to many places and carefully observed them with keen eyes. With its gaudy colours, it could have been quite a chirpy bird, but it is rather transformed by the loss of one ear. As a result, it seems now a rather sad little bird, as though it has seen too much, with a little too much wisdom. Some things it would rather have forgotten. It is the one faithful witness to history – but history can be a burden for a man of forty-two at a time when it starts to weigh more heavily on the scales than the promise of a future.

PORTRAIT **22**

THE ORIENTALIST

In Britain it is often hard to separate out the relationship to one's parents from the relationship to the class of one's parents. Ben epitomises the way these become inseparable. On the one hand, one could consider his parents working class, while Ben's own current occupation of acupuncturist is generally regarded as an almost quintessentially middle-class concern. He currently doesn't have a single patient who is not both white and middle class. On the other hand, his parents, too, in their own way, struggled to develop themselves and represented a generation in which most people felt that they were moving upwards in terms of the British class system. So Ben's own clear alignment to the middle class could be seen either as a repudiation of his parents' class origins or as simple continuity of a trajectory that they began and he completed.

While for his parents this movement was a gradual process, Ben recalls his own life as one of quite dramatic steps upwards, in a manner that hints at the complexity of his class affiliations. Someone born into the middle class would most likely have described becoming an acupuncturist largely in terms of spiritual enlightenment. Ben retains the more practical working-class sense that this was, quite simply, a successful career change. After a limited school education and several dead-end jobs, Ben decided in his twenties to make a second attempt at what he had originally missed out on and went into further education. This re-launched his career at a significantly higher level within management. Although this looked promising, in his thirties he decided once again to re-start his career, following a chance meeting with an acupuncturist. In retrospect, this demanded a rather different kind of 'higher' education: a new form of knowledge and skill, which he regarded as rising above the materiality of formal education. While he is quite open about the fact that this shift represented a career change, the ethical and intellectual uplift he associated with this new direction were just as important to his feelings about himself and his future.

In his embrace of refined middle-class values, spirituality lies in opposition to mere sentiment. So Ben had no problem disposing of his own past, including a suitcase of childhood objects which his parents had carefully preserved for him. He is pretty detached about this process of distancing. His years as a student and then after leaving home, in various subsequent assorted jobs and accommodation, have cumulatively acted to separate him from these vestigial links with the place and memories of his childhood. Nevertheless, like many others, he still seems to find his parents' home useful as a kind of half-way house, a place to leave larger objects. Things that would clutter his present environment but, you never know, might one day regain their appeal: his guitar or perhaps his ski equipment.

Becoming an acupuncturist necessitated a radical re-thinking also of Ben's basic relationship to material culture and the environment. His new relationship to Chinese holism and technologies for securing health became centred on the de-materialisation of space. He no longer has carpets, curtains, or pictures on the wall. His furniture is elegant, Eastern and minimal. Most of his previous life went to charity shops. There are no books or CDs on display. As he puts it, 'I try to make an effort and maintain a sense of order and tidiness by keeping things away, hidden away in cupboards and wardrobes'. Whether these are vitamins or small change, along with the books, they remain out of sight. He is averse to clutter, which he describes as 'energetically consuming for the mind'.

But, in his own way, Ben reiterates one of the fundamental contradictions of the Buddhist philosophy to which he ascribes. Formally, Buddhism is thoroughly anti-materialist; it constantly yearns to transcend matter in order to reach enlightenment. Yet over the centuries one of the principal ways it has come to express this spiritual opposition to materiality is through its fabulous statues, temples and reliquaries, which have created almost a landscape of monumentality. The desire for, or claim to, transcendence is inevitably expressed through material form. Ben has a similar desire for transcending mere materiality. He has a horror of superfluous ornaments and material culture. Nevertheless, he doesn't live in emptiness. His rooms are tastefully decorated with paraphernalia that symbolise his commitment: figures of the Buddha, ornaments from China; a manifest orientalism that has not so much repudiated materiality as replaced one version with another. He ensures that his room contains representations from the four elements of earth, fire, water and air, including, for example, a water fountain, salt water (that takes away the negativity in the atmosphere), plants (for the wood aspect they represent), and crystals (for calm). It is a very selective material culture, but it is still material culture. All other extraneous and unsuitable objects, such as Christmas presents, which try to invade this space 'end up being filtered back to the charity shop, very discreetly, at some stage'. In short, like Buddhism itself, Ben has to express his devotion to immateriality precisely through material forms.

As many others on the street, Ben sometimes has to compromise his core aesthetic in order to accommodate particular relationships. There remains, for example, a pair of ornate candelabra which clash with everything else he possesses, yet they come out at dinner parties when the relative who presented them is invited. His main memory of his parents' ornamentation is not that it was particularly poor in quality or taste, but rather that it wasn't what he calls cultured. It was simply in keeping with the northern tradition of a front parlour with the appropriate mantelpieces and objects. Many of the items on display would have been meaningful rather than simply decorative; for example, objects reflecting his father's hobbies such as collecting model cars.

So when Ben talks about a re-alignment of the things in his life, we can see this as reaching well beyond the immediate order of his room. At the core, certainly, is this new sense of order that takes its specific form from a Western interpretation of Eastern philosophy and which has become central to his career. But this in turn helps to create a consistency of alignment with his life as a whole. It fits precisely with his

notion that the middle classes possess a refinement, or a cultured relationship to things, which stands above the clutter of working-class ornamentation. This refinement is the culmination of his own process of
self-cultivation. The concern for order also accords well with the
Austrian origins of his wife, with her own inherited ideal of a tidy room.
She is just as happy as he is to have things put away and out of sight. In
some ways, though, he has now gone beyond her in disciplining their
environment. She retains a fondness for what he describes as the odd
piece of kitsch – which he feels needs to be suppressed, in obedience to
the dominant aesthetic. Even more of a problem is the presence of one
or two heirlooms from Austria. The couple compromise by retaining
them as possessions while banning them from display. This tyranny of
calm order affords benefits also for his wife. While for him it has become
an environment that facilitates his work and creates the appropriate setting for his patients, for her it represents a welcomed site of relaxation
and calm, which represents a wonderful antidote to her own work. As a
management consultant, she suffers from the kind of stress and drama
to which the peace and serenity of the home environment act as an
essential counterpoint.

Ben has also applied the general, stripped-down effect to himself. He
looks like a middle-class English acupuncturist. He wears a white top –
quasi-doctor-style – but with plunging neckline that reveals his chest
hair. He keeps his hands and nails immaculate. He wears black, slim-line
trousers with slip-on, eco-friendly chunky black shoes and no socks. He
looks the embodiment of holistic healing. Most of his patients are
women. He sees himself as possessing an aura that forms an integral part
of his work as a healer. For him, as for many of his patients, acupunc-
ture is inseparable from the holistic treatment of problems many of
which derive from the stress of London life. He views his patients as
'over-stimulated' and 'hyper-aroused', so that calm is a major part of his
treatment. In effect he sets up his own body such that its visible
appearance and invisible aura will radiate a personal calm that offers
sanctuary to his patients. Proximity to him as well as the surrounding
calm and uncluttered space allow his patients also to re-align themselves
mentally and counter London's disorienting effects on mind and spirit.
Normally he cycles, but when he has to use the crowded underground
system he would 'use energetic techniques about creating an energetic

form around you, an aura for instance, and sending out positive thought processes to the other people in the carriages and letting the energy flow go in . . . I'm aware of the energetic mood of the people, the anger, the frustration and that distance between people.' He does not use or like other people using machines such as an iPod, which cuts off their aware-ness of one another.

One might have thought that this indicates an all-embracing attach-ment to a single set of values, but actually the aesthetic retains something of Ben's ambivalence about class. What he believes in is not just a spiri-tual holism, but a spiritual holism that is efficacious, achieves things and helps to transform people's lives. He believes in it because he believes it works. What comes across is this mixture of practicality and spirituality; a practicality that Ben sees as stemming from the common sense attitude of his own upbringing. He would not regard his discussions of auras and energetics as airy-fairy. They are more like science. It is this practical application of spirituality that works for him and, he feels, helps him work for others. So, while for non-believers New Age ideas would appear to represent the complete opposite to common sense, for Ben they are actually more like his own common sense view of things. Spirituality becomes a form of functionalism. His bathroom, for example, is deco-rated entirely in the functionalist aesthetic of white, black and stainless steel, from the tiles on the walls to the toilet seat. Functionalism as an aesthetic movement repays the compliment; there was always something mystical about it. Its own tyranny of order has always had an eloquence and expressiveness that spoke to a higher function than mere technology. Functionalism flying on the wings of modernism often reached the heights of spirituality.

The same common sense attitude is found in his relation to other people and their things. Take, for example, the contrast between him and his sister: he is not inclined either to take or to display photographs, while his sister's house is absolutely full of them. She has children and he feels it would be entirely natural to have plenty of photographs in a house with children around. But he does not have children – so why would he have photographs on the walls? Similarly in his relationship to his own past, he could not relate at all to the theme of our project. He tried to rack his brains for any instances of objects associated with mem-ories, which were now important to him or might be relevant to a sense of loss. He drew a complete blank. This holistic enterprise works horizontally, as a given order of the moment; the only relevant objects are his oriental ornaments and his overarching minimalism (a minimalism which has nothing at all in common with that of Dominic). What is required is internal consistency between all the elements of his life; his home, his occupation, his relationships, working at peace with each other in the present. The past is just the clutter he has either repudiated or put away in wardrobes. The vertical dimension of time is sacrificed to the horizontal dimension of space. Because right now it is essential that he himself, and everything around him, should consistently express the same basic harmony.

PORTRAIT 23

SEPIA

It was one of those extraordinary contrasts. We had just spent two hours with a long-term resident of Stuart Street who plied us with evidence that this was about the most dangerous place in London to live. He talked about the destruction of cars outside a home; how his own flat had been squatted for a period; how he had several times spotted, through the window, the red eye of a rifle, sight-trained on him; and how careful we needed to be during our work. We left feeling somewhat shell-shocked, although the risks seemed modest, given that, at that time I was alternating research on Stuart Street with fieldwork in Kingston, Jamaica. We then walked a few doors down to our next port of call. On knocking at the door, we found ourselves being welcomed in by a frail, elderly and almost entirely blind woman, who scarcely bothered asking who we were before inviting us in, because, having lived for over forty years in this street, she knows it to be entirely safe. Jenny was one of the first people we came to know, and we learnt a great deal from her. Up until then we had tried to talk to people through the medium of particular objects that might be important to them, but after a while it was clear that, for Jenny, it was not any particular item that mattered, but the overall sense of order and the larger aesthetic that united all her things and all the places where she kept them. She thereby helped us to crystallise this concept of an aesthetic.

As with several of the elderly residents in the area who were born in Britain, the home interior became for us a way of relating a highly intimate and particular life to the wide sweep of twentieth-century British history. Looking at her things felt rather akin to listening to those radio programmes where an old soldier tries to convey how it was to fight on the front: you can tell from the tone of his voice how names which for so long have been mere crosses in a vast cemetery suddenly once again become poignant and bitter. But such programmes tend to focus on major historical events, war, the rise of women's rights, or the decline in farming. Here, in this house, in the objects to be dusted and stories about bringing up a family, and cooking, lies all that remains in-between such major issues: mere padding to history, but the substance of the year-in, year-out, of a long life.

It's just as well that old photos tend to be sepia, because this kind of old-fashioned English working-class interior seems rarely to deviate much from a dominant brown. The central picture on the wall, representing a rural scene with a hayrick, looks out onto a commemorative royal mug and tins, all of which seem to be reflected in the dominant French polish of the furniture. There is plenty of gilt and brass, but, between carpet and sofa, wooden photo frames and wooden light-stand, the dominant colours are all shades of brown. There are newer items, such as little ceramics with splashes of colour, made by grandchildren in school classes and given with love to 'Gran'. Such pieces now rest beside old decorative plates, or on the television set; but even these are muted and tamed by the sobriety and antiquity of the room as a whole. In most respects, Jenny gives a simple functional explanation for what she has and what she does. But she is quite clear that the long-standing order of things around the house is not a result of her blindness and need to know what has been placed where. As her tale unfolds, it becomes evident that this internal order long predates her disability and that its constancy has been both a blessing and a curse in her life.

With such a house, you know almost as soon as you enter that things, once placed, are destined to remain more or less stable for decades. The worn upholstery and the position of the cushions tells you not only which are the favourite chairs but how that same individual habitually sits on them. Commonly, also, in older English working-class houses you soon sense that, although you have been shown into the sitting-room first and this is the resting-place of many key possessions, some-how the sitting-room has never managed to inveigle itself into the heart of the home. It has been forced to remain more a façade turned out-wards, as a presentation to the stranger. It's only when you come into the kitchen that you are asked to sit down in a more meaningful, kindly, tone. Only in the kitchen do you feel the warmth of the householder, who can now relax and chat and make tea, having accepted you into her real home.

The kitchen is dominated, a least aurally, by the sonorous deep tone of a very large clock hanging on a wall: an old-style pendulum clock with dark wooden casing and a rounded top. This is not a clock that just tells the time. This clock stands for time itself; it was purchased early in her childhood by her dad and brings a distant echo of still earlier genera-tions sitting around their Yorkshire farmhouse, with people rather than television for company. Today it tolls for the resting-place of ancestors, to whom Jenny has perforce come nearer as her eyes close around this world and start to search instead for that which lies beyond. Not that she is giving up on life any time soon. She may be in her nineties, but she tells a story of one of her grandchildren enthusiastically informing his gran that the two of them would live together in the farm in Yorkshire 'for a hundred years'; and when she asked him how everyone else would fare, he replied, 'they can look after themselves'. While at times she has that frail, almost transparent look of the very elderly, on another occasion Fiona spotted her just emerging, her hair freshly done, from the modern-style hairdresser, who is clearly more visited by teenagers.

This kitchen is the place where Jenny undertakes her single most important task of the year: the creation of her Christmas puddings. This is a mammoth task, especially given her age. Every year since she married she would make twenty-one puddings and steam them, two at a time. Jenny needed to create a Christmas ritual, because Christmas was also her birthday and she never really overcame her resentment at having only one special day, when everyone else had two. Last year was different, however: she finally broke with tradition. For the first time she stayed at home, on her own, over Christmas, refusing the calls of her affronted family. She also made twenty-four puddings instead of the usual twenty-one. Somehow she needed to shift both traditions at once, and making the extra puddings somehow balanced the relinquishing of what had been a leitmotif throughout the years but one that she knew it was time to let go of, in her own controlled way.

Some of the kitchen equipment goes back to the time she first developed the recipe for these puddings; a recipe she has, to this day, never told to a living soul; though she does reveal that they have salt and pepper but no suet. It was also a way she brought her work into her home, having been employed as a cooking manager for most of her life. She is using saucepans that date from 1924 and she works on a table from 1923, which was second-hand even then. Next to it is another ancient inhabitant of South London; a stool, one of three she bought for a half-crown each. In the hall are more of her old Quality Street tins, somehow quite obviously the best and most worthy receptacle for the storing of these puddings.

Although the kitchen holds some of her earliest memories, it is also where she keeps up to date. It includes the most recent photos of her family, showing them as they are today. In her bedroom are more of her oldest photos, those that have become most deeply sedimented within her own memory, so one suspects that her blindness is no barrier to her seeing those images. Like those in the sitting-room, these photos belong to another world of time, where people and images remain of one age and are not updated. The sitting-room has the formality of a shrine, the careful, respectful and proper obeisance to time passed. But a different quality of time is created by the grand old clock in the kitchen which has the power to transcend ordinary passing time and to link the most ancient past with the present, practical, immediate time of the kitchen. Sadly, during the year and a half during which we knew Jenny, the clock was given to one of her children. We felt that this was perhaps a pity. It should have been allowed to sound out her years, as it had seemed destined to do. It's one of those difficult tests of family life. The gesture of handing it down was genuinely meant, but the appropriate response might have been to promise to treasure it after she has passed away. It is within the family, in particular, with its strange mixture of conventional and personal relationships, that every so often one person needs another to refuse their gifts, and yet cannot let them know.

Jenny had come to London at the age of nineteen and, having met her husband there, she stayed put. The day she moved in to her house, a neighbour came round with a cup of tea. She had four children at the local school, and at that time made friends with many other parents. She also regularly frequented the local pub. Her neighbour, who had a car, used to take them out into the country on weekends. She couldn't stand the neighbour's husband, but put up with him because she was fond of the wife and loved the outings themselves. Today, not a single one of those friends has remained in the area. As she puts it, 'people come in and out of properties like rabbits and there is no time to get to know anyone in the area'. But she is fortunate in that one of her sons comes every day to help her and to keep her company, and she appreciates that this is not something one can take for granted these days. Indeed, the only time we saw her become exceptionally frail and downcast was when this son was away on holiday.

Over the years, one hears endless remarks against 'the council'. As the arm of the state closest to people's lives, it tends to get the stick for their frustrations and sense of powerlessness before the still more anonymous central government. Very few people have a good word to say for 'the council', especially left-leaning councils. But when one looks beneath these complaints and annoyances, one can see, in home after home, something of the much underappreciated humanity which is in fact a bastion of British local government. Equality is intrinsically bureaucratic and the best we can ever hope for is a balance between necessary anonymity and individual sensitivity. Here, after all, is a ninety-one-year-old living in a large, many-bedroomed house, built for a large family. She has the protection of her tenancy and she has had the offer to move into a small flat, but as yet no serious pressure to move. After forty-four years, she has reason to feel that her joints and the joints of the house are entitled to ache and age in unison, and that feeling has been respected. The house, in any case, is not entirely unused by others; sometimes one of her children will come and stay for a weekend in their old bedroom.

Jenny's house is one of those where the gaps can be as eloquent as the presences. Jenny experienced more pleasure from being a mother than anything else in her life. As for many parents, there are those particular moments – giving children a bath, or putting them to bed – which remain exquisite in her memory. As each one left home, she wanted them to take something of the earth in which they were nurtured to provide continuity as they planted themselves in a new household. So, even if this meant buying new beds for her own house, they took from their respective rooms their own beds and as much of the bedroom furniture as they wanted. They bickered, though, over those half-crown stools; they all wanted one. It is clear from the remaining furniture that Jenny always had an eye for high quality, good solid wood and brass. Even in the war and post-war periods, she disdained Utility furniture as not quite good enough for her standards. Her bedroom wardrobe is a treat, with its unfolding sections, secret drawers and well-oiled hinges that could last for centuries. Inside this wardrobe are equally high-quality garments and suits which have also lasted for many decades. There is a fur coat bought for her by her husband and two suits from Aquascutum. Sadly, these days she is as likely to need good clothes for the funerals of her siblings as for the weddings of her descendants. Out of eight, only herself and one sister are left. But she has by no means lost her pride in her appearance or in that of her house.

While the people who once dwelt there have gone, the house has been repopulated, as far as she has been able to accomplish it, with at least the reminders of many significant relationships. A vase she wouldn't part with, a gift from a sister-in-law, now dead; ornaments from a favourite niece who used to come on holiday with Jenny and her children. Some small something from each of the grandchildren: an object made at school or, at least, their photos. A wall piece of hammered copper, made by her sister as part of her rehabilitation from arthritis. These gifts blend with items from different stages of her own life, such as a bottle of whisky from the Queen's Jubilee – but then this is a woman who remembers the coronation of King George. In the kitchen are wares such as the tea set she bought during the war for a sixpence. Many of these are now destined for inheritance by chosen descendants.

While each of these items has resonance with particular people, times and places, they also form part of a larger whole. Jenny's kitchen and sitting-room could also look like a generic stage-set representing her as a period or type. There is just the right balance between ceramic figures of swans, the glass pill-box, and the various brasses – the candlesticks and the gilt mirror. One can anticipate the kind of tea sets which will be housed within the wooden dresser with its leaded glass front. It's as though you have already seen the calendar in the kitchen hanging on the wall next to the decorative souvenir plates, or noticed other details, down to the mug of tea on the kitchen table and the drying up cloth suspended over the chair. The same goes for the backs of the wooden chairs themselves, with those two basic period designs: the one, a sort of *faux* column, the other looking as though it has a miniature ship's wheel in the centre.

Yet Jenny is entirely herself: an individual with her own, very particular, history and ways of relating to the world. What people forget today, in their cultivation of difference as a kind of cheap substitute for individuality, is that this very ordinary, repetitive sameness was itself what sustained relationships. In those days Jenny always had someone around to talk to about their children at school. To go out with for a drink at the pub there were neighbours, or perhaps most commonly her own family. Each person who came into this sitting-room and kitchen would feel instantly at home. One glance at the wallpaper and it could have been their very own sitting-room and kitchen; this was integral to the hospitality, the inclusive spirit in which they were taken in, given tea and invited to chat.

It is difficult to know the significance of each particular ornament just by looking around. The person living there may go for years on end without thinking much about them. The objects are really a form of decoration, a defence against the emptiness of space. So, just because they can recall stories about them when you ask, doesn't necessarily mean that objects hold any great significance for them. The stories may be not much more than an artefact of your own enquiry. But, as one comes to know people better, there are ways of discerning the significance of things and of appreciating what really matters – which is not their presence as objects, but the consequence of their presence.

In Jenny's case the key is dusting. There is dusting which is a chore inherited from the tyrannical domesticity of past times, a form of work for work's sake. But dusting can also be more like an excuse for a repeated re-acquaintance with each and every object in the home. For Jenny, in her blindness, one can feel that dusting is just such an opportunity. It is the way she can pick up, touch, replace and recollect each item in turn. That's why she says she can only dust when she feels like dusting. For example, when the family have been around and she has been talking about the old days. Then dusting became this point of physical re-attachment, filling the emptiness after the family has left. This is echoed in Jenny's stories which are told with feeling, with a sense of the presence of the person whom Jenny just recently recalled. It's entirely different when you listen to some people, when it is soon apparent that stories, as well as objects, can get musty and lose their immediacy. This becomes clear when they are brought out again, only half-remembered, for the telling.

Many of the best memories and relationships leave no material trace. Jenny has wonderful stories about a budgie which would dance to music, and was allowed to fly down and greet her husband every day when he returned from work. She recalls the budgie saying: ' "Martin's a naughty boy", I said, "what are you talking about?" And he said: "Martin no school, no school today." So I thought that's funny and so when he came home I said to Martin, "You been to school?" "Course I've been to school, what are you asking me that for?" I says "Joey says you haven't been to school", and he went to his cage and he says: "You been telling tales about me? I'll pluck every feather out of your body if you've told tales about me!" '. There is no trace left of Joey, although another couple down the road keeps a gaudy feather on prominent display, to help them recall a particularly irascible bird.

In her ninety-one years, Jenny has had her share of happiness; she might well say her fair share. But she has also had almost unimaginable crosses to bear. Three times in her life she has suffered a loss or separation that was so unbearable at the time that one feels, when listening to the tale, that one is still looking into a gaping wound that will never close until she herself is gone. Their presence is an essential part of understanding the happy memories and the care for the things around the house, because these are a part of what gives her this continued appreciation of such things. The high points of her life stand out still higher when viewed from some of the depths she can still recall.

The first of these separations occurred when she had only been married a year. It is vividly recalled in a photograph of her husband, taken when he first received his call-up papers. Then she didn't see her husband for four-and-a-half years. After his initial training he came and visited her for one day, not even a night, before he was sent abroad to fight. That he came back at all was a miracle. He was a sniper who fought in the front-line with bayonets, and volunteered to fight in Japan when the war in Europe was over. Even at D-Day he was on the front line. You have seen such individuals being killed a thousand times in a hundred films, as mere background to some star. Not many could have come through all that and returned home. Nor is this just hindsight; it was something that he must have known throughout that period, and probably she did also. It is a chilling recollection, which leaves you exposed equally to your own fear and to their courage.

The second appalling separation occurred when 'I went into hospital for an operation and I was in seven months and I never saw my children the whole time I was in, because children weren't allowed in hospitals. It was very hard; I wish I'd never gone. I kept saying to myself, I wish I'd never gone in hospital and had the operation. I didn't see my children and I had two sisters-in-law who had one each and the other two my husband had to put into foster homes – the two eldest.' While the stories which precede and follow are about her husband, there is something especially painful about Jenny's separation from her children at this time. Something in her voice conveys how, at this time, to have one's own children looked after by others, must have seemed a betrayal of her place in life. It doesn't help that this was through no fault of her own; because, if the children themselves, in their terrible naivety, can still feel this as a betrayal, then to the parent that is exactly what it is, irrespective of anyone's intentions. It was one of the factors that made it so difficult when each child finally left home. She remembers that, when the youngest left to get married, she cried for days.

The third such separation was appallingly hard because this time it was not an absence, but rather the experience of a loved one fading from recognition right in front of her. Jenny's husband had Alzheimer's. Jenny can still convey its horror, when she tells us: 'The boys used to come in and see him every day and he took it the other way. He says "Who are all these big men coming in everyday eating our food? Who are they? What are they doing? Where do you get these men from?" I couldn't stand it.' He would be up at night raving in the house, or getting lost out on the street, after insisting that he had to get out. Then there would be a summoning of the family to scour the streets for him and to find him like some dog, hanging onto a lamp post. At least death has a certain indiscriminate nature and inevitability to it. But having to look at, and care for, her husband. There was such an injustice, such a gulf between what he had done and what was now being done to him.

At the end of such tales one cannot help but regard Jenny to some degree, as a kind of 'everywoman', rather like the core figure in the film *Mother India*: the generic bearer of suffering through which the reproduction of humanity is somehow accomplished in the travail of childbirth. But this is nonsense. In another house a few doors down, there is a woman who had all the luck in life and no such suffering and she is no less authentic or personal. And there are those such as George (in the portrait 'Empty'), for whom there is no such transcendent wheel of nemesis, or balance between periods of suffering and happiness. There is certainly no natural justice or nemesis. Things do not even out within one life or between many. Jenny is not everywoman; she is Jenny.

AN UNSCRIPTED LIFE

James is not particularly tall, certainly not imposing, but he conforms to a particular English look, which seems to come into its own when one is white and whiskered. He sits where he always sits, in a certain chair, with a certain orientation to the room. He has his chair, as does Quentin. This is in no sense a possessive claim to territory. It is one of those little rituals of relationships, an object in the room which seems to be moulded to the individual's shape, stance and feel. So that, after a while, one can imagine the two chairs looking lovingly at each other, day and night, irrespective of whether their habitual occupants happen to be seated in them at that time. This was originally Quentin's house, and James only finally sold his own flat seven years ago. But they have been a couple for thirty years, and, as James notes, about the only thing fully separated out now is their clothes. Everything else gets mixed up.

James is charming, in the deepest sense of that word – where to charm is to induce, magically, a more benign view of the world. You are simply delighted to be in his company, because there is an aura of interest, concern, dignity and politeness that acts to make the room warm and welcoming. He is solicitous, and puts you at ease, but there is nothing remotely obsequious, because politeness comes across as his strength not his weakness. He simply prefers life in the company of others who are relaxed and friendly, and if he has a charm that can facilitate such a situation, then why not use it? You therefore can't help feeling that you, too, have at least a little more grace and charm than usual, simply because you are in his company.

James also has a certain kind of dignity that goes with his charm. A certain kind – since there are different kinds of dignity. One tends to come from effortless success, an aristocratic demeanour which is inherited and may put others in awe. That kind of dignity can also come across as aloof, cold and excluding of others. Then there is another kind of dignity that comes with failure. When you watch on television an elderly impoverished black woman, rescued from Hurricane Katrina's assault on New Orleans, you are almost in tears of empathy because of the way she retains that aura of dignity, however undignified the circumstances of her rescue. There is a gentle acceptance of what cannot be and will not be, which gradually transforms itself into the cultivation of, and pride in, what can be and is. This kind of dignity is as respectful of others as it commands respect; it is modest and pleasant. James, by good fortune, lives in a house as charming and dignified as he is, unpretentious but learned, middle class but classless in its inclusivity. In this setting he, too, commands a certain vague and general feeling of pride in what human beings have managed to be. One somehow senses that there has been in the past some suffering, some failure, or perhaps tragedy, which gives this humanity its depth and fullness of dimension.

James has had his share of suffering and failure, but these are put into perspective by the sheer good fortune of what he has. Above all, he possesses that one core relationship that gives life so much meaning and for so many people becomes the yardstick of whether life has been 'worth it' or not. His failure sounds like the inverse of so many Hollywood films: the founding myth of that industry, the tale of how a star is born. As in most such films, James starts from the bottom. His origins lie in a solid working-class background: a family, one branch of which worked on the railways, others in various respectable occupations. They had limited means, but were rich in appreciation of the countryside and in an abundance of extended family relations. They may not have been well educated, but they were smart and informed. A very pretty mother and a slightly odd father, who doted on his wife. From such origins there came forth a son who always seemed not quite to fit – who always had stars in his eyes and an artistry in his hands that seemed to speak to another destiny. In some black-and-white film, he would have been the unexpected winner of the talent contest, the chance discovery of an impresario. His art would have become his fame and fortune, and the wonderment of his family.

There are not many films dedicated to the great many more who share a fate much like that of James: those who don't win, but, because they come second or third still look as if they might yet become a star. In the end, they just carry on coming second or third. This is the person who struggles to gain the specialist training and blossoms in the freedom and bohemian atmosphere of the arts, who is certain that this is indeed the life for them. We see them start to develop a career, appropriately, as in many of those films, with those small parts – in the orchestra, in the chorus line, as the film director's assistant. But after a few years they are still there, in the chorus line, and it gradually becomes clear, quite clear, that this is where they will always be. James bears witness to all the films that should have been made about the understudy who is not discovered when the star is ill and just remains the understudy.

If it wasn't for the pressure of all those films, all those miraculous stories of how the stars came to their place in the firmament, maybe it wouldn't be so bad. But this is a world in which myth and expectation are deliberately blurred. So James became increasingly depressed, and then other things followed inevitably; the ones which usually are just an interlude in the star's making, to give the audience an illusion of struggle. First there is the drink, then the stage fright, then the limited career. In the films, you know full well that this is the token period of descent before the rousing climb to an unscaled peak. But in James's case it was a limited career that then became no career at all, just looking for a job – any sort of job, to keep body and soul together. Yet, in our story, James remains the artist, because it is the sensibility to the world of the arts that turns out to be critical in understanding the aesthetic formed by his relationship with Quentin. In the privacy of his home, James remains the artist because, irrespective of the highs and lows of any career he might or might not have had, he was correct from the start; an artist is simply what he or she is.

Quentin doesn't quite repudiate his name, but he has done his best to repudiate the causes of his name: that particular type of outer–outer

London, middle–middle class, whose conservatism is matched by its pretensions; where respectability is competitive rather than shared, because one is let down by neighbours, because 'things' and, worse still, 'people' affect property prices – and, if anything is bedrock in such places, it is property prices. Fortunately, the one thing such a family wants above all for their son is precisely that which gave Quentin his means of escape. The son must, if at all possible, go to Cambridge. So Quentin's parents certainly did all they could to ensure this appropriate trajectory for their son. Quentin, for his part, took whatever opportunities he could find, even before university, to gain some independent experience. He went abroad, he worked, he developed his independence. Quentin went to Cambridge, and forged a life there which embraced the freedoms of being a student without compensatory angst or loneliness. Something quite difficult for those undergraduates, emerging for the first time, from under the wing of powerful parentage. Fortunately this was in the seventies, a time when even Oxbridge saw a certain degree of left-wing radicalism as the norm. And politics was, above all, the means by which Quentin continued to foster his repudiation of the values of his upbringing, a process completed by his gradual acknowledgement and understanding of his own sexual orientation. Both of which fitted reasonably well the time and the place.

Quentin took up law and found the balance he wanted between using this career as a means to achieve social justice for others and a decent livelihood for himself. It was also a well-trodden path to becoming a foot soldier, then a middle manager in Labour Party politics. But, just as James found a certain sensibility to the world through his art – perhaps an oversensitivity – which created this larger aesthetic he brings to his relationship with Quentin, so in turn Quentin recognises that even to get into Cambridge required certain skills, and these became further cultivated in his career. As he puts it, 'in a sense it is a circular thing. I probably had something of that in me in the first place. So, as I said, in the beginning I didn't think I desperately wanted this career, but having got there I found it quite congenial, partly because my mind already worked like that, but it has obviously been reinforced and disciplined over the years.'

What Quentin is trying to convey through conversation, the sense of what I am calling an 'aesthetic', is not one simple trait. It is more a combination of ordering principles. Firstly, Quentin has a fantastic memory for details, precisely as required for a consideration of precedents or to identify discrepancies in witnesses' testimony. But this quality flows into other domains of his life. When on holiday, while James is more inclined towards the countryside, Quentin loves visiting old buildings. He is an inveterate collector of postcards of such buildings, which he now keeps in folders. Keeping postcards in folders – something everyone means to do, but hardly anyone does – is part and parcel of Quentin. He is a very ordered man. As he tells it, he once lost a holdall with half of his record collection and this meant that music in the latter half of the alphabet, such as Velvet Underground or Van Morrison, faded from his life for a while.

Such an aesthetic, a synthesis of memory and order, will inevitably have negative as well as positive consequences. Take his work for example: this combination is brilliant for recalling things, because it stores them well in his own mind, but he may be negligent about leaving the clear 'paper trail' that others in the office would like him to provide, in order to help them share his cases. There is also a potential negative quality in its application to his home life, because one of the sources of this neat and tidy mind was his neat and tidy family. He accepts this up to a point. He has even allowed his parents to buy him, over the years, new sets of cutlery and glasses to replace the mix-and-match disorder of the kitchen he retained from being a student, which they so abhorred. But that is the point. This same order could easily drag him back where he really doesn't want to go: the reproduction of the narrowness of his parents, where order is restriction and prejudice. That is precisely where James comes into the picture. Around the living-room, while Quentin files things, James places them. James has a feel for things looking good in unexpected juxtapositions. Theirs is a particularly English idyll of slightly quirky positioning and original sequencing. James has brought to the living-room the little homely vistas of an English garden, culti-vated but with that hint of wildness.

So in trying to understand and appreciate the material presence of a relationship expressed in their house, one has to engage individually with both Quentin and James. Each has to be properly excavated, sepa-rated out archaeologically as layers from the past, with an understand-ing of how each stratum is influenced by the one below. But that is only a half of what is required. Because the final result expresses not only the person, but the complementary nature of the relationship between them. What they really love is the way, as a couple, they can cultivate arts that bring out the best in each other while softening the worst. For example – cuisine. On holiday they follow James's love of nature and Quentin's of architecture, but most of all they follow their mutual love of really good meals. Quentin can remember very precisely what they eat, where they eat it and how they felt about it. He can recall details of meals he had when he was seven. So he can work out the degree to which this current meal adds some little nuance, the effect of one particular herb that detracts from or completes a taste. This blends perfectly with James, who on most days looks forward to cooking for the two of them, employing that creativity essential when cooking is not just interesting because it comes from a good recipe but even exciting. This may be achieved through some unexpected re-presentation of a classic form of a dish not served for quite a while. Why not a dash of chocolate in the curried sauce, or bread and butter pudding with cranberries instead of sultanas? Like one of those tiny tiles in a Roman mosaic, each meal takes its place in the culinary composition of their world.

It's the same with gardening. They both love to do it, but Quentin will provide the 'slash and burn' radicalism, the political economy of gardening that sets the parameters, while James, inspired by some immediate colours and textures in the garden, does that careful pruning and weeding which allows one thing to set off or complement another. Their aesthetic is also present in the way they make everyday decisions. There is a certain kind of maturity in some long-term couples, especially those who have brought up children together, where each takes equal responsibility for coming up with positive and negative reasons for a decision. Because the fundamental commitment is to gradually move to the one they can both live with in the long term. As they put it, 'I'm going to work out how we'll decorate it or I will leave it to you, it's very much a game, which is why it takes longer to decide, because we keep on; one of us will say something which makes the other one think a bit differently. It doesn't quite go in circles but it takes longer to get to the right place . . . I'm sure we will be much happier with the result than if it was just left to one of us.'

Indeed, an amusing aspect of listening to James is that he will start to talk about how he is so different to Quentin and why that's the reason they get on so well, and ten minutes later he will be listing all the things they have in common and showing how that's the reason they get on so well together. 'The two of us do get on incredibly well, we like quite similar things, we like pubs, we both smoke, we both love people, we are both gregarious – and then we have opposites, I love country and Western music . . . I absolutely hate opera, I just hate it and when I first met Quentin he took me to sixteen operas and I just thought – I can't be doing with this.'

The house shifts imperceptibly to accommodate the subtle dynamics of their dialectic. The blue glass collection assembled by Quentin from gifts and antique shops is matched by the brown glass collection developed by James. They themselves don't quite realise the way this has led to certain parts of the house matching the respective colours. But, even if Quentin cares a great deal that James should regard this as his home as much as he does, the history of the house, as originally his, inhibits this. Fortunately, in the last few years they have developed a new project, which is quite remarkable in the degree to which it seems to mark the further stage upwards from a mere earthly state to a kind of heaven on earth.

This being England and James and Quentin both being, in their own ways, very English, this image of paradise clearly has to be an English country cottage. It has meant cutting back on the holidays abroad a bit, because two mortgages and one salary has its limits, but the result is a project which is finally and fully joint. The cottage is a means as much as an end. Because, for them, the social life that comes with it is equally valued. They certainly didn't do badly when it came to their local, The Troubadour, close to Stuart Street. While other pubs are modernised and lose their particular form and genre of sociability, they have played their role in making The Troubadour a transition point to their country home. At least three evenings a week, Quentin will phone James to let him know he is on his way home, and they will meet first at the pub. Most Saturday lunch-times they can be also be found there. This is a pub with real ale, no sports on the TV, and a regular crowd, who all know, and are known by, the landlord.

But even The Troubadour cannot compete with the pub next to their country cottage. A pub where, as they relate, every single person who walks in greets the others, and there is a sense of community that comes with commitment. James insists that even food must give way gracefully to society. If dinner is going to be late because you are in the pub talking to friends, then, well, people remember that, after all, it's only dinner. The project of the country cottage has completed James as much as James has helped to complete it. He had still retained, even at the worst times, when his struggle for career looked hopeless, that ability to be convivial and to make good friends. So, even if Quentin has the salary that provides for the mortgage, they both know that the building of this Shangri La is founded as much upon the way the village in its entirety recognised the charm and the dignity in James's inclusive relationship to people and welcomed them accordingly. The process was surely completed this year when, in the village home-and-garden produce competition, James won a prize not only for the best roses but also for the worst scones.

The fact that the cottage is ridiculously tiny posed various challenges, which together with their labour have matured their own relationship into a vintage one, whose bouquet still retains its undercurrents of their respective individuality and character. James has been busy with the stripping and painting and Quentin in dealing with that extra bit of land they have to acquire on account of what is happening to the farm next door. The cottage adornments include James's photographs from his childhood and his painting of Quentin. Now, even when they return to Stuart Street, they spend much of their time talking about the cottage, their plans, the people there, and the people they are going to invite to stay with them. It is a place where Quentin's knowledgeable but socially concerned friends, who once intimidated James but do so no longer, can come down for a weekend away from the stress of work. But equally, it appeals immensely to James's artistic circle.

These friends represent the final contribution which completes James's sense of redemption. Whatever the problems of his career, he never lost his friends, the very good, firm friends he had made throughout his life as an actor. And gradually, as he had to confront the failure to become all he wished to be in order to realise himself, he came to realise that he did possess an art in considerable measure, one that was masked by the privileged position held by the 'arts'. This was his art of making and keeping friendships. Ironically, the final failure to be an actor left James with himself as his finest role – the man of charm and

dignity: the solicitous, self-deprecating James, with his appealing qualities that brings others out of themselves and, with hardly noticeable
gentleness, escorts them to the end of an evening. He possesses a rare
ability somehow to capture a certain ideal of convivial community that
most people search for, but often need considerable help to realise.

As one version of the disassociation from objects and materialism, it
was quite common in our fieldwork to hear people say that they don't at
all relate to photographs or taking videos because these get in the way
of the authenticity of direct experience. Despite this, in conversation
with these same people, we were often able to establish a detailed discussion around a particular set of images. Once James took out the
photo album of his sixtieth birthday party held at the country cottage,
there was no stopping him. Cousins from childhood, friends from his
early training, people they met on holiday, local villagers pour out in
profusion.

Mostly, therefore, these portraits have concluded with an affirmation
of the way people relate to objects and images as a positive aspect of all
their relationships. For example, once we talk about the specifics of
music, Quentin will go on for hours almost without pause, remembering events, giving opinions, comparing sounds. Yet there are some dis-
tinctive aspects of the relationship that this couple has developed to
objects as mediating their relationships with each other and with other
people. Both Quentin and James have cultivated particular versions of
an immaterial apprehension of the world. In Quentin's case, he really
has an exceptional power of memory. Although he has that collection of
postcards of buildings he has visited, it soon becomes evident that they
are there more as an ordering process than as aide-mémoires. He possesses far more detail through recollection and recollection, unlike a
postcard, includes that vital element, his own opinion. His opinion completes the sense he has of the look and form of the building itself. This
use of recollection is even more obvious in the case of food, which leaves
no trace and whose taste cannot be captured by postcards and photographs. If the enjoyment of cuisine is to be built up through experience and comparison, it has to be through a sensual memory, a
phenomenological experience of the world.

With James, the reason why he would find insufficient meaning and
comfort in objects and images is in some ways quite the opposite. His

skill at friendship relates partly to his own fragility as an individual. In his relationship with Quentin, in particular, but with others, too, he finds himself largely through the affectionate gaze of others. In fact, this affection may be generated partly by other people's own unconscious appreciation that he needs them in order to be himself. When James was feeling at his lowest, although he had the paraphernalia from his more successful career moments, these remained largely in suitcases under the bed. The one object he found helpful in those times was a letter from one of his best friends, brimming with fulsome appreciation of James as a friend and reminding him how many good friends he has and how much they appreciate him. This was a letter that could remain like the voice of an actual friend, repeating something whose truth he could not deny about his own worth in the world.

There is both continuity and displacement here. James is, at one level, still seeking applause, still working an audience; but, instead of the grand audience of the arts, he has the intimate audience of his friends. James has about him something of the contradiction conjured up by the image of a dignified puppy: a potential exuberance of giving and wanting affection, but held in check, so as to include and not overwhelm those more reticent in these matters than himself. For these reasons, this is one household where the comfort of things has but a small contribution to make to the comfort of persons. In this respect they are both matched and complementary. Since this is true for such entirely different reasons. Quentin's unusual autonomy of mind matches James's unusual dependence on the presence of others. But what they need above all – and what they now have – is their relationship sculpted from their complementary natures and mutual dependence, and which here takes shape in the form of their love.

OH SOD IT!

Di reveals her strength through colour. Her hair is bright, often also her lipstick and her clothes. There is usually something red, but other colours will also work for her. She might match gold mesh slip-on heeled sandals with orange nail varnish, or a chunky necklace with a multicoloured top. Brightness of colour is ridiculously rare amongst British-born Londoners. Despite its easy availability in the shops, the vast majority retreat to an extraordinarily drab attire, which seems as dismal as the weather. So, when an individual somehow manages to break through into full blossom, you know there is something behind this. The particular variety of strength exemplified by Di is best accompanied by the very British exclamation, 'Oh sod it!' Because it is the kind of strength that gives insistence to one's presence in the world in the face of disapproval, disappointment, possible disdain, and finally age. Di is certainly not old, but she is by no means a teenager either, and her brightness and breeziness carries an edge of someone who has experienced heartache, not just read about it in novels. She can be pretty sardonic too, when occasion arises.

It certainly is a strength. This particular version of 'Oh sod it' is generally seen as the kind that won wars, dug deep, and saw off adversity. Though winning wars is probably not the analogy of which Di, who has the general left-leaning sensibilities of a modern social worker, would

approve – unless of course 'wars' refer to personal struggles in relationships; in that case she would probably acquiesce in the idea that
she's had her fair share of the battlefield. Quite commonly, it's an 'Oh
sod it' that can also mean 'Yes, let's have another drink, why not?' But
Di has the kind of heart and the kind of head that doesn't forget that
'why not?' is a genuine question. When faced with clear reasons for discipline, she acknowledges them. She will, by all means, have a good
time, but not at the expense of her writing up her case work, or anything where her conscientiousness to the people she serves is involved.
The reason why 'Oh sod it' won against all sorts of adversity was that
it always contained a particular blend of pragmatism and morality that
gave it its determination and perseverance; and blending pragmatism
and morality is what Di is all about.

Di has seen the world, and brought enough of it back with her to
make for a very worldly house. In her time she has smoked, drank and
cavorted with fellow sorts of largely now ex-hippies from Thailand to
Afghanistan, from Sri Lanka to Istanbul. Her house is a museum to the
expansiveness of such times; it has its own 'Oh sod it', aimed at the relative parochialism of the present. She has the cheap beads, the gaudy
fabrics, the kitsch pictures, the amulets and the various godlets; serious
and silly stuff made from fibre, straw, stone and wood and the odd
remarkable plastic. She has enough symbols of luck, omen-taking
instruments, appeals to spirits, and games of chance to have cast her
future to a dozen different fates. It may be that 'ethnic' isn't in fashion
as much as it used to be, but – 'Oh sod it'. In any case, this is no shrine
to the past. It may have the Balinese batiks and masks, the African
gourds and soapstone, the Penguin books and the Ché poster. But it also
has plenty of recent materials, through Mandela to current Afro-pop,
plus the mugs, cushions, plants, tins and modern artworks which integrate the world she has seen with the world she now inhabits.

This miniature world in a house, this celebration of colours, textures
and experiences that cheer her up when she comes in at the end of a day
spent in dreary, cloudy London has been her bulwark. When she separated from the husband, who had shared most of these early journeys
with her, what mattered was that the best part of their life together had
attached itself to the walls and was staying put. Unlike many other divor-
cées, she was fortunate in that his leaving meant not an abandoning of

this possession of home, but, if anything, a further drive to appropriate it as her own. The house became the project, the devotion to herself that was allowed vicariously, because it was a house, and so did not appear as self-pity or conceit. It was an expression of herself as still just as interesting, still the source of good stories; good stories that only worked after a few drinks or a smoke, and some that even worked cold sober. No other person, even if they repudiated her, could do so in the form by which she had distributed herself throughout the house. Fortunately, her ex understood the nature of this thing they had made together. He never asked for anything, never tried to split such possessions. They had an integrity that transcended them as people, and he respected that. To be fair to her ex, any divorce lawyer will tell you just how rare this is.

The objects that mirror us along the walls and surfaces of our rooms can be surprisingly capricious. You can no more take their support for granted than that of people. For all that she had invested herself in it, making every little niche and windowsill a positive reflection of whom she had been and might yet be again, the house could still be an empty house, a lonely house, a dark house. The bright sparks of the past could fire her up, but also depress her, as she feared she would never burn so brightly again. Yet at the least the house could still remain a secure retreat from the hurts of the world. It could still remind her of her own worth when there was no person willing to take on that role. So now, with her current partner, it makes sense that he retains his own apartment, even when he is living some of the time at hers; because the house is now so much part of the way she presents herself to the world. No one else could hope to lay their hands on the right photos – that particular ornament that adorns her tales, makes her point, makes them laugh.

Di's mother disapproves. She says she has all her own past in her head, in memories. Why should you need so much stuff? Why keep the old wedding telegrams, the out-of-date passports? Why would an ex-hippy be so materialistic? But her mother misses the point. Being a hippy was a commitment to having experiences of the kind one's parents never seemed to have. Because this was your emancipation from merely suffering one's fate in the world. You didn't just go to school, get a job, get married, do what you where supposed to do. You said 'sod that for a life' and you sought out and had experiences that you chose, that you trekked to, that you spent your last penny on. You thereby knew, and could attest to, there being so much more to the world, and there was no shame at all in bearing testimony to that. Indeed, the problem now was that the next generation seemed so unambitious by comparison, so limited, so parochial – frankly, so boring.

The expression 'Oh sod it', at least as it relates to Di, implies a particular mixture of benign shrewdness and sadness. It's a mature, realistic sense of the contradictions of all relationships, taking the rough with the smooth. Di is shrewd in that she feels she can appraise people and situations pretty clearly. Although almost all her life is devoted to 'good works', and she really cares about the people she works for, she has enough experience not to idealise such people, especially people who are suffering. Being a victim is rarely in and of itself that which builds character and compassion for others. She is not necessarily expecting gratitude, or imagining that she has been able to make them into better people. She is simply content to play her part in redressing some of the basic unfairness of the world that has led these people to need her. And it's a job.

'Oh sod it', has also been born out of the parallels to all this in her personal relations. All the men she has known have at least as many problematic aspects as good qualities and the same goes for relatives too. When she was younger, she was more concerned with her personal freedom and had the energy to take herself out of any overly restrictive relationship. Today, however, she would accept much more of the sacrifices that seem inevitable if one wants to keep any sort of relationship going, because the alternative is lonely and depressing. Her sense of 'Oh sod it' expresses something that younger people very rarely perceive, about the awful burden of freedom. Now she can decide that, sometimes, just having the obligations of a relationship helps relieve the pressures of choice and the emptiness of individual freedom. This, she understands, is not weakness or a denial of herself. Just looking at her clothes and the way she presents herself, one can see she is more, not less, confident about her own crafting of an individual presence in the world. With plenty to be proud of, and to give, and enough strength to acknowledge past mistakes more than most, she can afford an unusual degree of realism, without it degrading into mere cynicism. There is a defiant feeling of 'let tomorrow do what it will – I have lived today'.

Whenever Di wants to cultivate this same, resigned but smilingly bemused, perspective on the world, her favourite pub provides constant reinforcement. Di doesn't go much to the pubs in Stuart Street, but, not far up the high street, there is a pub that seems to attract the 'characters'. Endless stories from every part of the world. The typical 'trickster' stories of people who as immigrants have had to suffer the indignities of being at the bottom of the pile, but can have endless pints on the memories of how once or twice they put one over on some toffee-nosed authority or cold-blooded establishment. Sure, this doesn't tend to end quietly of an evening; someone will always get bloody-minded, empty a glass over someone else's head. And yes, it can get repetitive – the same stories, the same arguments and sometimes the stupidity and ignorance as well as wisdom and experience. But it is full of life in a way that staid dinner-party conversationalists, probing each other about the best schools and the 'in' restaurants, will never match.

Undoubtedly, the one constant support that has helped Di to retain this sense of facing full-on the truths of the world is the house itself. There is the self-respect she carries with her, the fact that she still looks good, slim-waisted, well toned. Yet, could she have kept that up without the house? Probably not. But it would be far too simplistic to see the house as some kind of nest or lair, or the other empty clichés, inspired by clumsy analogies with animal worlds. Di's relationship to her house is just as complex and contradictory as it is with people, and just as realistic. She is the kind of person who will embrace sentimental attachments and joys, but doesn't try to distinguish them from knowing the monetary cost and worth, or the practical logistics of keeping things going. That's her point. You can actually afford to get maudlin or ecstatic occasionally because your feet are still on the ground and nothing is taken for granted and there is no pretence. So when Di contemplates her wall stuck with tickets from gigs she has been to, she simultaneously knows what she is and what she is never going to be able to do again. Yet that sense of loss is ameliorated by the feeling that she still manages to do more than most people, and that she can therefore still afford to celebrate what she has been in the past. When she listens to her favourite music, this doesn't exclude thinking about how things could be better, whom she could be making love to while listening to it, or whether there should be one more wild house party. But that doesn't mean she can't sit back with a glass of wine and enjoy the lyrics she knows so well. She would never put it so complacently, but there is something about her work that at least tries to do good for others, day after day; so that, whether you succeed or fail, you can live with yourself in a way that people who do not give of themselves never seem to understand.

Around her are dozens of photo albums she can share, cringe over, burst into laughter at and be tormented by. There are all those ethnic items which she much prefers to high 'culture', because they seem warm and inclusive of people, not clever art which excludes and intimidates. There is not one single thing in this room that doesn't testify to contradictory feelings of simultaneous gain and loss; of both other people and their absence; of places she has been and the fact that she hasn't had a holiday in three years; of intense intimate shared joys and of vicious quarrels and separations. In a few cases, the objects reflect back on family and on those extraordinary frustrations that come with it. People like her mother, whom she loves so much and yet finds so infuriating; the original contradiction, on which maybe all the others were modelled. The things it was impossible to say to her, which ended up as things she regretted having said to others. But the house itself is a means of dealing with contradictions, not just a reflection of them. When she came to take away a whole bunch of stuff from her parents' house after they moved, she had to decide what to do with them. Putting them in her own house would compromise her hard-won autonomy as a child, but she had taken them precisely to have them close. So most of the stuff ended up in the garden shed; this achieved the right degree of nearness, and yet at the same time the distance she needed in relation to her mother.

On reflection, there was a kind of consistency to her life, things that built on each other in ways she would never have expected. What she has inherited is a strange mixture; a kind of spiritual pragmatism. There is a certain kind of British non-conformity in her background somewhere. There was a religion in which you were expected to accept your fate and get on with life, deal with practical tasks like repairing furniture and clothing, and not complain – not even talk much about stuff. But at the same time there were the church traditions that spoke to a higher spiritual dimension and an ethical concern with sharing, fairness, and how the world ought to be. She had become a hippy, she thought at the time, in repudiation of all this; but, in retrospect, perhaps it was the only way she could have continued in the same vein. There were a load more logistical practicalities about being a globe trotting hippy than anyone of that tribe ever admitted to. Sorting out the transport, getting a place to stay, keeping going on very limited funds, dealing with strange, often absurd, situations, and plenty of repairing and upkeep. Even at the time, they couldn't just be swept under a magic carpet woven from exotic Eastern spirituality. That is why she didn't just come back all New Age. Rather, the exposure to the sheer inequalities and desperations of the world affirmed a growing empathy with all its diverse populations. Eastern spiritualism and non-conformist religion didn't seem to have much to do with each other, but somehow for Di there had been continuity. She now recognised that, in the end, this seems to have left her with a more truthful acknowledgement of the contradictions that she saw around her than most people seemed to want to admit to or cope with.

She would have liked to have used this maturity to develop certain kinds of relationship, with a man, then with children, but this had only partly worked out. Maybe you needed a different, more simplistic fantasy to get on better in relationships. So in the end she was expressed most truthfully, most fully developed, through her house, in its almost baroque exuberance of decoration that spoke to the richness and colour of the world – her house, which also was the place she looked after with the same practical attitude with which she had learnt to repair greenhouses in her youth. Now she could mend things while listening to a fine CD system and post-feminist ballads, or an old Neil Young track. In those days, fixing things was more likely to be accompanied by Radio Luxembourg coming from a tiny beat-up radio. Maybe she does still often come back to an empty house, but any self-pity is momentary. There is that 'Oh sod it' moment, maybe a quick drink, and then she gets on with making dinner. So finally there is the house itself. More of her personality lies around its walls than she can ever inhabit at one time, but, if she needs to trade it in to pay for an early retirement because she is never going to get a decent reward for her work, well then – Oh sod it, she'll sell.

JOSÉ AND JOSÉ'S WIFE

José has a distinctly Mediterranean air about him which seems rather too enclosed by a bleak sitting-room in a cold London street. One feels instinctively that we should be meeting him in a sun-drenched café over a glass of something. It would be so easy to just change the setting, because the man himself could remain as he is. There is something about the leather jacket and the leathery swarthy skin that makes one feel he has spent a life in the fields. His mannerisms also convey another world. The way he keeps a rolled-up newspaper in his hand as he speaks and bangs the table in front of him with the paper whenever he wants to emphasise a point. He is of that age also – the children grown up and left – when you feel he would be so much more content sitting with a group of men, talking about the news, sports or nothing in particular, but enjoying the company. As with so many people in the area, he has sacrificed the life that once may have seemed predestined, precisely because there were opportunities abroad – later on, more specifically, opportunities for his children – that, he feels, he would not have found in his homeland. But he deeply misses the sun, and one can feel his barely suppressed sighs when he hears of others taking their retirement as an opportunity to return and to eke out at least their latter years in a sunnier climate.

The street itself could be worse. Residing there for a quarter century, he has found some of the neighbours have been fine and friendly; others have those bad habits – creaky doors, or inconsiderate tossing of cigarette ends into his garden – that become infuriating after a while. He is not reconciled to that lack of civic interest or pride, that make an English street so dirty but whose presence he claims, make a Mediterranean street so pretty. If you can't have the sun you could at least still manage a few windowsills of red geraniums. We never met his wife, who was working despite a series of operations, after spending long periods without work, so we never heard her side of a story which, more than almost any other in this street, divided along rather old-fashioned fissures of gender.

Listening to José and, in particular, looking around his house and garden, what struck you was not so much a distinction between a Mediterranean and an English aesthetic, as a realisation of how older distinctions based on gender have disappeared in recent times. When this did emerge in the form of José's house, it appeared as a curious mixture of differences in region and differences in time. Just by remaining the same, some people become something of a museum, an evocation of things past. It may often be the case that migrants remain the most conservative of all: since while people in José's homeland may have shifted with the decades, and certainly the English too have shifted with the decades, José and his wife reacted to the separation from the land of their birth by remaining staunch adherents to the daily habits of their childhood. Ironically, some of their habits are probably also more characteristic of the customs of England at the time when they arrived than of the customs to be found today in their original homeland. The sitting-room with French polish, gilt trimmings and various shades of brown reinforces this feeling of age rather than place.

The most evident anachronism is the basic relationship between José and his wife. We are sitting with José, but we are overwhelmed by the material expression of José's wife. To call her José's wife, irrespective of her name, seems an appropriate domestic nomenclature. 'Domestic' as in a devotion to family that is inseparable from devotion to the home. Looking after the home becomes the act of a devotee who sacrifices herself to this architectural altar to her family. She gives her time, her labour and the suppression of self-interest in order to look after husband and children. What she expects in return is not reciprocity, not that they should look after her in return for her care. Rather, what she craves is their respect and appreciation for what she does and what she has become. Both husband and children should acknowledge her labour by eating together at meal times, by their love for her, by enabling her to become, in turn, the respected grandmother and matriarch of the family she has nurtured. Her husband in his turn should be properly masculine and devote himself to the labours and pursuits in the world that she respects in a man.

This devotion is only partially directed at her family as persons. There may be close emotional times, embraces and warmth. But much of the day-to-day effort is directed to cooking, shopping, ensuring that no one runs out of the basic things that are simply assumed to be present in the house. In addition, the aesthetic of this relationship is embedded in the house itself. Just as José's wife never wants to be taken for granted, and always wishes her labours to be and to remain appreciated, so the house cannot be for her simply a finished construction, which is there to be enjoyed. It needs to remain an object of constant, endless devotion – even when the children do not need her. The house stands for the family; its demands should be insatiable.

So José's wife creates the conditions which ensure that she will always be needed and that her labours will never end. The house is absolutely stuffed with ornaments. The most common are those china figurines, which in their most upmarket version are probably Royal Doulton or Royal Worcester; but, for this family of limited means with two workers but in relatively menial occupations, a less exalted make must suffice. More Royal Dalston than Royal Doulton; a copy which can be purchased at the local market but looks pretty much as good to all but a connoisseur. Since every nook and cranny is filled with these and other ornaments, cleaning the house is an incredibly time-consuming occupation. Each ornament has to be removed, dusted and replaced. Not surprisingly, given their delicate nature and the awkward manoeuvrings imposed by their sheer quantity, they constantly fall and break. This has two very considerable advantages for José's wife. Firstly, it means that she can go to the local shops and market fortnightly, to buy replacement ornaments, as has become her well-established custom. Given that there are absolutely no free spaces left, the survival of this practice entirely depends on a reasonable rate of attrition amongst the present china occupants. Secondly, it gives her a chance to command José to apply his masculine DIY skills to the careful gluing and repairing of the ornaments which, perhaps unfortunately (because then she could buy some more), are not completely shattered.

If china figures dominate all available horizontal surfaces, the vertical spaces are fully colonised by a settlement of family photos. The organisation of these photos represents her hierarchy of value. Pride of place goes to their own wedding photographs followed by those of their children's weddings. Visitors to the house are left in no doubt that these weddings were splendid, crowded, rather overwhelming occasions, which will always remain the highlights of their lives. Second to these come general family photos, the grandchildren, and also those portraying earlier stages in their lives. But, just as with the ornaments, José's wife could not bear for this process to be static or seem complete. As soon as anyone in the family has been on vacation, they are expected to provide some idealised holiday photography which can then be set up on a wall somewhere further up the house – perhaps in a bit of the hall outside the bedroom, which still has some available space. Each little picture ensures that the big picture remains up to date, an image of the family which grows and changes, but also remains.

This endless replenishment of the home with appropriate domestic images is the mode of José's wife's endless devotion to her family. Her daughter understands this only too well, and for some time now she has been trying to call a halt to these activities. The independence of the child is much harder to achieve if the parent continues to find ways of appearing to extend their labour on the child's behalf. Never mind that the children haven't been living in this house for many years; they still know that, back in their natal home, their mother dusts and reorders daily; and, when she dusts, she dusts for them.

Not all – perhaps not many – daughters are so churlish as to deny altogether the love that is dusting. José's daughter, judging from José's account, is in fact still very attached to her parents, to their house, and indeed (quite possibly) to their aesthetic of gender distinction. Although the children moved out many years ago, José and his wife have never really undertaken the full re-decoration they supposed they would soon get round to. They replaced the wallpaper and the carpets laden with the smells, tears and stains of the children's early years. But the rest remains to be done. In particular, their daughter's room is still always called her room. Just as it was gradually cleared of her children's early possessions, so more stuff seems to have come in to fill it. Most recently, their daughter's wedding dress and unwanted wedding gifts had to mingle inside the wardrobe with photographs and the remaining clothes and tokens of her childhood – things she has never quite got around to taking to her own home. The room and its possessions still beckon the daughter, who may still give ear to their call. On occasion, when José returns from work and his wife is on shift duties, he finds the second lock on the front door open. Their daughter, who has retained her own keys to the house over the years, lies asleep in her own room. She had a headache and there is still something comforting about the place – this respite from marital duties, which draws her and relaxes her.

One can sense José's own contentment with this scene. Does he go up, glance at her though the door as she lies there tucked up, and fill himself with the almost unbearable intensity of parental love and care? He doesn't say. Surely José's wife would find it even harder to resist. It is actually their daughter who most often phones up and asks her mother to come shopping with her – or just phones up. It is unbelievable how much those two can talk. I imagine his wife somehow ending each expedition, overcoming her daughter's remonstrations, and coming back with some little china figure she has fallen in love with, which echoes her love for the now not so little figure accompanying her. José is quite clear about how much he misses his children and how happy he is to see his daughter in the house again.

José himself may have the weathered skin of the fields, but it has been hard for him to maintain quite such a devotion to the skills, roles and values of a man. But he has done his best. In the house, he has accomplished far more than simple DIY. Both his daughter's and his son's room retain the wall-to-wall cupboards of his own making, each with its set of seventeen doors. But his world is really outside of the house, and here, in the middle of a South London street, is a southern European garden. This is not a grass lawn bordered with honeysuckle and forget-me-nots. This is a working market garden, a productive feast of fruit trees, tomatoes and vegetable patches that require the labour of a man as much as dusting requires that of a woman. Even the limitations of such a garden were accepted as a challenge. José had to make wine, and, if he could not grow the grapes, he and a friend who lives nearby could at least buy the grapes and make the wine from that: a good two hundred litres of strong red wine, produced in a wooden barrel outside in the garden shed – something of which José was greatly proud.

The wine matters because José is not trying to be conservative as such, just to retain the customs of his homeland; above all he is trying to be true to the values inculcated by his own father. He recalls: 'I know how to look after the wine because my father had a lot of wine. Sundays we got ready to go to church in the morning. You have lunch and after lunch my father would say, "here boys we have to go to change the wines". So I said to my father, "please not Sundays, please, can we do it week days, because Sundays is the day for us to play with friends, why must we do it today?" So I am a little boy behind my father all the time and I could see the way he looked after the wines . . . I never forget what my father told me when I left when I was eighteen. My father started to cry when I said goodbye to him and he said, "listen, my son, never go with bad friends, never go with people who smoke, don't live with people who drink, don't go with bad girls. When you decide, find someone you like and marry, but don't involve bad friends". I never forget what my father told me that day.'

In the end, José's conservation of the traditional male has not perhaps gone quite as smoothly as his wife's conservation of the female. Most important has been the disparity in the behaviour of their children. Within the different environment of contemporary London, the continuity across the female line was easier to maintain than across the male line. Their son left home quite young, and relatively abruptly. He had no desire for this ambivalence to his natal home that his sister retains. Within a couple of years, he instructed his parents to get rid of anything he had left there, which they duly did. At one level this seemed natural. José expects women to have sentimental attachments to their things that men do not. But they lacked other, analogous forms of bonding, and the separation was much more complete. Partly this was fortuitous. The son has had two daughters, and so has no interest in the legacy of his own childhood things, and he lives relatively far away. So José needs that sun-drenched café and the men to talk with. Within the house, while his wife dusts and cooks, his main solace is music. There is the Elvis Presley he heard as a child, there is the music of Brazil he is fond of, and above all there is *fado*, the mournful genre of Portuguese music which speaks directly to those forms of loss that can never be entirely repaired but must always be revisited. For its aficionados, it is the pure sound of longing.

Decades of feminism have taught us to be anything but romantic about the traditional asymmetrical couple, as this was symptomatic of inequality. But it is still worth discriminating between an asymmetry based on power which is resented and one which represents a mutual desire for complementary distinction. One time, when José had a crisis at his workplace and stayed there overnight, his manager was completely bewildered by the sheer amount of weeping, worry and desperation of successive phone calls from the females in José's family. It says a good deal about which kind of asymmetry is at stake. We may not wish to romanticise such relationships but in this case it is the rigid differences in gender, within which they discern the very meaning of the word 'romance'.

The different trajectories may still make for many differences in opinion and desire, and this matters now, because there is a critical decision to be made, which is whether now finally to return home. The word 'home' may be an odd one, given José's wife's devotion to the house they live in, but there has always remained another house, also belonging to them, also stocked and cared for, that stands for another home that is their homeland, and a much sunnier one. For José, this also means another house where he has to pay the utility metres, pay a man to check it when the alarm goes off, make sure that his wife's beloved plants are watered. Although he has some pension, in truth they probably won't go until he reaches full retirement age, but for José that can't come soon enough. When they do go, there is little that he would probably take with him. His wife would have more problems; all that silverware, all the things she has invested in. I wonder about the items which came from their country in the first place: all those lovely tablecloths. Who has the time to clean and iron them? In any case, no one uses them any more; it is more fashionable to leave the table bare. All these years they remained in cupboards upstairs. And yet I have a feeling that, when José and his wife go home, they will go with them.

Portrait 27

WRESTLING

When Sharon first opens the door, she comes across as an ordinary look-ing housewife – but then, perhaps, just a bit too ordinary. Sharon was impressively unconcerned to make anything of herself, even though she was expecting us, her visitors. This was not mere indifference, but that very different thing – studied indifference. Her hair wasn't just not par-ticularly neat; it didn't even look brushed. Her clothing could almost have been nightwear. There was certainly no form of make-up. There was no attempt to create a façade, or a representation of herself. She simply presented as the non-descript of middle-age. The reasons became evident not just from the content of her tale, but also from its manner; because there was the same clear, slightly brutal, honesty about her narrative – not just the events of her life, but her explanation for any-thing we touched upon. Everything was there, exposed, without any call for sympathy or attempt to impress; perhaps because Sharon's story and Sharon herself were quite impressive enough. There was no need for elaboration or staging. All that needed to be conveyed was the play itself, the characters of tragedy and redemption.

Sharon never had it easy. At school, she was highly dyslexic at a time when such things were paid little regard. So hers was a childhood with plenty of school but very little by way of education. Her parents were extremely conservative and strict; both had strong views about traditional gender roles and what was and was not appropriate for a young girl. Her mother was, and is, highly self-conscious about her own appearance. She wouldn't dream of going out to the shops without first spending a considerable time applying make-up and accessories, to ensure that she looked good, but, more particularly, as young as she could. But this was precisely where Sharon soon strayed from the path chosen for her. Along with everyone else, Sharon took gym at school, and it soon became clear that she excelled by far over her peers as a gymnast. Like many of those Olympic gymnasts one sees on television, she was quite small but stocky, and she found that a careful regime and sustained application could help her become, not just the best in her class, but of champion level. As she put it, 'I was the youngest and smallest kid in my year, and it gave me a great sense of myself and a sense of confidence . . . which was a great disappointment to my parents because it wasn't feminine'.

At least gym was still appropriately associated with school and lessons. But then, under the influence of magazines and television, Sharon became intrigued by what her parents regarded as a far less palatable version of the female physique, that required for wrestling. As this developed into a serious preoccupation, she found it was not just her parents' norms she had repudiated. Her exceptional ability and the effect it had on those around her gradually drove her to embrace wrestling's associated sub-culture. Her transformation affected even the question of whom she could go out with: 'I'm seeing this particular guy at the time, who is a little bit smaller to me build-wise, and I went like that, to cuddle him, and I cracked both his ribs on each side and it was a sheer mistake. I had no intention of doing it, but after that I flatly refused to go out with any guy who was smaller than my particular build at the time.'

She found that others simply couldn't cope with the regimes associated with her love of wrestling. 'So you don't put yourself in the position of socialising around "normees" because they wouldn't understand.' She also discovered through hormone testing that she had some quite masculine elements, and felt that learning to control any aggressive tendencies formed part of that process of self-discipline. This could also have its positive side, as she soon started earning money as a nightclub 'bouncer' dealing with troublemakers – something that still helps complement her day job. Hearing all this, one tends to look again at Sharon, expecting to see something rather more special in her appearance. But her ordinariness is too complete. There is nothing obvious in this slightly dishevelled housewife that would signal the significance of her own body to everything she became.

Under these conditions, forming relationships was anything but smooth progress. Twice she became engaged and twice this fell through, making her feel she had to constantly pick up the pieces and start again. Then, at the age of thirty, she married. A year later she gave birth to her daughter Tate, somewhat traumatically, through a ninety-six hour labour. By the age of thirty-two, however, everything had fallen apart. She broke up with her husband and then divorced him. He then set about systematically destroying everything she had built up. He burnt all her photographs, smashed her trophies, even burgled the house she had moved into and stole her electrical goods. Finally he moved out of London, and since then neither he nor his family made any contact with her or Tate, their daughter. Then she lost her job and her house and developed Bell's palsy. Her life and her body had fallen apart – 'I found myself sitting in the ashes of what I used to be'. For three months she camped out all day, every day, with her baby, in front of the offices of the local council, demonstrating her plight as a homeless single mother, sleeping at friends' and relatives' houses. Eventually, the council housed her in the property off Stuart Street in which she was still living at the time of our fieldwork.

This move allowed her effectively to re-start her life. When they moved in, they had only a single mattress and two chairs from a skip in the road. The initial furnishing came from scouting around the neighbourhood, to glean goods which resulted from the common London activity of putting surplus materials outside one's house when moving to a new location. But gradually things accumulated. Given the fragility of her sense of possession, she began hoarding and accumulating well beyond her needs. Even today, she can rarely bear to buy new clothes, preferring the bargains of charity shops, and she still finds it difficult to part with the accumulated stock of her wardrobe.

Things improved further when she found a charity which helped her with child care, and then a unit which specialised in re-education and hence understood, and could deal with, her dyslexia. She discovered books and education, and took to it like a duck to water. She started courses in social science and excelled in her exams. Finally, she reached a level of achievement which led to her tutor asking her to cover the same classes she had once attended. She found that she had become established as a qualified teacher in sociology within adult education and special needs teaching. She developed her own sociological interests mainly in theories that related to re-empowerment and psychodynamic ideas concerning people's ability to take control of their lives – 'which I think is sometimes quite a laugh really as here I am being dyslexic and I'm teaching adults how to do the job I did'.

On the other hand, she wasn't entirely enthralled by her new colleagues. Sociology purported to have considerable concerns with issues of class and a positive and empathetic stance on empowerment. Yet in practice she found far too many academics also used their skills to put people down and disparage them. There were elements of her working-class background that still could be alluded to as common. In particular, for all their avowed radical feminism, their image of femininity could become quite restrictive. Sharon's renewed devotion to wrestling didn't fit well within the canons established amongst her colleagues. Nor did the fake-blond-with-handbag look she had recently adopted, partly to compensate for what might have been seen as the less feminine aspects of an appearance which comes with high-level wrestling. She may not have dressed up for us, but she could present herself pretty well if she chose.

By the time Sharon was nearly forty she had started to develop concerns about her daughter and, more especially, about the environment her daughter was growing up in. Her own background was pretty rough, and she knew all about the behaviour of very young girls at London night-clubs. She felt her daughter was starting to get hassled by some of the youngsters in the area of Stuart Street. Sharon had found the neighbourhood to be very friendly when she first moved in. All the houses around her, in her little cul-de-sac, had been built and occupied at the same time, and the new tenants felt that they represented a new community. This was expressed in an unusual amount of house-to-house socialising and the development of plenty of mutual interests. But London's population is also unusually transient, and, gradually, many of those initial tenants left. There was an increase in vandalism, which was related to the problematic influence of an established crack house in a nearby street. The street cleaner had changed, the milk round had gone, and the local kids were looking for trouble. As it happens, the only actual unpleasantness experienced by Sharon in eight years was the theft of a stereo system from her car. But quite a number of residents in the area developed a narrative about how bad the district had become, although most of them had very little to report by way of actual problems or incidents. Nevertheless, during the period of our fieldwork, she became increasingly desperate to move out. Eventually she achieved her goal and re-located in the north of England.

This desire to move house seemed to have deeper roots in what emerged as a quite consistent, though particular, relation to change and movement. Although she referred to the way she moved things around her house as occasional, later on her daughter insisted this was something that took place every couple of days, something Sharon subsequently confirmed. For example, between our first and second visit the couch that looked out onto the garden had moved to a completely different position, opposite the TV. The chairs which had been by the window against the wall, where she sits and smokes and Tate sits for her dinner, were now placed in entirely different parts of the room. This constant movement was highly unusual. Most households have a strong sense of spatial routine with long-term positions, where things stay and people go. There might be the occasional re-siting of furniture, perhaps when other re-decoration is carried out. Sharon's frequent moving of basic items of furniture, which led to constant change in the daily routines of walking through and sitting within this space, was certainly most rare.

Meanwhile, there are other elements in this interior space that help to create stability. When she thinks about moving house, her first priority is now her books – especially her textbooks on sociology, from which she can't bear to be parted. She has also developed a small collection of dragons, ranging from glass to pewter and china. This fits in with her interest in Celtic mythology and wicker (a sort of benign New Age version of witchcraft). Tate has her own extensive collections. As with many nine-year-old girls, her assiduous collection of dolls and bears has increased through the commercial exploitation of children's tendency to mimic the virtues of devotion and care in their play. She has cabbage patch dolls that need looking after, and even a bear from the Croydon factory where you come to the factory itself, stuff the bear, add a message which gets placed in the 'heart', and then have it stitched up. The bear follows you home, with its own clothes and your own commitment to its future. In Tate's case, however, these exercises in care and devotion have never been restricted to bears. For much of her early childhood, her mother was still having a pretty rough time. As a result, the relationship between Sharon and her daughter has tended to be rather more 'grown-up', with Tate often discussing and sharing problems with her mother, problems that other girls might have remained sheltered from. Their situation had not been helped at all by Sharon's own parents. Despite her own desperate state and Tate's need of active grandparents, Sharon's parents would not renew their parental role in order to help Sharon; they continued instead to regard her as someone who should be helping them to cope. But then Sharon never intended her relationship with Tate to bear much resemblance to her relation with her own parents.

Sharon is clear that her parents had quite doctrinaire ideas about what kind of person she should be, and that her launch into professional wrestling was about as close to a systematic repudiation of her parents' ideals of femininity as could be imagined. But things are not so simple, because there were other influential factors, from quite early on in her life, which don't necessarily bear on her relationship with her parents. There was the fact that she was the youngest and smallest in her class. This often makes a big impact on schoolchildren and could of itself have created enough of an incentive to shine. But there again, she didn't expect to be that good at gym; she followed this trajectory more or less by accident rather than design. So one could see the relationship to her parents either as incidental to her adoption of wrestling or as essential and formative. But it is much more likely that the conjuncture of these two factors – conditions at home and in school – really sustained this direction of development. Thinking in retrospect about these narratives of lives as a whole, the most common phenomenon seems to be that what people become is determined by multiple factors: one cause is reinforced by another, or by several factors which often are quite independent of each other.

Sharon has recollections of what might have been 'key' moments – moments which had the effect of making suddenly clear to her what she did or did not want to be like. At one point she recalls a vision, which took place when she was nine, of a much older woman, closer to the age she is now, dressed in pink and with pink lipstick and orange blusher. She claims that this led directly to her sustained aversion to women dressing younger than their age. I don't know, but I can imagine that this memory is significant because she could see the consequences of such a 'denial' of age in her work at the night-club, and because her own daughter Tate is, after all, nine too. This is not to deny the memory and its enduring impression from the time it occurred; but its impact also seems linked to her fear about the forthcoming sexuality of her daughter, undoubtedly one of the reasons she is about to leave the area.

A similar combination of factors seems to account for her powerful ambivalence towards images of femininity today. There is her devotion to wrestling, in an age obsessed with super-thin models *à la* Kate Moss. Wrestling offers a deliverance from the tyranny of such standards, but not a simple one. Sharon seems to compensate with the potential for glamour found in, among other possessions, her handbags. At least one would have seen the handbags in this light if there had been only say five of them. The fact that she has thirty-two may mean that this is a medium in which ambivalence remains expressed rather than resolved. Finding her own form of femininity is not just an issue of self-perception. She quite recently developed a temporarily successful and satisfactory relationship with a man. They broke up only shortly before we met her.

So between glamour and wrestling, Sharon seems to fluctuate between two radically opposed ideals of being female. She might have possessed a more balanced or compromised middle way. Perhaps this polarisation is influenced by her continued relationship to her parents which also tends to fluctuate between repudiation and reproduction rather than finding a stable place in between. An illustration may be found in the way she described, first her parents, and then her own relationship to hoarding. While both her parents hoard, they each do so in quite distinct ways, which she regards as partly accounting for their divorce:

My mother has a thing for the Egyptian stuff. You walk in and her living-room is just with bits and things. And to me it is just clutter and her bedroom is like a shrine. You could walk in there and, if it wasn't for the dressing table and the modern bed, it would look like a tomb. It's her comfort, that's her way. She has always hoarded as long as I can remember – candles, ornaments. When she goes to dust it's a major event, because she's got so much.

But her father is a 'mass hoarder':

The attic is the length of the house and it's packed, and in one of the bedrooms you cannot even see the bed. To give you an indication, he buys tea bags every week, and there is only him in the house, and there is a stack in the attic of 200 boxes of tea bags, because 'you never know when you are going to run out', and there are boxes for stuff which he no longer has but you never know when you need a box. The day he moves out we are dreading having to try and pack him. He has a carpet that has been up there for four years that's never gone down anywhere, but 'you never know when you are going to need a carpet'.

She is quite resigned to the knowledge that, whenever she visits her father, they will come back with something that she and Tate call their 'red cross parcel', usually teabags and milk and some great bargain her dad has picked up at the supermarket. This hoarding is, then, a significant characteristic of her parents' relation to order – or rather disorder. In certain circumstances, whether she liked it or not, Sharon found herself reproducing their behaviour. This is exactly what happened when she moved into her current house. Under most circumstances, Sharon abhors this hoarding, which she regards as irrational and intensely irritating. But she couldn't help responding this way under the extreme conditions of homelessness, followed by poverty. So she understands that, when the occasion demands it, she will end up reproducing, rather than repudiating, her parents' relationship to things.

Sharon's parents' relationship with her is just as ambivalent. They still maintain a constant critical commentary on how she looks and who she has become and why she hasn't been able to settle down successfully with a nice man. But her evident physical strength has now become a resource. It's not just that when they buy a new fridge, she carries it upstairs; they lean on her also as a source of order and common sense, and continued to do so even when she had vast troubles of her own.

Take a third example – Sharon's relationship with her own child. Sharon has no desire at all to reproduce her parents' forms of parenting. Indeed her problem is rather that her parents are themselves reproducing their parenting, this time in their role as grandparents for Tate. These days, Sharon's mother's less than comforting comments to Sharon about 'how pretty you were once' are accompanied by niggling remarks that Tate seems to have more leggings than skirts or dresses. So Sharon is torn between the desire to be a good daughter and the need to be even further removed from the nefarious influence of her parents for the sake of her own child.

This produces an almost terrifying sense of responsibility in a single parent with so much knowledge of what she does not want to happen to her daughter. Sharon constantly refers to teenage pregnancies and other misfortunes of young girls in the area, in direct reference to Tate's early puberty. She sees Tate as potentially forced to become the sort of person who might reflect the traumas of her own life. 'I don't want her having to be in a position where she has to be that tough, as it's not in her nature. The only way I can change that for her is if I change her surroundings . . . she is not tough enough to hack it round here with these kids . . . I have to move her out of this into somewhere different, where it's easier, where she doesn't have to be tough, like I've always had to be.' But, as a direct result of these concerns, Sharon now finds that this heightened degree of parental responsibility leads her to exercise the very control and constraint over her daughter that she was so desperate to escape from as a child. She is becoming controlling and conservative. So, whichever way she turns, she cannot escape reproducing some aspect of her own parents' influence, which she wished to evade. Tate herself is already starting to exercise her own understanding of the relation between material culture and control. For example, she collects dolls and bears and when one of them she has chosen to cuddle at night begins to become associated with bad dreams, she throws it away and selects another, which seems to give her good dreams.

Sharon sees this issue of control in everything, from wrestling to relating to her living-room. With wrestling, she notes: 'I can exercise my need for control over things by my training, without affecting anyone else, without anyone else being pressurised or pushed into

something or anything like that.' She also appreciates that being a
single mother places a premium upon control: 'You don't have a
choice, and when you become a parent you have even less of a choice.
I don't have the luxury of just being able to fold.' So Sharon has
no problem identifying her own motivation for constantly re-ordering
her room:

> I'll move things around and change things, if I need space in my head,
> if I've got a lot going on. I need to clear my head, I need space in my
> head, then I'll sort out my environment. If in here (the room) is sorted
> then in here (her head) gets sorted . . . Instead of having enforced
> change, because I didn't have any control over it, this way I can control
> . . . until the next cycle sort of thing – the next cycle comes up when I
> might feel stressed or under pressure. Then I think, OK, and I have a
> mad fit again. And if I'm going to do it, it will always be late in the day,
> late afternoon or early evening, because I function better at night . . . A
> few months ago I split up with my boyfriend. I couldn't do anything
> about that, but I could do something about the room, so . . . frenetic
> moving of stuff about.

To everything she does, Sharon brings what is now a highly self-
conscious and abstract knowledge, based on all her academic training.
She knows that this activity of extensively moving things around every
other day might be regarded by others as obsessive or irrational. She also
sees the rationality of vicarious control: asserting herself with respect to
a genre of things that she can control might perhaps help her deal with
all that she cannot control. Yet none of this self-knowledge reduces one
iota the actual efficacy of moving the furniture, or her need to do it. Just
as her knowledge of why people need to hoard – which she also
described as irrational – didn't at all save her from needing to hoard
when her own circumstances fitted her theory of hoarding.

On the contrary, as is clear from her anxious discussions about how
she should act as a parent, such knowledge, experience and reflection is
a constant aspect of the way she engages emotionally and practically
with all the daily decisions of her life. According to the post-modern
perspective Sharon has been teaching in sociology, we are increasingly
abstracted from some real world and lost in a virtual world. But none of

this rings true for Sharon. For her knowledge does not alienate from experience. She is not ironical or distanced. If anything, knowledge just gives her a sense of responsibility which leads her to decisions and to act, though in the presence of reasonable doubt. But then while Sharon teaches sociology, her lessons have come mainly from life.

THE CARPENTER

Since so many people today regard *Absolutely Fabulous* as indeed absolutely fabulous, it has become one of the dominant images through which we consider the legacy of the 1960s. It captures a particular kind of English version of the hippy, one that attaches itself to older versions of English eccentricity; a half-demented, half-creative, arty flakiness, which in that series was marvellously complemented by the daughter Saffy, who struggles to create firm order and a return to rather more common sense. But *Absolutely Fabulous* is certainly not the only legacy of those days. There is another form of idealised Englishness, which also takes its tone and texture from a core set of hippy values crystallised around the themes of 'peace and love' – a key expression of that time.

In stark contrast to the TV series, the theme of peace and love ambles its way back to the equally English ideal of 'nice'. This became, over the subsequent decades, the gentle return of at least a part of that generation to a set of values expressed in their desire to become potters or carpenters, ideally associated with some attachment to the land and its cultivation, if only of their own supply of 'weed'. Later still, most of these sixties ideals faded away, but they left for some a commitment to gentle craftsmanship. This is what seems instantly recognisable in Daniel: a certain mild-mannered, gentle paced, patient form of 'nice'. I have always envied the laid-back relaxed attitude to life which comes with it. This version of the ex-hippy days produces a very different style of parenting. I have no doubt that, although she is only ten years old, Grace already appreciates that she has a really nice father. Perhaps one day, if she comes to watch *Absolutely Fabulous*, she will be much relieved that her father took the opposite route to Saffy's mother.

Daniel was reminded recently of some of these early influences when he watched the re-formed Pink Floyd as they played in the Live Aid concert. It immediately transported him back to the time when he first heard *Dark Side of the Moon*. For many years, he continued to go to rock concerts at places such as Reading and Knebworth. Over the years, however, there have been breaks as well as continuities. Much of his record collection disappeared in a fire, and much of the rest was sold at a time he was stony broke. In any case, he was never one to keep much by way of mementos. The style of music, to a degree, defines the man. It is hardly surprising that Daniel never took to heavy metal, but preferred the gentle integration of rock represented not just by Floyd, but also groups such as early Genesis. Someone once told him that the strings of DNA are a mixture of original sequences and repetitions, which meant that everyone is coded in the manner of a musical score. This idea appeals hugely to Daniel. Music, he feels, has an innate genetic quality which links the generations and links the separate times of his own life. Currently, he remains a bit frustrated that he is going to have to wait for a few more years before he can introduce Grace to the music he loves and wants to bequeath to her. At the moment she is into the pretty and somewhat plastic pop created for ten-year-olds. Daniel is normally a very patient man, but the desire to replace her current music with what he sees as its much more authentic roots is clearly testing that patience.

Daniel would never be one to repudiate his past entirely nor to reproduce it fully. He prefers to see things in terms of a more constant flow across the generations. It was his father who first helped to develop his other main interest in gems and minerals, which is evident in the living-room of his house. These items are placed mainly in one extensively filled display cabinet, but many are also scattered in other areas, as isolated specimens. At the time, his father worked in a shop selling magazines, and suggested Daniel subscribe to a monthly devoted to this topic. This was the foundation of his subsequent collection. But then, more recently, Daniel's enthusiasm for mineralogy spilled over to his mother, who started to develop an interest in it too. Equally, Daniel loves to involve Grace in any way. There is one place in his display cabinet where a model dragon sits proudly on top of a pile of gems, and Grace talked to us about the different touch and feel of these objects, as well as about their look. Listening to her, one can hear echoes of Daniel and guess at his craft in parenting. By making her see the gems in terms of these sensual qualities and by linking them to children's lore such as fairy tales, he has, with impressive success, found ways to involve Grace in something which, under a different treatment, could so easily have appeared to her as an intimidating science of minerals that excluded her.

Of all the things Daniel learnt from his father, the one he appreciates most is the craft of cabinet-making and, more generally, carpentry. One of the best times of his life was the years he spent working with a partner as a professional craftsman in wood. With this skill, he joined some others who were able to live that idealised lifestyle, at least for a while. Those values that filtered down from the sixties, may not have achieved peace on earth, but they did instil a certain peacefulness. In stark contrast to the trajectory represented by *Absolutely Fabulous*, Daniel's love was for craft rather than any pretension to high art or high fashion. He simply doesn't have the kind of egotism and self-centredness that sometimes tends to be associated with becoming an artist. Certainly, he had his own way of doing things; indeed he could be quite stubborn and pedantic about making things in one particular way. But this was not in order to cultivate his name or fame.

His is a modest craft, which develops naturally out of his respect for the people he serves with his skill. His ideal work is highly personal and specific and, typically, has as much to do with a deep concern for the wood as for the client. Daniel has very clear ideas about the qualities of each type of wood. He is particularly fond of wood from fruit trees such as apple, pear or cherry. Most of all, he loves the eccentricity of wood that comes from burrs, which he can use as veneer, to make his furniture special. His bedroom contains one of the few pieces of furniture crafted by him which he has kept for himself, and it is quite stunning. When one inspects carefully the insertions of burr veneer, which mark the edges of drawers, and other surfaces, the craftsmanship appears to be completely flawless and inspiring in its perfection. Typically, this piece is stored in the privacy of the bedroom. There is hardly anything in the living-room to display his craft. Nor does he readily speak of it, until it comes up in other conversation.

Daniel doesn't just relate to the potential qualities of each variety of wood; he also shows concern for each individual piece of wood. It is said by anthropologists who have worked in the Arctic, that the Inuit look at some raw material such as a walrus tusk and pray to it, hoping that it will reveal the imminent figure or design that lies within, waiting to be released by the craftsman. In a similar manner, Daniel and his partner used to come across particular pieces of wood in workshops, or a loft, and patiently consider and discuss what form should ideally be made from this particular shape and texture. The carved product is a kind of homage to the potential of the wood itself. Although they could turn out a regular product such as CD holders, they much preferred bespoke carpentry. The items he mostly recalls are those commissioned for some slightly eccentric or particular purpose, such as the special cabinet made to hold someone's medals, or the construction designed to store and display an old ship's bell. He is also just as appreciative of other people's handicrafts. When his mother had to move house, the only things he took from her were gifts he himself had once given her, hand-crafted souvenirs from East or South-East Asia, where, unlike most tourists, he fully appreciated the degree of craftsmanship invested in their making.

So whatever he inherited from his parents, Daniel took further and developed. This was certainly true of his mineral collection and his cabinet-making; it was also true of his marriage and his parenting; the latter, in particular, he clearly understands as a craft. To be fair, his parents had to deal with seven children and he only has one. The seven of them grew up in poverty and with very little by way of resources. While he may not have been well-off compared to most people in Stuart Street, he appreciates that he is extremely wealthy compared to the previous generation. So, when he regards himself as going beyond his predecessors, he attributes this not so much to his own abilities but more to the resources, which give him the possibility to do more things, and different ones at that.

One of the most obvious signs of this increase in wealth is the sheer amount of possessions to be found in a contemporary home. Daniel owns almost nothing from his own childhood, simply because he had practically nothing of his own as a child. As one of seven, everything tended to

be handed down; he possessed things only as an interlude between older
and younger siblings. The contrast with Grace is huge. She has loads of
everything. In particular, she has a massive collection of soft toys, so
many that at any given time half of them need to be stored at her aunt's.
Grace carefully cycles them between the two sites, so that none of them
should feel neglected.

Those she retained at the time of our visits were piled high up, on
the topmost shelf of the bookcase in her bedroom. There one confronts
a hundred smiles and two hundred eyes. This is Grace's collection, her
array of teddies – well, perhaps half of them are actually bears. There
are also seals, dogs, giraffes and other species. Some dressed in uniform,
some wear sunglasses, some have pink embroidered feet, some clothes,
some ribbons. Some are orange, some white with black splodges, some
brown. They are piled up so high that one can count up to seven layers
of soft toy. A closer look can perhaps reveal a certain aesthetic, which
works its way through this household as a whole. It's not that there is a
particular order, but rather a logic by which the mass of toys are
arrayed. In essence, the medium-sized ones lie nestled into the cracks
and gaps left by the biggest ones, and then in turn the smaller ones
nestle in the armpits and perch on the shoulders of the middle-sized
ones. As a result, no space is neglected; every inch is populated. This
ten-year-old comes into her room and is faced by a soft, appealing mass
that looks down upon her in a single, overall expression of comforting
and cuddling.

When one glances more widely across the bedroom, one finds this
aesthetic repeated in other ways. Again, every surface, niche and possible platform is populated by figures, no place is neglected, and each toy
is just the right size for its place in the room as a whole. The living-room
upstairs is also crammed with ornaments, mineral collections and many
souvenirs from Daniel's wife's country of origin. There are some fine-
quality retro turntables, which, clearly, are possessions of pride for
Daniel. But in the interstices of all these adult things are a whole set of
Grace's own productions. All those drawings, the little papier mâché figures, and other, more or less successful, efforts which have returned with
her from school now have their own place in the public room of the
house. In a similar vein, there are photos of Grace that are clearly kept
up to date, with her latest looks placed in front of earlier versions of this

evolving person, capturing many moods and adventures. Overall, the effect is, again, one of *horror vacui*: that leaves no gaps or empty spaces. A material expression of the way one feels that Grace is completely cuddled and cultivated. No aspect of her goes unnoticed or un-encouraged. Any little piece crafted by her will immediately have earned its place somewhere in the house, which has nothing so self-important or valuable that it could refuse the companionship of a little papier mâché cat.

This is not spoiling, it is not attention that leads to self-absorption. On the contrary, what Grace learns through being loved in selfless ways she is expected to give out in her turn. She proudly shows us the various tokens which relate to the help she gives to the 'Save the Children' charity. She is hugely loving to her various pet rabbits and guinea pigs, not to mention the family cats. Some children are bought pets, but the parents do most of the work. That is not Grace. She can speak for hours about every little task she performs to make her pets' lives comfortable and complete. The care she has learnt in recycling a mass of soft toys now develops further, in the more rewarding care for her soft animals: these seem already to have learnt the trick of escaping her clutches just far enough to be chased around the living-room but nowhere too far or too dangerous. For a child of her age, Grace also appears to me unusual in the degree of interest she shows in her own parents: how much she seems to know about them, what they enjoy, what they did on their holidays. She is already developing an affection for their frailties that is testimony to her growing maturity.

These frailties form part of the way love operated in this household. Daniel does not wish to make himself complete, or self-sufficient, or accomplished in too many things. If anything, he seems to cultivate his faults and his failings as much as his skills and his labours. This seems particularly true of his relationship to Roberta, his wife. Daniel appreciates a great deal about Roberta, starting with the very fact that she cares for him. Daniel was never confident in his relationships with women; he didn't experience his first kiss before he was twenty-one. Roberta does the ordering, he cultivates his need to be ordered. She takes the photographs, and knows all the details of each image; he remains incapable of remembering to take a camera, but he enjoys and acknowledges her memory for detail. He bakes the bread every day; she does the serious cooking. His passion for gems and mineral collections makes it extremely easy for his wife and daughter to know what to buy for him for Christmas or birthdays. This concern for others extends further. It is typical of Daniel that, when he dreams of winning the lottery, he thinks first of buying a really large house in the countryside; with a wing where he could house his elderly mother, to 'bring her back into the family fold'. So what started as a reflection on the way teddy bears are ordered on a shelf then gives rise to our understanding of the overall aesthetic that gives form and pattern to the relationships which constitute this house. The way the differences between two parents create complementary relationships, so that each tries to inhabit the gaps left by the other, and this in turn creates a more complete and effective relationship to the child.

Some of what Daniel says about his relationship to his parents has to be taken with a pinch of salt. On several occasions, he noted that his parents were never sentimental. As I have already remarked, this seems to be a theme in English families: an insistence upon a traditional English working-class pragmatism, which simply could not afford sentimentality, given their struggle to raise seven children on very little income. Daniel claims to have inherited something of this. He accounts for his lack of interest in mementos and photography as evidence for his own pragmatism. But I strongly doubt this. I suspect that his parents were a great deal more like the Mr and Mrs Clarke down the road, who also lay claim to this pragmatism. But you only have to mention the cat, or a grandchild, to find them as mushy as old raspberries. The same goes for Daniel: you just allude to some relationship, his wife, his daughter, his gems, his wood, his house or his music to see this would-be rock of pragmatism washed away in a flood of sentiment.

Though modest, Daniel is not without the quality of self-appreciation – the proper complement to modesty, if it is not to become self-deceit. Not pride, but rather acknowledgement of his good fortune in what he has done and what he still can do. But it is the latter, what he still can do, that is most sensitive and comes closest to a genuine sense of loss. Daniel loved his early days of freedom; that early post-hippy aura. He loved the spontaneity with which he and a bunch of mates could suddenly decide to peel off from any fixed commitment and go to Scotland for an undefined period of time. He still feels he could handle the mud and the Spartan conditions of the pop festival's tents. He has willingly put all this into abeyance in order to concentrate on his beloved daughter. The problem is, rather, how he envisages life when Grace will have grown up and gone from home – something he admits, will not take too many more years.

He always imagined that, somehow, when the time comes, he would pick up from where he left off. Maybe a little more by way of comfort than the old muddy tent, but not a whole lot more. Yet in his heart he knows that that probably won't now happen, since by that time, in his late fifties, it's more likely to be the way it was this year: watching a re-formed Pink Floyd, but watching on television; seeing documentaries about Bob Dylan rather than seeing Bob Dylan, reminiscing, with new experiences limited largely to some new summer-holiday destination. The failure to be able to return to that youth, the inability to take up the freedoms sacrificed in order to look after his family – these are things he will regret, probably always. Part of him feels strongly the irony that, when young, one doesn't really have the depth of understanding or the time to realise the fantastic nature of these experiences. Now he would have an altogether deeper appreciation, but the opportunities are probably gone. So there are shadows behind the lights, but they are hardly paramount. For now, and hopefully for always, there will be plenty of people, and wood worth crafting, and plenty of gems still to collect.

THINGS THAT BRIGHT UP
THE PLACE

It's Christmas time, and the Christmas grotto, that is otherwise Marcia's front room, has sprung into action with the flick of a few switches. We three sit, almost cowed into silence by the sheer cacophony of sound and light. One can just about make out 'God rest ye merry gentleman' emanating from her singing Christmas tree, before it is drowned out by two saxophone-playing Santas with their Good King Wenceslas, in turn, competing with an entirely different carol from an even more jazzy Santa, who moves his hips in a manner suggesting that he has been avidly listening to Marcia's favourite reggae carols. But the sound is mere background to movement and light. We have already met the strange wizard figure holding a crystal globe with purple light, flickering in lines that splay out around the inside of the glass. The tree lights pulse off and on, and above them is a lighted star. Other figures sway, turn in circles, jump up and down; but, again, this is mere background. Because, after switching on a dozen figures – some of which respond, others of which have run out of battery – we turn to Marcia's latest purchase that, placed on top of her dresser, effortlessly dominates the mass of figures writhing and playing beneath her.

Behold Marcia's angel. The body of this angel is a fair-headed female, rather older in years and more buxom than the type usually found on Christmas trees today, with a vague Victorian grandeur. Her huge wings gradually beat back and forth and, as they do so, their 'feathers' change through a remarkable series of intense colours, purples, reds and blues, constantly catching and throwing off light from different surfaces, punctuated by little tufts of fibres whose ends compete with their own displays of equally bright light. These fibres festoon the base and parts of the dress of the angel herself.

Christmas is a time when the inhabitants of Marcia's room get to party. The room itself is an extraordinarily populated space throughout the year. There must be dozens of ornaments and figures on the central table. Many of these battery-operated clowns, or figures in the national clothing of a country she has visited, have tasks to perform that have nothing to do with Christmas and can be called upon to entertain guests, or Marcia herself at any time of the year. The dresser, other side-tables, and every raised surface have their own share of figures. And, while there are quite a few typical souvenirs, for instance mini bottles and ashtrays, it is the figures that dominate. Black musicians who, as Marcia put it, 'bright up the place', jostle the Santas, the religious icons, and the toys. In Marcia's room, Jesus looks out from the midst of the Last Supper and his eyes fall on Humpty Dumpty, in turn overawed by a three-foot Matador, whose arms are now laden with a bunch of pink plastic roses. A litter of six china kittens plays at the feet of a Japanese lady. A Red Indian joins a beach party of almost naked figures, including one well endowed sunbather, whose modesty is barely saved by a carefully positioned bottle of sun lotion. There must be a dozen saxophonists strategically placed around the room to serenade a picture of Marcia at her wedding nestling respectfully below another portrait of Jesus holding his own sacred heart. Fairies nibble on tropical fruit three times their size. Pixies play with peasants. Goats look amazed at basketball champions, while plastic lilies protect Puritans who read epistles to pigeons. Marcia has brought tolerance, though not exactly harmony, to not just one world, but many.

So the room is not just populated, it is unbelievably crowded; and Marcia herself hardly needs to tell us about the overwhelming cause of the suffering that afflicts her now and has afflicted her for so many years: her loneliness. One of the more poignant themes in the room is ornamental telephones, china copies of old-fashioned phones, with discs to be dialled: phones which can never ring. One phone does, not that rarely. People do make contact, they do visit, but never as much as she would like. And those visits merely punctuate the long sentence of being on her own. Yet there is something else about the phone that rings. It is itself highly ornamented, its function almost suppressed by the group of figures at its base, which swing round and light up. It is remarkably difficult to reach; one has to push past the dining table and three chairs without knocking over any of the table decorations. It's almost as though the issue of lack of contact is only half coming from those who neglect her; there is at least as much emphasis on her making it difficult, resenting it when people do contact her as much as when they don't. Partly because the person on the phone is often, of course, someone who hasn't rung for far too long. This ambivalent phone suggests that juxtaposing the crowd of ornaments and her loneliness is much too simple. Many more complex forces are in operation here.

Sitting with Marcia for our 'closure' meeting, when we were explaining that our work was coming to an end and that therefore we wouldn't be able to visit her again, it suddenly struck me that there was a profound truth to much of what she had been saying to us, a truth that I hadn't previously appreciated. Marcia tends to punctuate her conversation with homilies of the kind that seem undressed unless given with appropriate sighs: 'the Lord will provide', 'only time will tell'. Up until then, I had never really paid much attention to these phrases, waiting for her to resume her conversation with other words that seemed to contain more information, something we could learn more from. But then, at this final meeting, the background sound suddenly came to the fore. I realised that when one is elderly; when arthritis competes with trapped nerves and sores in a shifting landscape of pain and frustration; when one never knows if family will come and visit, and then whether they have any real interest other than hoping for money or gifts; when friends have their own problems, and the church is a bit far to walk to regularly; when the only real relief in the last few years has been the trips organised by the church, from which Marcia has gleaned so many souvenirs (but she missed the last few, because there is just no point when you can't really walk); when one's capacity to make one's own life has ebbed away – well, then homilies become the real truths of life. When you can do nothing, then only God, fate, or luck may bring something or someone to ease your situation or to add to the burden. Perhaps, for a change, someone will pay a call, perhaps the herbalist or masseur will live up to the rumours about how they dealt with Mrs R's creaking joints and soothed Mrs M's headaches. But there have been too many disappointments; you have been let down too often. All you can do is wonder if some wheel of fortune, some stroke of fate might almost by accident alight upon you, just once more. The Lord alone knows.

For now, as Marcia looks to the horizon, it is mainly storm clouds that are massing. News has arrived about another land dispute, which will take away her last rights to the family inheritance in Dominica. It's OK that the money to which she might have been entitled is going to a sister in the States, who genuinely needs it more than Marcia; but it's a pity that nothing of her stake is left. All those cousins who, over the years, only ever responded to the things she sent back home with more demands for yet more things: they are the ones who now threaten her rights. Even when she made an effort, and sent back more than she wanted to, the thank yous never followed until months after her gifts had arrived, and there was always something grudging about them, that she has tried to ignore. But things in London weren't much better. Yes, the insurance would pay, but why did the leak from next door have to flood her basement, and why with sewage? Maybe she could move. Those Victorian houses are so much better built than these modern buildings, they have real bricks. The family in London hardly paid her much attention. The grandchildren were now too old to be much amused by the plastic and plaster population that waited patiently in this room for someone to entertain. They could still surprise her, though. During the time we knew her, she 'discovered' a granddaughter, nearly twelve years old, whom her son had never previously admitted to. She even met the mother, a white girl, pleasant enough. Maybe she would visit this Christmas. Surely she would.

But, with her hips, Marcia wasn't up to making much by way of preparations. A traditional West Indian black cake, certainly; maybe a sponge or rock cake; and visitors were at least offered some alcohol at any time of the year. But the punch bowl she's had for eighteen years would not be holding punch again. The anthropologists were paying a last call. We had helped with odd jobs around the place during the year: tying back a rose that threatened to scratch passers by, helping a bit to clear a way in the room – nothing much, and then Marcia would sit and talk. She kept up with the news; would grieve at the situation in the Middle East, or tell us the real reason some politician was behaving badly. She would relate a host of alternative remedies, some from Dominica, most of which seemed to involve castor plants, and plenty more from hearsay in London. We would hear of God's graces and the need to listen to the Lord, and always some stories about church visits to Malta or Madeira, to Poland or Portugal, to the places her heart was still set on visiting – South Africa or Brazil. She would laugh at her own wonderment: the time when she saw the mist descend from mountains in Switzerland and asked in consternation where the fire was that was causing all that smoke. Stories are constantly evoked by the population of souvenirs, which bring into her home memories of Cuba and Spain, Cyprus and Florida. As she often remarks, these things are light and bright, perhaps they bring back something of that brighter sun that has never yet shone on those fated to live only in London.

Looking around at the ornaments, it is only too easy for people from another background and a different system of values to dismiss these things as kitsch. Plastic and plaster, bright colours, not a single flower that is real. Yet to think in terms of kitsch is simply to condescend, to fail to engage with the materiality of this assemblage; what precisely she has and why. Because, as one comes to understand her and this scene within which she has centre stage, the whole re-forms itself, once again, into a very different kind of aesthetic, one that holds considerable meaning and populates the landscape with clues as to who she is and the contradictions that life has created for her. Indeed, after a while, one comes to realise that it is probably those very tasteful art and craft works, characteristic of middle-class living-rooms that have the emptiness and shallowness we try to project upon kitsch: mere purchases, often expensive purchases, to fill a space on a wall. The pieces in this room are quite the opposite. Some are saturated with humanity; some, with the transcendence of the divine; some are the face of brutal and inhumane treatment, while others the form of consolation and peace. Above all they offer some form of companionship.

To start from the beginning, from her beginning, there are some, but only some, elements in this bricolage that allude to her homeland in the Caribbean. They are nothing as superficial as figures that look overtly Caribbean. Indeed in Trinidad, for example, by far the single most common ornament in people's sitting-rooms is the ceramic swan – while far and away the most common wall decoration is an imitation tapestry, usually of some pine-forest scene with glades and snow. It is these two, the very opposite of tropical symbols, that would be the ornaments most reminiscent of Trinidad – and I speak as one who once counted and recorded the ornaments in one hundred and sixty sitting-rooms in a town in central Trinidad. In Marcia's room there are almost no objects that come directly from her homeland. She says 'There's nothing there that would interest me. You have to look forward not back.' Where there is continuity, it is not in the individual objects but in their mass. What is familiar is the sheer number and variety of ornaments. There is commonly, in the Caribbean, a set of wooden open shelves. This is called a space saver and it does precisely the opposite of what its name implies. While it might include a television in the centre, most often it simply uses up a good deal of space and fills it with a wide range of ornaments which serve no apparent purpose other than to decorate the room.

Marcia actually has a dresser rather than a space saver for this purpose, and the objects that stand most clearly for her Caribbean origin are the flowers. None of these are real, but many of them are paper flowers she has made herself – an art form she learnt as a child; not as a hobby but as a way of earning a few cents, because she had to. One influential early experience was poverty, and if the crowd of ornaments invokes all the places she has been able to visit, this is partly a trophy – a token of where she has been, of how much she has thereby achieved in her life against initial expectations. She comments that, 'when you progress, you stop and you look back at your past and see what I have achieved. Where I am and where I came from. Because when I came in this country I just came with my suitcase and my shoulder bag.' She is someone who has not only known hunger, but had to endure it with little sympathy. Certainly it wasn't hunger of the kind that endangers life, but it was a sense that one couldn't rely on getting to eat even what one considered to be normal daily provisions. But no sympathy. You were told you couldn't really be hungry when there were so many fruit trees around. But try stuffing yourself with green mangoes and see how your stomach feels the next day.

This poverty, and the feeling that one had to make do, had more subtle and longer-term effects. Her mother had been a schoolteacher, probably not very different from the figure of Hortense in Andrea Levy's novel *Small Island*: the kind of female Caribbean schoolteacher who doesn't just teach, but for many decades was somehow burdened with being the external embodiment of a particularly rigid and authoritarian concept of respectability. These were the figures who brought discipline not only to their charges but to the community as a whole. If they neglected that role, say, by becoming pregnant at the wrong time with the wrong man, this was a betrayal not just of family but of the values of a whole community. So Marcia's childhood was a strict one, and the overriding ethos was to learn how to look after oneself and remain stoical about the heavy domestic responsibilities of a woman; to be able to sew, to cook, to provide, to keep things not just clean but crisp and spotless. As one grew, one also took on the larger responsibility of budgeting, finding ways of keeping body and soul together not just for oneself, but for husband and family. Marcia started by making paper flowers for sale. Her son was born while she was still in the Caribbean, from a babyfather she soon lost touch with. The boy stayed in Dominica with Marcia's mother until he was twelve and she was sufficiently settled in London, with a husband, to send for him.

Making a living also carries with it a certain Caribbean inflection that remains important in understanding Marcia's room. Its not just a job, but a continuous obligation that seeks opportunities wherever they emerge. Few people in the Caribbean, unless they come from wealth, merely go on holiday. A holiday abroad is always an opportunity to engage in what is called the suitcase trade: buying things cheap, to sell on one's return home. Many of the things Marcia has in her house were originally bought in threes and fours, even more so with the clothes she has in her wardrobes. On return from her church holidays she would sell most of these items to friends, relatives and neighbours, keeping one for herself if she particular liked the object. In fact, the choice of what to buy was usually based on what she wanted for herself and the assumption that, if she found something that looked fun or beautiful, then hopefully others would see it that way too. She built on a network she had already formed as a seamstress, making and selling clothes, in addition to whatever job she had at the time.

So the first, deepest layer that emerges in the excavation of Marcia's living-room is that of her Caribbean origins. But the next layer is much more turbulent; it betokens the fact that, in many respects, everything she learnt there and the skills she derived from her origins proved singularly inappropriate and ultimately betrayed her. In the Caribbean, such devotion and dedication to work and budgeting could bring a reward. Many such people there end up, at Marcia's age, effectively the matriarchs of a large extended family, fat with respect, ready to meet their maker having kept faith with a hard life, but one that could bring love and devotion. This respect gave such an older woman genuine authority and power and recognised the wisdom evident from her accomplishments. Marcia certainly did her duty. She scraped and sacrificed and took her place in this order of things. She suffered from inequalities that made her the provider, but also the abused – when it came to relations with men. She took her skills of making do and used them to sew cloth and curtain and whatever else was needed for her home, her relatives and others. She was dutiful as a daughter to the day her mother died and beyond. Her last visit to the place of her birth was in 1976 when she returned with her mother's ashes. She also tried to respect her mother's dying wish for her to live with her sister, even if this meant at the time losing a promising partnership with a man. When she worked, she worked hard, and, when others took holidays, she just saw these as opportunities to earn more by doing overtime.

So Marcia has done her part, has fulfilled her side of the bargain, has made her sacrifice, and, by all that is fair and just, she should now be what she had seen others become before her: the matriarch. She has tried to keep a respectable home. She would meet neighbours, even have a little drink, just so that no one would think her snooty. But she was very careful to keep this within strict limits, so as not to become what in the Caribbean is called 'social' – someone who spreads gossip, is too keen to swap stories with those living around her, and thereby loses respect and comes to be seen as a source of trouble. Marcia has kept well away from this path. She followed the straighter and narrower road her mother had set before her. As she puts it, 'you show me your respect and I show you mine, that is my policy'. Her mother's portrait still looks down at her from a photograph on the wall. Yet God moves in mysterious ways, and life is not simply the meting out of justice and fairness. Again and again Marcia felt that her generosity was merely abused. Her husband was the worst – well, actually his sister was the worst. It was she who had come to live with them at her husband's insistence when he brought her from Dominica. But who stole Marcia's clothes, took every advantage of her, and made sure to turn her husband against her. Marcia divorced in 1971.

Then she had to fight again for her rights. Her husband kept the property and would have left the country, without her receiving a legal settlement if she hadn't been on to him. She struggled again, to fund her own property at a time when no one was giving a mortgage to a West Indian divorcée. This turmoil had done no favours to her son, who left home early and couldn't be prevailed upon to have the patient educational ambition that might have brought him the kind of success and honours his mother planned for him. Even here, the repetition of her own childhood probably did her no good. When her son left, she made him take absolutely everything. She thought it was her duty to teach him at least self-reliance, independence. He took the lesson, and became so independent that, from then on, she hardly knew what was happening in his life.

So one of the main sources of tragedy for Marcia is precisely that legacy she has inherited through the generations. Whenever people talk about roots, the legacy of one's homeland, we automatically assume that this is a positive asset which will help to give migrants a good foundation in their new land. But why should this be? Isn't it just as likely that this legacy may be unsuited, ill adapted, debilitating in this very different setting? Marcia's legacy was one that was formed by, and worked well within, a certain condition of poverty associated with a close extended family. It worked a whole lot less well in the isolation of a South London street, where it seemed to retain the harshness but less of the benefits. Keeping a proper distance only ensured loneliness. Being a good strict mother only caused alienation. Being a bit less respectable and more convivial might have served her better. By nature she could have been, would have been, but by upbringing she could not, her roots would not let her. By now, however, Marcia is who she is. Even though she may regret now the discipline with which she brought up her son, she can't but feel that it is her duty as a grandparent to teach her grandchildren proper behaviour. It seems almost incredible that, with six grandchildren, not one of her ornaments has ever been broken by them during play. But, as Marcia observes, she used to give them such stern warnings that they just wouldn't dare.

Marcia's mother taught her the pride of respectability, a trait that makes her look for opportunities to give; but the one thing she finds really hard to do is to receive. It's symptomatic of the way she is layered with drapings of respectability so that she has no place left which could make her vulnerable to others. And that includes the ability to act as the recipient of other people's kindness. If a grandchild wants one of her ornaments, an object she believes they can cherish, she will give it to them. But when her son wants to buy her things for the house, sensible, useful things like a new Hoover, she finds fault with them, wants to take them back to the shop. Even with us, the anthropologists, if we give her something, it comes back double-fold.

The degree to which her roots and strategies have failed her becomes evident when one looks more closely at the plethora of things around her. At a superficial level, the sheer crowding of objects makes this living-room a quintessential example of Caribbean front rooms. But then, one comes to see that it is almost the exact opposite. Apart from one or two photos, there is almost nothing in the house that portrays any relationship with another person. While an actual Caribbean house would be full of paeans to one's mother, educational certificates and family photos, such things are absent here. Every object and image is something she has bought or made. Apart from one single photograph of her wedding, one of her mother and another of the grandchildren, there are no things that relate to the memory of others. There is absolutely nothing in the whole room to tell you that she once had a husband. There is no material evidence at all that she has a child. Apart from the one photograph, there is no other evidence even that she has six grandchildren. The place is not just crowded with stuff; these ornaments have crowded out, obliterated the presence of people. Furthermore, unlike any Caribbean home I can recall, there were simply no things in this room that anyone had ever bought for her – no gifts, except in the sense of gifts she had bought for herself. The place was utterly devoid of relationships. Once upon a time she made photo albums, but now she couldn't remember where they were, nor had she thought to show them to her grandchildren. She simply remarks that they would be far more interested in computer games. The telephone which is so hard to reach makes more sense now.

The room is rather a homage to Marcia's self-reliance. Too many people, men and women, husband and husband's sister, and others beside, seemed to offer something, only to reveal later the ways they could thereby hurt her. The only things Marcia can trust are those she has bought for herself or made for herself. Her aptitude for the suitcase trade reflects the way she tries to keep control over relationships. Most people view the market as alienating, while gifts are what form relationships. But for people like Marcia, the fact that she can sell things rather than entering into relationships of giving and receiving, suits the distance she seeks to retain from others. As she puts it, 'I like to buy and sell because I don't like to ask nobody things'. These inanimate people who populate her room are much less of a trial than real people; they are at your behest alone. 'When you're alone these amuse you. These are like your companions. Because I don't want any headache. If you've got a husband – I'm a divorcée – if you've got your partner, it's "where you've been so long?" You're being accused of things you don't even know about. I just want to come in and no problem.'

So, although the objects in this room look quite extraordinarily diverse and unrelated in theme and form, actually, compared to most people's living-room, this one has exceptional integrity and homogeneity. Because she has consistently refused the gifts of others, everything ultimately relates to her own personal taste in things. This collection is an uncompromising expression of herself and the personal integrity she feels she has preserved. Ornaments, unlike people, reflect back directly the care you give them. 'It's a lot of hard work but I always do it. When you see lots of dust you take it down and you shine it. And then you wipe the place down and then you put back the furniture. I wipe it down and then you feel happy. And that is what I like.' Even the idea that ornaments are there to entertain the grandchildren has faded, as they have got too old for such things – the youngest is twelve. Now it is only Marcia who is kept company and entertained by the world she has created for herself, a world within which she can be relatively at peace.

Most importantly, in the end Marcia did find a way to make a little happiness for herself. She found some rays of sun that she stored as a squirrel hoards nuts, till they filled every niche and crevice of her house. Once she was retired from work, she became more involved in the church, which took her under its wing and flew her from a damp chilly local hall to sunnier climes. For decades the world had been her solace, through its presence in her room on the TV screen. Marcia loved the news, and she could be as much an authority of the politics of international relations as on the bush medicines of her childhood. Now the church magically transported her, directly to all those places she had heard about but never expected to see in real life. There is still some bitterness, some contradictions. All those holiday periods she gave up while she was at work, in order to earn money: what for? Now she was too old to enjoy holidays with a partner or even in good health. But better late than never.

It is the tropical sun, the Mediterranean sun reflected in these myriads of objects that 'bright up the place', brought back from a dozen holidays with her church. The scenes of beaches, the bikinis and the sombreros, the rum and the palm trees, the matadors and the dancers: these have come back to evoke her stories of where she went and what happened to her, the stories that she can attest to and not just hear from others. Marcia keeps the room itself at almost tropical heat, with the windows closed and thick net curtains, as though to keep her population comfortable in their original climate. There is one more element of the display that gives her the capacity to make gifts and entertain others. Alcohol is a clear theme. All those miniature bottles, or those special ceramic shapes, with brandy, rum or some fluorescent liquor. The contents have been, and continue to be, offered to any adult visitors that come around, including us. This is the most recent layer of her life and, at present, her deepest concern is that, with fading health, she may start to miss out on the opportunities for further church visits to places she has yet to travel to – places she has now a great ambition to visit. So her room is a repudiation of most of her life, that is, of sacrifices that were never rewarded by others. It is filled instead with this unexpected after-life the church has already given her in the form of trips abroad.

Occasionally things have worked for Marcia: they have come together and made sense. The fact that these visits were all organised through the church is critical, because it helps to explain one final factor, which at first seemed odd. The objects that populate Marcia's room are not just strangely juxtaposed girls in swimsuits nestling against penguins; there is also a definite mingling between what anthropologists tend to separate out as the sacred and the profane. It is clear that for Marcia this distinction does not hold. Quite the contrary. When Marcia talks about how this collection of things developed, she starts with the most sacred image. She says: 'I like ornaments. You know, before I started to work, the first thing I bought was a chain and my crucifix. I didn't even buy clothes. But I just liked these sacred things. And from then on, that's it. And I love ornaments. Now I sit down and look.' Marcia has no issue with thinking about all manner of sacred images as 'ornaments'. The whole ensemble was dominated originally by the image of Jesus holding in his hands his own sacred heart. Most recently, though, he has been joined by her angel, equally high up, standing on top of the dresser. The rays that appear to radiate from Jesus actually do radiate from the angel. The incandescent colours and the kaleidoscope patterns make it seem like a figure winged with stained glass.

So, while all other gifts are spurned, Marcia has always allowed herself to be infused by one gift giver. To accept her own life, its hardships as well as its blessings, as coming from God. So far from meaningless kitsch, this living-room is a diorama of the meaning of her life. A collection of universal images representing the great diversity of humankind, infused, as it should be, with the image of its creator. It was more than apt that the very first of her travels was to Israel, where she felt it was suddenly revealed to her the bliss that travel could bring. This room is testimony to one of the most ubiquitous and powerful Christian injunctions: that the task is always to find ways to bring Jesus into one's life. Looked at carefully, the room tells us how Marcia has done just this. The final clue lies in her images of the Last Supper.

The Last Supper is probably the single most common picture found in houses throughout tropical Christendom. Through Africa, Asia, Latin America and the Pacific, it has become perhaps the most predictable image on display. It combines the sanctity of a powerful moment in Christian theology with an ideal of the extended meal of fellowship and friendship, something which is often part and parcel of traditional communal life. In Marcia's case, the conventional, white Last Supper is complemented by an Africanised version, with the disciples looking resplendent and pretty 'cool' in bright colors. This Last Supper is no longer the aloof, cold English vision of the conventional tapestry; it has the conviviality and warmth that, Marcia feels, is far more appropriate to the way the divine gives warmth to humanity. What might have been seen as kitsch is actually here a striving to convey directly, and to include, any visitor in Marcia's own vision of how the divine may be present in people's most ordinary, inexpensive things. Although brought up in other churches, it is no great surprise that Marcia ended up going to a Catholic one, for this is a quintessentially baroque room, not simply in the profusion of ornamentation but also in the way it engages with all the senses.

When Marcia's room is experienced as a whole, there is ultimately another figure that more than either the angel or the Last Supper effectively mediates the way religion inhabits her life. There is, above all, one moment when the divine is brought down to earth and Marcia is alive in a heaven whose image she has painstakingly created: this is Christmas. Because, of all the figures in the room the one that truly links her ideals of the Caribbean life, the life she may never have had but whose promise she would never betray, with her sense of Christian fellowship and faith, is Santa Claus. Santa Claus, the inverse and complement of Jesus, the rotund and the ascetic, the jocular and the serious. Jesus and Santa Claus together preside over her living-room, making it the meeting place between Israel and the Arctic. The final image of Marcia must be the one we began with, a vision of her sitting there drinking a little alcohol under the benign gaze of a dozen Santa Claus, from the place where Santa himself must be happiest, the Caribbean: where Santa can play his saxophone to a reggae beat, swing his hips, wine his waist and bring the joy of the Lord on the celebration of his birthday to all the peoples of the world.

HOME TRUTHS

If my own life was inspired by any one single figure from early childhood, it was probably the DJ John Peel. I've had a ridiculously happy adulthood, blessed by far more than my fair share of good fortune; but my childhood was lonely and miserable – not so different from that of John Peel himself, as it seems now, after reading his autobiography. There were weeks when the only thing I really looked forward to was the John Peel show. Through him, I had an early enchantment with musical dissonance, whether the weird American dissonance of bands such as Captain Beefheart or Frank Zappa, or the quirky English dissonance that John Peel tracked down across the land, in bands which flourished in some gawky exuberance for a few months and then disappeared. This was the music to which I would flail my limbs about in what was then called, quite properly, 'idiot dancing', though fortunately this was largely in the isolation of my room. Between the heavy metal and the transmuted folk or the silliness of the Bonzo Dog Doo Dah Band, I could dance through my childhood rages and jealousies and sadness and hatred. Most of all I danced through my frustration at not being able to talk to girls. Well, in truth, at not being able to find a chance to have sex with girls, except every half an hour in my own imagination. Somehow John Peel's music not only expressed the dissonance between desire and actual life, but did so in a manner that mined the deep enjoyment and humour to be found within the sheer absurdity of a frustrated life.

Then for many years I had to do without John Peel, as my work led me to try to comprehend the dissonance of the world. Spending two years in the Solomon Islands, then a further two in India and finally two more intermittently in Trinidad, my research was devoted to understanding the diversity of contemporary humanity through its material form. There were few places with as little in common as the Solomon Islands and India. As an anthropologist, I was instructed to avoid making judgements; to use these ethnographic experiences to question my own stance and expectations; and see these as just as fortuitous as the happenstance of being born a Jew or English, when it could just as well have been Trobriand Island or Kwakiutl. The expectation was that one spent sufficient time with some other people until there was at least the beginning of empathy; a sense of why they might understand the world in the way they do, believe what they believe, feel what they feel and take so much of their own world for granted.

Then, in view of my wife's ever more demanding work and our responsibility for two children, I could no longer spend these extended periods abroad. On my return, I found that John Peel had apparently transformed into two, at first seemingly irreconcilable, people. There was still the radical John Peel insisting on playing for us the most extreme, experimental, imaginative, music; anything but mainstream. Some of this was magically good and some so excruciatingly awful that somehow it was magical too. But then, on Saturday mornings, there was the same John Peel hosting another radio show, called *Home Truths*. This became a programme which starred everyman and everywoman: people who appeared on the show precisely in order to express the quirky charm of a certain ordinariness. A programme where being ordinary was itself the virtue – the virtue of being able to respond to events, rather than people who claimed to be extraordinary or who precipitated events. Thereby courage was revealed as instant and unthinking; humour consisted in appreciating an absurd yet unavoidable sequence of events. People marvelled at the way a bureaucratic process, or some initially simple car journey, had led to a landscape of experiences vastly beyond intentionality or intelligibility. And all such moments had become stories that John

Peel sanctified with his own all-encompassing humanity and concern. A benign transcendent being with a Liverpool accent who could accept and embrace any form of humanity with the blessing of simply being interesting.

My response to the apparent contradiction was to apply what I had learnt about anthropology to John Peel. On the surface, a life-long attachment to the most difficult and radical otherness of music seemed the very opposite to this focus on the ordinary life of every person. But such contradictions were the meat and drink of my own academic life. Very often, when one encountered things that seemed at first to be entirely contradictory, one searched, to find conections and often found they expressed an underlying structure of values. Explaining social and cultural contradictions was part of the fun, crossword-solving aspect of anthropology.

It was evident that, for John Peel, there was no contradiction between his two radio shows. Underneath was a consistent logic, a willingness to embrace the creativity that could be there in music but also in responding to the unexpected possibilities that life constantly throws up in one's path. John Peel saw that the everyday consumption of unexpected events was active rather than passive. This creative response could produce its own forms of quirky dissonance, which we enjoy celebrating because on the one hand it echoes the everyday rhythms of life, on the other it creates from these all sorts of unexpected developments. Something that he seemed to see equally in the music. There may be thousands of people fishing, fetching children from school or buying tickets for a train; just as there are thousands playing base or keyboard. But once in a while some variant on the familiar theme produced something that sounded extraordinary, whether in the form of a song or a tale of an experience. Something you would never have thought could emerge from those repetitive foundations. Thanks to John Peel, I would get to hear new tracks from Led Zeppelin through to Radiohead, but also what turned up unexpectedly when someone was digging in their garden or going on a date. Most recently there has been something of a rapprochement to these forms. Reflecting on the music scene at the time of our fieldwork, it progressed from Franz Ferdinand and Kaiser Chiefs through to Arctic Monkeys and Lily Allen. There seemed to be an increasing delight in lyrics based on everyday encounters. Not a conscious tribute, but a trend I think would have met with John Peel's approval.

So the holistic ideal of reconciling opposites may be applied to societies or to individuals. It certainly seemed to be required in the case of Murray, the hedonistic Buddhist. Murray had led quite a peripatetic life, living in a whole variety of squats and council estates, mixing with a wide variety of women in largely uncommitted relationships. Somewhere along the way he had a child, who doesn't live with him. It's not that Murray was incapable of commitment; it's just that much of that commitment had been to drugs, motorbikes and music. It's hard to be specific about the drugs, but in terms of music it was, above all, the Clash and the Stranglers' albums that remain high points of his life. When we first met Murray we entered into a very long conversation about pop music, because, when we broached the topic of loss, it was the loss of his musical heros that swam into view. It also seemed to create a kind of triangle. Fiona and Murray mourned at length the loss of Joe Strummer from the Clash and reminisced about the way he had been memorialised at Glastonbury. Murray and myself mourned with equal passion the loss of John Peel who had been a key figure for him, as for me. Between Fiona and myself there was in retrospect, a mutual envy: on my part, of her contemporary Glastonbury experiences; on hers, of the bands I had seen live when a teenager.

Music formed an essential part of Murray's relationship to his own family influences. He talked about his father's passion for Bob Dylan. Murray was always impressed that his father had loads and loads of albums – a commitment to musical accumulation which was much rarer then. And the commitment to Bob Dylan became a constant, a leitmotif in his life: any kind of anniversary and he would play Bob Dylan. The ideal of a memorial to Bob Dylan is a little problematic. After all, Bob Dylan isn't even dead. He recently popped up very much alive, as an author, and previously as the subject of Martin Scorsese's documentary. But that didn't stop Murray's dad from appropriating him as memory and a mourning for past times. And that, in turn, gave Murray a model for caring for the loss and change in the music that dominates much of his life. So in their own way these musical figures are turned into objects that stand both for the death of times and for the continuity of times. Murray describes the monument made out of car exhaust spares to Joe

Strummer at Glastonbury and, as we talk, a monument to John Peel forms in my head. A collage of everyday objects, but juxtaposed in a way that exposes and confronts us with the creativity and dissonance that lies there in ordinary things, perhaps Marcel Duchamp let loose in Tesco.

Murray was not unappreciative of the sound quality and convenience of CDs, but certainly missed the covers of vinyl, of which there were still around two hundred in the room. With the shelves of vinyl, CDs, the loudspeakers and the music system, music seemed to have a material presence commensurate with its importance to Murray. For him, as for so many others, it also represents a collation of his own past, since it is through music above all that he relates to particular women he has known, times he has been through, the best parties and the weirdest places. Many of these, given his experience with drugs, were places he encountered somewhere within his own head. Yet this materiality of music stands oddly juxtaposed with the other primary presence in his room, which is that of images and paraphernalia connected with Buddhism. Just as Murray could spend hours talking about his favourite bands, so he can talk with considerable knowledge about the attributes of a particular Bodhisattva or incarnation of the Buddha: precisely how they catch demons and protect people, how and why the artist must finish by painting the eyes. Some of the ornaments are junky tourist pieces of the kind you might pick up from Kandy to Kathmandu; others more serious pieces, which their creator might have seen as worthy of spiritual consideration.

Buddhism is the other side of Murray's life. At least to his own satisfaction, Murray is a full-on Buddhist. As the winter closes in on London, he migrates south, to spend up to several months at a Buddhist retreat, somewhere in a warmer clime. The fact that this behaviour serves equally as an expression of his hedonism and as its complete rejection is just what makes it entirely plausible. There he will chill out, living in a cave or simple hut, with only solar power for electricity and virtually no possessions; with water only from cisterns, and heat from wood-burning stoves. Helping to construct a stupa (Buddhist reliquary), he gradually releases himself from what he calls the neurotic cravings of the world. Freeing his head from the news, which, in its daily manifestation at fixed points of the day, whether in newspapers, on radio or on television, has increasingly lost its content and turned instead into a kind of incessant ritual in his life. Instead he will be somewhere that is nowhere, contemplating rocks and sky. To be honest, it never quite sounds as the Buddha intended. When Murray contemplates the sky from his Buddhist retreat, he is as likely to be trying to recognise each planet (a technique that he picked up from a relative with a PhD in astronomy) as contemplate possible endless rebirths. He has a sense of transcendence, but he has never quite left his physical body – at least not to the degree that occurred with that incredibly strong, US-imported acid he tried in Glasgow. Murray couldn't possibly say if his retreat was a cheap holiday, a hard discipline, a muck-about, or an excision of desire. A bit like the English weather from which he has escaped, it's probably many things, often on the same day. But, if enlightenment requires complete detachment, then Murray still has quite a few rebirths to go.

So it seems entirely appropriate that Murray should tell us about these Buddhist retreats while nursing, along with both of us, a succession of pints. This was after trekking some distance to find a pub which possessed what we could agree was a decent beer – pretty much my ideal fieldwork setting. My own convoluted means of legitimating the strange mix of discipline and hedonism, egotism and empathy that is my life is rather different from his, but I have no problem at all in recognising their common nature and contradictions. Murray lives in modern times and has been able to encounter a vast diversity of experiences. The drugs went from uppers to downers; he has seen the ecstatic and the casualties, including the fatalities. But he also knew his beer, and his fags, and his mates, and his Saturday nights. And his friends might work in garages or never work at all, or they might have PhDs from Cambridge and know people who know people. Out of all these myriad possibilities and experiences, which, in their mere expanse, could have left him blasé or wasted, he has developed certain commitments. For instance his music and his Buddhism have become as rich as his ability to spend time cultivating them at the expense of those other interests, which necessarily had to be sidelined and become mere backdrop to the genres in which he has chosen to invest himself. Using resources from his family background in Ireland, from his father's relationship to Bob Dylan, from his own experiences of music and silence, he has found ways of reconciling the particularities of his interests, allowing them to form balances that enable him to visit certain extremes without falling off the edge. One can only try and struggle to piece together his unique jigsaw from these continuities and discontinuities. Is there a link between the original Irish Catholic religiosity of his family and his relationship to Buddhism; and if there is, is this evidence of continuity or of discontinuity? I have no idea.

All his passions for experience, material and immaterial, cluster around him in his room. The CDs, the brass icons, the photographs, all talk loudly about him without prompting. Other objects only start to sound when they echo his narrative, for instance the rocks that have come back with him from one of his retreats. But then here, as in all these portraits, there are also the light fittings, the bed sheets, the plastic bits and pieces above the fireplace, the teddy bear, the candle, the castor plant, the jeans and the sofa-bed, the glass and the box file. Given more time and space to paint his portrait, these mundane quiet statements would soften the more insistent signs, helping us to place him back in the domestic order of the day-to-day breakfast and dinner, pub and shop, work and television. And this would have been appropriate since Murray is settling now; this girlfriend may, just may, become *the* girlfriend. He now works regularly and it's genuine, good work, helping teenagers with problems that he, after thirty years of being a teenager, understands better than most. He uses a phrase from his Buddhism: the importance of a 'right livelihood'. He feels he has turned at least some lives around.

If Ben the orientalist married materiality with Buddhism, then Murray has gone one step further, to become the hedonistic Buddhist. It never occurred to me that a person would find their hedonism through Buddhism; officially, the two are not on speaking terms. But there was always going to be some bloody-minded Londoner who didn't give a toss about what Buddhism was or was not supposed to be, and, if making spirituality the conduit of hedonism (or the other way round) made sense in his life, then that's the way it was going to be. And Murray showed precisely that it could make sense. Doing ecstasy, or doing Yoga, or going on a retreat which doubles as a holiday are simply what works for him as experience; experiences which flow in and out of materiality, such as the relationship between listening to music and appreciating the CD cover, between the memory of a woman and her photograph, between a little pill and the dreams. The gaudy multi-limbed figure of a Bodhisattva is both inspirational and fun. An extraordinarily sensual image of transcendence. As in so many modern lives, Murray has achieved consistency through contradictions. But I can't help thinking that Londoners do this particularly well.

Epilogue

IF THIS IS MODERN LIFE - THEN WHAT IS THAT?

If this is a street in contemporary London and these are its people, what, then, is modern life, and what is the nature of that humanity which lives in these our times? My PhD thesis was set in a village in North India in the 1980s, which seemed at the time to approximate the traditional object of anthropological enquiry. No one within that village appeared to contest, though they did debate, the fundamental religious cosmology by which practically everything in life could ultimately be understood. Whether they were Hindus or Muslims, there was an overarching sense of God, or Gods, who determined matters ranging from why people lived on earth to how many times one should eat, bathe, pray, be married, and why the crops failed in one year but flourished in another. That was my first study in material culture. I discovered that, even though it was not evident to the villagers, the pattern and order exhibited by the range of pottery made in that village – for instance the shape of both the rim and the body – could be related to underlying religious and social orders of purity and pollution or the caste system.

The foundations of modern anthropology and the other academic disciplines were built on the terrain of secularisation and the Enlightenment. This has reversed the direction of causation. For these Indian villagers, the cause of this order of the world was divine, and they were merely one of its manifestations. In the social science founded by figures such as Durkheim, it is humanity which created religion and cosmology. It is not the Gods who demand that we undertake rituals; we create these Gods in order to justify the rituals which give us the fundamental bonds and obligations that allow us to live together as social beings and to legitimate the orders and laws by which we live in society.

Social science, whether consciously or not, aimed not only to explore but also to enact the Durkheimian view of the world. The phrase 'social science' affirms the existence of something called society, which can be the subject of scientific study. Durkheim himself was concerned that, if modern life was lived under the conditions posed by Nietzsche's death of God, then people needed to keep faith with some alternative transcendent object – ideally, society itself. Otherwise, as is implied by his study of suicide, there was a danger that life itself would seem, and indeed become, pointless.

As a result, while social science began in a spirit of Enlightenment radicalism, it has inevitably become the source of an increasingly conservative view of modern life. It has been practised under the auspices of this ideal of 'society', with the corresponding fear that, if modern life becomes, as it were, too modern, then it would fragment into mere isolated individualisms and lose any sense of purpose or order. There have been several candidates employed in fostering the mantle of a common identity. For example, nationalism bonded people through their common relation to the nation, while communism attempted to unite people under a global ideology of equality in labour. Modernism enjoined us in a common search for future progress. For social science the liberal market might be a threat, if it reduces us to individuals who merely express ourselves to the degree that we choose a particular commodity. Although perhaps we could be united by the ideological commitment to the market itself?

The street presented in this book does not, however, suggest that concepts such as society or community play much of an immediate role in the lives of people who reside in a modern metropolis such as contemporary London. In a way, the state operates too efficiently. The underlying forces which provide basic education, health services, public order, the media and the condition for the development of an economy can deliver our daily goods without us having to know anything much about how this came to be. We tend to be aware of these forces only when they break down and disappoint our quite extraordinarily high expectations of them. Politics is reduced to that which we blame for whatever and whoever lets us down. We do not seem to require any active allegiance to, or alignment with, some abstract image of society or community, which lies closer to our daily lives. There are some vestiges of collectivity in the street, for instance the church and the pub, but most people make limited use of these. Other areas not covered by this study, such as sites of work and collective leisure, may be more sociable; but equally they may not be. On the smaller side-streets, households give at least the impression that people know each other, while on Stuart Street itself this is rare. We need to face up to the degree to which in contemporary London, people do not live their lives in order to accord either with the cosmology of a religion or with the cosmology of a belief in society. For the most part, these are the random juxtapositions of households, as determined by forces such as house prices, transport systems and proximity to work, school and leisure. The political economy determines these circumstances, but not how people live within them.

It is not my intention to claim that society is dead, or that God is dead. It is, rather, that the goals we might attribute to religion and society are increasingly accomplished without recourse to any explicit symbol of either community or God. This is not, however, a portrait of a broken whole. The people of this street are no less ethical, or concerned to obey the basic laws of the land which protect each from the other, than the people of the Indian village I have studied, or the Londoners who lived through the two world wars. There are good people and evil people; lives that are full and empty; but that was always true. A religious individual may still argue that all our actions require a moral determination based on the constant re-interpretation of religious ideals to fit our historical condition. We accept, for the most part, the need for a state that should operate both with a measure of consensus and with a measure of tolerance of diversity; a state dedicated to arguable levels of redistribution, to welfare, and to the protection and education of citizens. We can argue vociferously for a balance between redistribution and autonomy, fairness, oppression and meritocracy, faith and science. But we seem to argue within the frame of an increas-

ingly accepted liberalism, which assumes that, inasmuch as actions do
not result in any harm to others, people are free to be and do what the
hell they want.

I think that this amounts to a repudiation of much of Durkheim and
of the initial premise of social science. People do not need to believe in
society; they may not even bother to vote and they may treat politics
more as a spectator sport, on a par with football. Their fundamental
allegiance may be to Ireland or Jamaica, or it may increasingly be split
between several different locations; but it is not necessarily related to the
place where they happen to live and whose laws they feel thereby con-
strained to obey. Many have allegiances that are either fluid or unim-
portant. Take, for example, Simon and Jacques: they seem to regard
Tallinn, the capital of Estonia, as in effect a distant London suburb,
which they might choose to live in next. Marcia may go to a Catholic
instead of a Pentecostal church because it is closer to her house, probably to the consternation of both branches of Christianity. We live in a
world where much that shouldn't be the case according to the rules of
social science and of competing ideologies is, and, more profoundly, it
doesn't seem to matter much that it is.

Where perhaps social science was also wrong – but then so was liberalism – was in assuming that the alternative to society would be isolated
individuals, defined through choices – whether of commodities or of a
political party. The very concept of the individual, constructed as the
other to society, was just as subject to ideologies, for example that of
liberalism. Under liberalism the individual represented a fundamental
unit that would function as a viable alternative to God or society, becoming in itself the basic point of reference. In different ways, sociologists
such as Nikolas Rose, anthropologists such as Marilyn Strathern and
philosophers such as Charles Taylor have explored the history of individualism and its consequences. But in the portraits presented here I see
limited evidence of any belief in, or cult of, the individual *per se*. On the
whole, most people seem to feel that being solely an individual is, largely
speaking, a failure in life. I don't want to proclaim that the individual is
dead either. There are some people, such as Aidan the exhibitionist, who
do see their individual lives as the project to which they largely devote
themselves. A project emblematic of modern freedom. Some of the
younger participants who also participated in this study seem to espouse

this ideal of individualism, at least in practice, while breaking away from their family. But, later on, most people seem to be individuals by default rather than by design. Many, such as Di, treasure some autonomy, but only to a limited extent. Individualism *per se* is most fully equated with loneliness. The extreme cases are older men such as George, Harry and Stan.

My inclination is to start from somewhere else. Suppose we put to one side the history of philosophy, social science and religion and turn to the real people living in the real street of our study and ask of them: 'Oh, people of Stuart Street, tell us what should, and what does, matter in life?' If we asked them what is the difference between a full life and an empty life, I suspect we would hear a surprisingly uniform response. It would focus upon whether or not they experienced a number of significant and fulfilling relationships. If we imagine this to be their response, then perhaps our primary concern should follow theirs, and begin not with society or the individual, but with the nature and quality of these relationships. We would then recognise that individuals are, in large measure, the products, and not merely the agents, of those relationships.

Were the people of Stuart Street to assert their allegiance to significant relationships, they would almost certainly have in mind relationships with other people. Their desire is for good relationships with children, with parents and the wider family, with lovers or spouses (sometimes lovers and spouses), with colleagues and with good and true friends. Beyond these, hopefully, some would also assert a desired relationship to wider collectivities as an ethical commitment; a relationship of responsibility to future generations, as in preserving the environment, or some concern for people from less privileged backgrounds. Although these portraits show some people acting strongly on these ideals, others pay them merely lip service. But this book is intended to highlight another set of relationships they would be less likely to mention and which only emerged because I chose to ask about them. That is their relationships with objects. The theoretical ideas I explore in my academic publications derive from a dialectical perspective, in which material objects are viewed as an integral and inseparable aspect of all relationships. People exist for us in and through their material presence. An advantage of this unusual perspective is that sometimes these apparently mute forms can be made to speak more easily and eloquently to the nature of relationships than can those with persons.

So the first two conclusions of this book affirm the centrality of relationships to modern life, and the centrality of material culture to relationships. This leads then to a question as to the larger context within which such relationships are constituted. In my PhD on pottery in an Indian village I showed how the order of everyday objects was systematically consistent with the ideal order of religious life. Whatever a person does, whether cooking or moving from one room to another, the order of things in time and space reinforces their basic beliefs about the natural order of the world. In this way everyday ritual is also an aesthetic, something which gives order, balance and harmony to the world people live in. The anthropologist Pierre Bourdieu argued that our orientation to everyday objects was one of the main reasons why we accept as natural and unchallenged the routines and expectations of life. He, too, located a systematic order in everyday things among Muslim Berbers in North Africa. More importantly, he argued that the very same underlying order could be found in their use of agricultural implements, their calendar, or their expectations of marriage partners. People do not need explicit educational systems or schools in order to learn how to become a typical Berber or Inuit, because everything they touch and do is infused with that underlying order that gives them their expectations of the world, and which are characteristic of their particular society. The order of things – how to sit, be polite, play and dress – is their education, socialising them to become typical of their people. An anthropologist does not start from individuals who create their worlds. We start from the historical processes and material order which create those characteristic individuals and their expectations. In short, material culture matters because objects create subjects much more than the other way around. It is the order of relationship to objects and between objects that creates people through socialisation whom we then take to exemplify social categories, such as Catalan or Bengali, but also working class, male, or young.

Having established this for societies that justify themselves by tradition and religion, Bourdieu argues much the same for secular French society of the 1960s. We are taught to believe we are free individuals who each choose what we like because we possess individual taste. But actually, as market researchers could tell us, so-called individual tastes are highly predictable. People in manual labour with limited education predictably favoured substantial food that fill you up, art that depicted intrinsically beautiful subjects, identifiable celebrities rather than more abstract film directors. Middle classes, such as a schoolteacher, by contrast preferred explicitly moral foods, that today might be organic produce or wholefoods, while someone in advertising favoured an aestheticised *nouvelle cuisine*. Each class defined taste in opposition to the other. So, just like the Berbers, French people of the 1960s had preferences and expectations which reflected their original socialisation into what they were supposed to like, together with the values and tastes inculcated by formal education, while still believing, largely incorrectly, that they, as individuals, have chosen their personal lifestyles on the basis of individual taste.

On the evidence of research in France in the 1960s, Bourdieu could still assume a certain degree of homogeneity and norms that could be defined by systematic opposition. This has not disappeared. There are still many traits and behaviours which similarly characterise contemporary English society as a whole, and may sometimes be quickly adopted by new immigrants. This is true especially in England outside of London. But, if ever we lived in a post-society, whose primary focus is upon diversity rather than shared or systematically ordered culture, then the London street of this book is such a post-society. In other writings and research I have considered the surprising generalisations one can make about Londoners. This book, however, has deliberately focused on diversity rather than homogeneity. Some of this diversity reflects that of plural, or multi-cultural, societies. People who still carry with them expectations based on the long traditions of particular cultural orders. José has his Mediterranean way of doing things, and it is quite likely that these remain closer to the customs of the time of his childhood, than those who remained in the land of his birth but have since changed. Similarly, the way Elia gives out her emotions and is hurt when these are not reciprocated by others in the same manner was immediately recognised by a Greek reader as quintessentially Greek. The way Mrs Stone gives her life to the building of a house in Jamaica is not simply a return to Jamaica but a continuation of the way the home defines life as a project for most Jamaicans. The way Mary and Hugh relate the dead to anecdotes told in the pub, has continuity with traditions of behaviour in Irish pubs. Again, the way Jenny decorates her house with brass and china or her old grandfather clock, and Charles continues traditions learnt in his boarding school, or James and Quentin enjoy their gardening and their pubs all illustrate orientations and orders we recognise as English or British.

Such general characterisations accord with that – now rather abused – term, 'culture', where it implies a generalised set of customs and orders that pertain to particular people of a specific time and place: Irish culture, English culture, French culture. We can even apply these labels to unprecedented actions. A principal point in Malcolm's portrait was to suggest that the use of his laptop remains consistent with the beliefs and customs of Australian Aboriginal societies. In other recent researches I have studied the impact of the mobile phone on low-income Jamaican families and the way the internet is used in Trinidad. In these publications the emphasis was on surprising continuities in the way people deal with new objects. However, in Jamaica and Trinidad culture remains, relatively speaking, the common possession of neighbours, who all continue, for example, to celebrate Christmas in an almost identical fashion, while on Stuart Street there is a juxtaposition of a whole host of different cultural expectations.

In a London street, Jamaica, India and Australia are no longer thousands of miles apart, but just a few doors away. For some, ideas of traditional culture have become optional identity markers. Jorge will cook for others, on occasion, an exemplary Brazilian meal, but he derives part of his Englishness from the pop music he was attached to as a child, while still in Brazil. Class or gender identity may be primary, or may be something to be asserted only in certain circumstances, and actually shifted because of a change in occupation or sexuality. Overall, then, identity and culture, in the way I have just used these terms, increasingly look vestigial rather than determinant of the order of things.

So, while some portraits show continuity with categories such as region of origin or class, others seem to take delight in not according with any such general traditions, but more or less make up customs as they go along. Ben, with his Feng-Shui, takes culture as a kind of off-the-shelf system, which does not accord with any specific older religion, but is an amalgamation of generic Eastern ideals. He creates not only something he can believe in, but something which may well be efficacious in his treatment of others. Even more impressive are those who seem to start from scratch (pun intended), such as Charlotte with her tattoos. She has created her own material order, seeing the potential of her increasing attachment, successively, to clothes, piercings and tattoos to devise something which is as internally consistent and as meaningful to her as a religion. Marcia, betrayed by the failure of her personal relationships and of cultural continuities between London and the Caribbean, has built her world from souvenirs of her travels. Sharon, through her wrestling and her child, has repaired a life torn from under her. Di keeps herself together through her home; and Dave would have fallen apart, almost certainly would have died, but for the same resource. Most such material systems are also forged in relationships with other people, such as between Ben and his wife, or between Sharon and her child, but some are constructed in isolation. In many, it is relationships to things and to the order of things that dominate – as with Daniel and his owl, Stan with his pornographic images or Marjorie and her living-room.

The term 'things' in this study is deliberately generic. There are whole schools of academic thought, such as phenomenology, that would privilege particular things, for instance the body or the house (or space), and would see these as the core to the larger material aesthetic described here. I do not share these views. There are portraits here, such as those of Dave and Di, which are centred on the house itself; without which their lives might have fallen apart. As in the case of Charles, this relationship can be equally emotional, moral and financial. Charlotte's medium of cosmological order consists almost entirely of what can be done to, and with, her body. Sharon found it hard to mix with people who didn't share her extraordinary commitment to the cultivation of the body. But I see no reason to highlight homes and bodies as against pets, lovers, kitchens, friends or religion. A clear conclusion of this volume should be that we cannot assume or presume the genres which constitute the relationships to which lives are devoted and through which people feel fulfilled.

A similar point may be made with regard to psychology. If anthropology has tended towards a cultural determinacy, psychology has tended towards a parental determinacy. In some versions of psychology and psychoanalysis, for instance in the writings of John Bowlby, the pattern of all attachment is determined by the first attachment. One is saved by having a secure base and doomed without one. At least in its vulgarised versions, this comes close to blaming mothers for bad children. It also ignores other societies, such as Bali, where children are brought up through systematic forms of separation and rejection by parents – a strategy deemed essential in order to civilise them properly.

As seen in these portraits, this relationship to parents is sometimes one of systematic reproduction, but just as often one of systematic repudiation. The children of Mr and Mrs Clarke seem unusual in their concern for basic civil responsibilities. They care about more people than is common. This seems most likely to reflect the example of their parents and the values they were taught as children. On the other hand, Marina uses the unlikely vehicle of McDonalds' Happy Meals to repudiate in systematic fashion certain aspects of her parents' values, as does Sharon the wrestler. Donald has more comfortable links with his grandparents than with his divorced parents. These people are all English by origin, and yet it is hard to see them as reflecting some common pattern.

In any case, unlike much psychology, this book allows for the possibility that parents are not particularly influential. The primary impact on Charles was not his parents but his boarding school. In growing up, the influence that supersedes that of parents and school may be lovers and friends, but it may also be the culture of rock music, a pet dog, or alcoholism. It may be one's work as a retail buyer, as a carpenter, or in social services. Any of these influences, just as much as that initial influence of parents, may be constructive or destructive. Finally, there is no evidence that people end up becoming 'fully formed' at some point in their lives. As in the case of Peggy and Cyril, the most significant influence of all can occur when one is in one's sixties and all previous influences become completely re-configured in order to fit better with a new and now determining influence on one's life. Marjorie stands out as someone who seems to just keep on growing with life's experience.

I do not see this street as a sample; these people are not representative of any group. There is no particular reason why in this street there are so many gay couples, or several catastrophic single men present. Social science too often just ends up with whatever category it starts with. If you study gay couples, then it is hard not to conclude with regard to sexuality. While, as far as I can tell, being gay has no particular bearing on any other generalisation one would make about these individuals. My main concern in this study is not what one learns from knowing the class, gender and origin of people, but primarily what one doesn't learn from these things. Because most of the diversity that is found in this book does not reduce to sociological categories or labels, or for that matter colloquial categories or labels.

The terms 'influence', or indeed 'relationship', seem rather too general to give much by way of insight. One evident finding is that, if we ask what leads to a more profound shift in a person's perception of themselves, it mostly occurs when several influences reinforce each other rather than as a result of one single cause. This, I think, is part of what accounts for people's uniqueness. Take for example Sharon. Sharon was the first participant I wrote about, in the quest to understand the hundred households that make up this study. Ever since, I can't help but think of Sharon as representing my 'typical' participant. This is significant because there is no way I would have expected to meet one individual who was simultaneously involved in professional wrestling, being a night-club bouncer and training teachers in sociology – not to mention the unusual relationship to her child. Sharon became my typical participant because, in an entirely arbitrary fashion, she stands for the astonishing diversity and uniqueness of all those who participated in this project. It just happened to be this street; these happened to be the people I met; she happened to come first in my writing up. In the end everyone turned out to be like Sharon – that is, typically untypical.

What makes Sharon typical is that her life is overdetermined, meaning that it takes a particular collision of factors to account for what she does and who she becomes. Was she a wrestler because she was smallest in class, because of her talent for gym, or because of her parents' oppressive ideals of femininity? Most likely, it is the conjuncture of causes that makes for the effects. Sharon is also typical in that she shows that merely to have ideas and insights about oneself and about such causes doesn't produce anything that could be called a post-modern consciousness – consciousness that distances you from yourself and creates some sort of ironic or alienated relationship to the world. Sharon teaches sociology, but still finds she has to move furniture around constantly, so as to clear her head. Knowing what she is doing doesn't seem to reduce the need to do it. Ordering and re-ordering things is the stuff of life for Sharon, an integral part of her relationship to her parents, to her child, and also to herself – which reminds us how Mead argued that the self is always simultaneously both subject and object to us. There is nothing particularly ironic, or alienated, or post-modern about Sharon, or indeed about the vast majority of these people.

So the next conclusion is that social science, and especially the version of it which took form around the notion of 'post-modern', seems entirely mistaken in assuming that the decline of society and culture would lead to disordered fragmentation. On the contrary, among the things once accomplished by religion or by the state but now increasingly delegated downwards, to individuals and households, is the responsibility for creating order and cosmology. It will sound cryptic when it is put so tersely (the sociologist Habermas provides the detail), but dialectical philosophy regards modern people as just as authentic as those of the past. An order, moral or aesthetic, is still an authentic order even if one creates it for oneself and makes it up as one goes along, rather than just inheriting it as tradition or custom. Indeed, for Hegel, having responsibility for creating the order one lives by was a mark of the authenticity of that order.

So people are not fully determined culturally, or parentally; but neither are they free agents who choose who they may become. Through the reinforcement of various influences at particular times, certain traits and styles develop which come to characterise them, not as individuals but as networks of relationships. This produces what I have called, at different times in this book, an aesthetic. I do not use this term to implicate the arts. Rather, it refers to pattern – sometimes an overall organisational principle that may include balance, contradiction and the repetition of certain themes in entirely different genres and settings. An example was the way I came to understand the carpenter Daniel. I started with observations about the manner in which his daughter displays her soft toys on the shelf. From this, one could see a particular order, which then seemed to hold for room decorating more generally, but also for the logic of Daniel's form of parenting and for the emotional repertoires of the household. Similarly, as one looked more closely at the walls of the hall and living-room inside the flat of Mary and Hugh (the former publicans), one could discern a particular way in which they bring together the dispersed elements of their lives, from religion to work to family, and make something that both transcends these categories and yet gives them their own integrity. Sometimes this seems more of a process than of an order; take for example the way Marjorie learns from life through accumulation – whether of foster children, clothes or images of her family – which, so far from producing materialism, refines her skill in making people feel loved. Often, as Elia with clothing, graves and jewellery, or Charlotte with her tattoos, a person creates an aesthetic by exploiting the different potentials they perceive in the specific properties of each material medium, to create an overall cosmology based on the complementarity between these genres. As an embodied expression, tattoos are more extreme than piercings, which are in turn more extreme than clothing. The critical balance, or opposition, may also be between people. This is very common in households dominated by couples; such as the relation between James's quirkiness and Quentin's systematisation, or between Simon and Jacques. Sometimes it looks more like a triangle because of the huge significance of a child, as in the case of Anna, Louise and their son, or Daniel and his wife and daughter. In turn, these triangles grow into more complex networks, as between the Clarke family and their wider society, or, for Dave, between photographs, music, heroin and the house.

The point is that household material culture may express an order which in each case seems equivalent to what one might term a social cosmology, if this was the order of things, values and relationships of a society. A very little cosmology perhaps, when it pertains only to one person or household, and one that will only in a few cases ever develop into an abstract philosophy or system of belief both to legitimate and to explain itself. Most people are not called upon to explain themselves with this degree of consistency, even to themselves. Nevertheless, such a cosmology is holistic rather than fragmented, and though holistic may include contradictions. Although the focus is on the interior space and on intimate relationship, these aesthetics are not isolated from the wider world. They may conjoin with outside influences, an occupation such as retail purchasing for Donald, school, as in the case of Charles, or one's larger responsibilities to the world, as a magistrate or school governor, as with Mr and Mrs Clarke. It remains the case that an aesthetic can be almost entirely religious, as for the devout Christians who appear in this volume, or a continuity of traditional cultural norms. But this book makes it clear that other people, who no longer follow religious or cultural traditions, may still demonstrate an integrity as to the form and pattern of their relationships; a style that we recognise as theirs. As such it is possible for them to be apprehended through the kind of analysis we would once have applied to a particular society and religion. In many cases, this aesthetic, with its repetitions and familiarities, provides a comfort to people on a par with the comfort that Durkheim associated with religion and society. But, in the same way it can also be a burden, a constraint, and a mystery.

This study is fundamentally anthropological rather than psychological. It concerns structures of relationships that are external, relationships to people and to things. It could still be regarded as the study of societies, but just of very, very small societies. These days, a household, and sometimes one individual, has to create for themselves something of the principles and practice of cosmology and economy, which we used to think of in terms of a society. This is possible because resources such as our material wealth, our relative autonomy and educational foundations give us means far beyond those of individuals in the past, and perhaps equivalent to those of larger social groups. Certainly, this volume reveals results that may be tragic, contradictory, oppressed and unfulfilled; but anthropologists have found that societies too can be tragic, contradictory, oppressed and unfulfilled. The innovation lies in appreciating that the creative possibilities of tiny instances of humanity rival the diversity of societies traditionally studied by anthropologists. So, for me, this street is New Guinea and every household in this book is a tribe.

To summarise: the first point is that the effective nature of the modern state and our increasing level of resources grant us a creative autonomy. We merge cultural and parental influences, normative social orders and other ingredients, which we add as we go along. This is essential in the conditions of modern life, where households may combine people from different points of origin or with very different concerns and tastes. Households have become more like societies which create a cosmology, to a greater or lesser degree linked to wider religious and cultural norms. So, even while anthropology may be losing one object of enquiry – a relatively coherent and consistent object called society – the same perspectives might be applicable to the household, or even to the individual.

The second point is that the alternative to society is not a fragmented individual but people who strive to create relationships to both people and things. These relationships include material and social routines and patterns which give order, meaning and often moral adjudication to their lives; an order which, as it becomes familiar and repetitive, may also be a comfort to them. I have called this order an aesthetic, although it often remains tentative, contradictory, multiple and constantly changing. But then this is true, if on a different scale, of larger cosmologies and aesthetic orders, such as society or religion. Anthropology may still construct generalisations based on observing a surprising homogeneity amongst people of very different origins, as I argued with regard to shopping in my previous study of a London street. But this book emphasises that attention to London's unprecedented heterogeneity allows us to learn from the diversity of people in the same way we once learned from the diversity of peoples.

Yet somehow all this academic debate remains cold. One of my reasons for writing in a largely non-academic style was my hope that the portraits themselves convey something of the warmth of this humanity. The aesthetic form that has been located in these portraits is not simply a repetitive system of order; it is above all a configuration of human values, feelings and experiences. They form the basis on which people judge the world and themselves. It is this order that gives them their confidence to legitimate, condemn and appraise. These are orders constructed out of relationships, and emotions and feelings run especially deep in relationships. Whether these are to a collection of objects, divorced parents, the landscape of a living-room, a pet dog, or the intricacies in the life of a stable couple. Participants in this study often used the encounter as an occasion to re-examine and, to some degree, re-evaluate their lives. This book tries not to judge people, but does recognise that they make judgements about themselves. They reflected on their accumulated possessions, to consider the degree to which their lives have or have not been worthwhile: or as termed here, full or empty. So the study of material culture is ultimately a study of value and of values.

The anthropology of the other has come home, to become here an anthropology of the home. What was once the creation of societies is now in part accomplished at a domestic level, under the auspices of effective but distant state systems. The result, as I hope this book makes clear, is neither homogenising nor bland nor superficial. These people are entirely extraordinary, as diverse as the diversity of societies. It is to that richness of a London street that this book attempts to pay homage.

Appendix

THE STUDY

The material upon which these portraits is based lends itself to several possible academic studies. The original research project was an investigation of the way material culture helps people deal with loss and change. This is intended to be the subject of another volume to be written in collaboration with Fiona Parrott. We also hope that our research can yield benefits relevant to the welfare of this population by helping professionals to understand how we can learn from observing individuals' own efforts to alleviate or express feelings of loss using their everyday material culture. The present book is an addition to our initial intentions and grew out of a desire to demonstrate that the humanity of the people we encountered in the street could be revealed by their material possessions. The epilogue is offered more in the spirit of philosophical anthropology.

There is absolutely nothing special about this South London street, where Fiona Parrott and I carried out research for a year and a half. It's a slightly odd task to look for a place which has no particular features and offers you no reason to choose it. But not a hard one. Most streets in London appear from the outside to be pretty ordinary. We had some criteria for selecting the place we have called Stuart Street: a location we could both travel to without taking too much time, and with a mix of properties implying a range of incomes. Stuart Street seemed to fit the bill. There are a few larger properties that are still family homes, although others are divided into flats. There is also plenty of what was once council property, now mainly owned by housing associations. Then there always seemed to be some building or painting work going on, which signified gentrification. By and large this is the kind of area people move into when they form couples and out of when they have children. This is reflected in the composition of the portraits, although, such is the diversity of housing, that every kind of household is likely to be represented to some extent.

At first we were pleased to have chosen such a long street, which promised a good mix of inhabitants, but within a few days the downside of this selection became apparent. At that time we didn't know anyone well enough simply to ask to use their loo, and the pub was closed during the day. So, initially, we were desperate to find people to interview, to gain access to their bathroom as much as to their insights. Knocking cold on strangers' doors has always filled me with terror, so perhaps this extra incentive helped. Gradually things improved. As we went from knowing ten, then forty, then finally one hundred people, it became more a case that we couldn't walk for five minutes without meeting people we knew and stopping for a chat. At this period we could be found inviting people for drinks in the pubs, going out for meals with them, helping to carry shopping as they pushed the buggy down the street, popping in and having a cup of tea, or asking the people we knew to help introduce us and vouch for us to their neighbours. Chatting was now rather about catching up with the latest developments in their lives – the job interview, the persistent illness, the new relationship. Fiona started to go almost every Sunday to one of the churches in the street, and then took up residence in a shared house on the street itself, while I continued to make the trek from North London.

Not all the people who feature here became friends to the same degree. Many remained within the confines of more formal interviews, people too busy to see us otherwise. But after seventeen months even the local corner shopkeepers admitted that we seemed to know more people on the street than they did, and we felt we had been able to achieve the kind of relationship which approximates to the anthropological ideal: an ethnographic study of an area. Yet the street as such hardly features in this book. Each portrait seems to be a separate encounter with a separate household. This is because, while we may have come to know a great many people on the street, in the main they did not know each other. They just lived by juxtaposition.

The research method, based on a single street, replicated a previous study I had carried out also with a PhD student, Alison Clarke. That study had concerned itself with shopping, the way people's acquisition of objects helped one understand love and care in families. On that occasion I used the method in order to avoid selecting people as tokens of categories and to include the sort of people who might never otherwise be selected for inclusion in research. This time I wanted to move from a study of how people acquire goods to one focusing on how they relate to loss. For this purpose I formed a team with Stephen Frosh, an expert in psychoanalysis, and with Clive Seale, a specialist in death, both personal friends, in order to try and obtain a grant. We failed completely. So I can reassure you that no research grant was used up or harmed in the course of my research. But, about a year later, an MA student at my department, Fiona Parrott, heard about the proposal and expressed an interest in undertaking precisely a study of this kind. So, I decided to dedicate to this task such time as was not spent teaching. We started by carrying out twenty pilot studies with a variety of people ranging from friends to other students.

Our primary research was carried out for seventeen months, with more intensive fieldwork in the summer. It was completed in September 2005. Then in order to ensure academic autonomy, Fiona Parrott started on an independent thesis, under separate supervision, on the topic of the relation between objects, photographs and memory, following completion of which we plan to write up the initial research topic on the role of objects in helping people to cope with loss. In the meantime, it seemed that the richness of our encounter could lend itself to a different genre of writing – one intended to share our experience with a much wider readership and also to introduce more generally the branch of anthropology I teach: material culture studies. So this present book is intended to demonstrate how one can understand people through the medium of their things. The term 'things' is used loosely; the focus can be on the house itself, or living 'things' like a dog.

In all but two cases, the thirty portraits presented here come from our fieldwork in and around Stuart Street. The other two derive from our pilot study of twenty cases, simply because I couldn't bear to leave them out. Also, the term 'street' is a slight misnomer. We included the little side-streets off the main Stuart Street as part of the project, and, on occasion, people we had met on the street itself, but who lived a couple of streets away. Nevertheless, this is not a fictional block of flats or neighbourhood; the people I describe here are real-life Londoners.

As well as trying to make this book a good read, I have also tried, where appropriate, to convey something about the manner in which the research was carried out. Within the text there are many examples of the struggles involved and of the tentative nature of my analysis and inter-pretation. Although several of the portraits are presented as life stories, this is not how we received this information. We concentrated on the possessions in the house. But such was the richness of background mate-rial that it has been possible to recast it subsequently in the manner of life narratives. The depth of these encounters varies hugely. In some cases we would meet these people often and we came to know them very well over many months; but in other cases, the portraits are drawn from just one or two in depth interviews, which happened to focus on a par-ticular relationship with objects that seemed important to convey.

The tone of the book in some cases (by no means all) could be described as positive. This may not be to everyone's taste, because such a tone can be taken as an expression of sentimentality, a concept I dis-cuss in Portrait Seven with reference to Mrs Stone. Partly this positive stance is an artefact of the nature of our encounter. In discussing their lives and their possessions, people tended to cast themselves in a better light. Then too I grew very fond of many of the people we came to know and empathised with their personal or collective struggles to make something positive of their domestic worlds. This book is also constructive because it is concerned with the craftsmanship that people bring to relationships, to people and things, and to activities ranging from parenting, to ordering their music.

The final issue to be broached is that of the ethical implications of writing a book so closely tied to the lives of real individuals. We made considerable efforts to ensure that all participants understood what we were trying to do in this study and that the results would include a PhD dissertation and publications. Hence no information was obtained by using any form of deception. We also made a commitment to respect the anonymity of each participant. Finally, we did our very best to ensure that individuals felt positive about the encounters themselves, which is something they constantly affirmed.

For this reason, the street bears a fictional name, and so do all the participants. Furthermore, any details which may lead to the identification of specific individuals have been suppressed. For instance, in most cases real occupations have been changed to analogous ones. I take responsibility for making all such changes, and I have tried to make them in a manner which (I hope) has not altered the interpretations and conclusions. All these changes are designed to protect the subjects of our research, while ensuring that this book remains a work of non-fiction. Anonymity and its preservation seem to me essential to contemporary anthropological research and its commitment to the welfare of those who have agreed to participate in that research. I would hope that this is something everyone can and will respect.